William Shakespeare
and
The Birth of Merlin

also by Mark Dominik
Shakespeare-Middleton Collaborations
A Shakespearean Anomaly

William Shakespeare
and
The Birth of Merlin

Mark Dominik

Alioth Press
Beaverton, Oregon

1000334670

Library of Congress Cataloging-in-Publication Data

Dominik, Mark
  William Shakespeare and The birth of Merlin / Mark Dominik.—
1st Alioth Press ed.
    p.   cm.
  Includes bibliographical references and index.
  ISBN 0-945088-03-5 : $25.00
  1. Shakespeare, William, 1564-1616—Authorship. 2. Rowley,
William, 1585?-1642? Birth of Merlin. 3. Arthurian romances—
Adaptations—History and criticism. 4. Merlin (Legendary
character) in literature. 5. Merlin (Legendary character)—Drama.
6. Arthurian romances—Adaptations. I. Rowley, William, 1585?-
1642? Birth of Merlin. 1991. II. Title.
PR2856.D66 1991
822.3'3—dc20   90-1188
                                                                         CIP

First printing, 1991

Published by Alioth Press
Box 1554
Beaverton, OR 97075-1554

Designed by Susan Applegate of Publishers Book Works, Inc.

Note

The text of *The Birth of Merlin* quoted in this book and reproduced in full as an appendix is from *The Shakespeare Apocrypha*,
edited by C.F. Tucker Brooke (London, Oxford University
Press, 1908).

All citations of, and quotations from, the works of Shakespeare
refer to *The Riverside Shakespeare*, G. Blakemore Evans, textual
editor (Boston, Houghton Mifflin, 1974).

Contents

Preface to the
Revised Edition

THE FIRST EDITION of this book represented an initial attempt by a layman to address an issue of authorship attribution in English Renaissance drama. Perhaps inevitably, it contained a number of rough edges and eccentricities—and some bald errors also—that compromised its impact and efficacy. Naturally, therefore, I am pleased to send to press this new edition, corrected and revised in the light of my own evolving views and in response to some of the criticisms directed against the first. I believe that this second version is substantially more successful at making its case than its antecedent was. The general hypothesis remains the same: the internal evidence of authorship in the play *The Birth of Merlin* provides clear and persuasive verification of the external attribution to Shakespeare and Rowley.

The years between the original writing of this book and its current revision have only left me more convinced that dismissal of the external evidence of the play's authorship is fundamentally unsound. Like any other historical documents, these attributions need to be treated with appropriate seriousness; while historians certainly recognize that any such evidence *might* be false and that any document *might* be tainted in a wide variety of ways, they normally do not reject the provenance and authority of historical documents without substantive evidence. Subjective opinions and speculative objections, it should be needless to say, are not valid grounds for decisions in such matters. These strictures apply to the study of English Renaissance drama as well as to any other form of historical inquiry; when we turn to Samuel Schoenbaum's guidelines for attribution studies (quoted in Chapter I), we find that he stresses the necessity of respecting external evidence, and of refraining from the use of "intuitions, convictions, and subjective judgements" as deciding factors. Yet the standard evaluation of *Merlin*, which denies Shakespeare any hand in the play, violates both of these basic rules of evidence. Consider two other late Shakespearean collaborations: critics of previous generations disputed Shakespeare's contribution to *The Two Noble Kinsmen*, and in a few cases even to *Henry VIII*; these rejections of Shakespearean authorship were radically defective, not least of all because they neglected these basic points of respect for external evidence and resistance to subjectivism. This same defective approach is no more valid when applied to *Merlin* than it is when applied to *Kinsmen* or *Henry VIII*.

Since my judgment of Shakespeare's presence in *Merlin* was formed independently of anyone else's work, I have not made extensive citations of earlier writers who have held similar views. (Fred Allison Howe's article on the authorship of *Merlin*, listed in the Bibliography, contains a useful brief summary of nineteenth-century opinions.) I certainly do not claim, nor have I ever claimed, any sort of priority in the perception of Shakespeare's hand in this play. An academically trained commentator would explore at greater depth this critical background, the work of Horne, Delius, Tieck, et al.; perhaps I may be faulted for failing to do so. Similarly, I have once or twice been criticized for relying on C.F. Tucker Brooke's 1908 text of the play, instead of editing it anew. My choices in these matters derive from a consciousness of my status as a lay reader of Shakespeare and the Elizabethans, and not any sort of expert or authority. (I write this wholly unapologetically—I think that a layman who reads Shakespeare and his contemporaries is rather a good thing to be.) I conceive of this book as a layman's commentary on one aspect of Shakespeare's work; it is more important for it to say something worthwhile about its subject than to conform in all respects to the academic model. Some might argue that the study of authorship questions in English Renaissance drama is now so specialized that laymen can no longer make any useful contributions. Respectfully, I have to disagree. Our concern is with literary works of the early modern era, written in our native language—an accessible area of inquiry. While a layman may not bring the full resources of an academically trained specialist to investigations in this field, a fresh viewpoint may have a more-than-compensatory influence.

Some materials in the original version have been omitted from this revision because they lack the most immediate relevance to the main business of this study—not because I have changed my views on the issues involved. I have edited away some paragraphs that are not crucial to the larger argument in order to achieve what I hope is a sharper focus on the essentials. The basic thrust of this book seems challenging enough to some readers; ancillary considerations can distract from the primary issue.

It is not my contention that this study "proves" that Shakespeare and Rowley collaborated on *The Birth of Merlin*; I feel that contentions of "proof" are conceptually treacherous. It is easy to claim that a case of authorship is "not proven," or even "not provable"—all one has to do is demand a more rigorous standard of "proof" than the available evidence can meet. I do assert that the hypothesis that Shakespeare and Rowley wrote the play is the best that has yet been presented—"best" in that it is dictated and supported by the vast weight of the evidence.

This contention is easy to refute in principle: one has only to present a superior hypothesis. In reality, however, that would be a very difficult task, given that an alternative hypothesis would have to counter the unanimous external evidence in favor of Shakespeare and Rowley plus the strong internal evidences of various types that confirm a conclusion in their favor.

Accepting Shakespeare as the part-author of *The Birth of Merlin* is no more unreasonable, outlandish, or eccentric than accepting Shakespeare as the partial author of *The Two Noble Kinsmen*, or, indeed, as the author of the acknowledged canon in preference to Francis Bacon or the Earl of Oxford or any of the other fifty-odd (sometimes, very odd) alternative candidates proposed. In all three cases, an objective and reasoned overview of the evidence favors a positive conclusion.

CHAPTER I

Method and Criteria of Evidence

THE CRITICAL and scholarly consensus, both traditional and modern, on the play *The Birth of Merlin*, published in 1662 as by "William Shakespear and William Rowley," is unanimous on two basic points: first, that the play is a poor play, and second, that it is certainly, or virtually certainly, non-Shakespearean. "There is nothing in the play to support the ascription to Shakespeare."[1] "The overall inferiority of both the verse and the dramatic conception precludes any substantial likelihood that Shakespeare had a major part in its authorship."[2] "The play is crude and lumpish; it is stilted and monotonous in the verse, gross and tame in the prose. It would be pleasant to think that Rowley had no more to do with it than Shakespeare."[3] Other, similar verdicts could be listed, if further illustration of the consensus were needed.

My purpose in this study is to challenge both of these judgments, and to begin the necessary task of refutation. I would assert that *The Birth of Merlin* is rather a good play, judging it against the general run of Jacobean drama—it is funny, colorful, fast-paced, entertaining, and at its best even charming, moving, and exhilarating, a rewarding work that deserves more attention than it has received. While far from being a masterpiece on the level of Shakespeare's great plays, *Merlin* is superior to any of Rowley's solo plays; I judge it a better play than *The Two Noble Kinsmen*, a far-from-great play that is nonetheless partially Shakespearean in authorship. I will also argue that there is indeed a "substantial likelihood" that Shakespeare contributed to the authorship of *Merlin*; the play is full of elements that support the ascription of the external evidence, as I hope to show in the ensuing chapters.

These two aspects of the play, its quality and its authorship, seem obviously related at first sight: a bad play, we would think, is hardly likely to be Shakespearean. Yet we should recognize that the two questions are fundamentally of different natures: the question of quality is one of subjective aesthetic evaluation, while the question of authorship falls into the realm of fact and historical evidence. A significant measure of caution should be observed whenever we are tempted to conflate these issues. (This is true, of course, for both sides of the argument: if my higher assessment of the quality of *Merlin* were accepted as sound, such acceptance in and of itself would not mean that the play is more likely to be the work of Shakespeare. Conversely, even the lowest evaluation of a play's quality should not be allowed to contravene legitimate evidence of authorship.)

The dangers of confusing these issues are amply well illuminated by the history of Shakespeare studies: previous generations of commentators often disputed the authorship of works in the Shakespeare canon, solely because of their subjective aesthetic responses—plays and poems that were judged to be too poor to be Shakespeare's had their authenticity denied, even though the evidence clearly was in favor of Shakespeare's having written them. *Titus Andronicus* and the plays of the *Henry VI* trilogy were most frequently and most consistently subjected to this treatment, though most of the other early plays, along with *A Lover's Complaint* among the poems, have been mishandled in the same way. (And if we consider the views of the more extreme disintegrators like J.M. Robertson, we see that virtually every work by Shakespeare has met with this same type of objection.) In the more sensible critical climate that currently prevails, such arguments are no longer applied to the works of the acknowledged Shakespearean canon;[4] they should not be applied to any works. It is important to realize that we must set aside our subjective impressions of the play in order to achieve an objective valuation of the relevant evidence of authorship.

Perhaps the key play for comparison with *The Birth of Merlin* is one already mentioned—Shakespeare's and Fletcher's *The Two Noble Kinsmen*. Consider some facts about the latter play: *Kinsmen* was first printed in quarto in 1634, years after the deaths of both Shakespeare and Fletcher; it was assigned to the two playwrights on the title page of the original quarto, though the play was omitted from the earliest folio collections of both men's works. Some early commentators like George Steevens and William Hazlitt rejected the attribution to Shakespeare, arguing that apparently Shakespearean features in *Kinsmen* were actually due to Fletcher's attempt to imitate Shakespeare. The attribution to Shakespeare was alleged to be either a mistake or an act of overt fraud by John Waterson, the quarto's publisher. Happily, other early critics (Charles Lamb being the best-known to a modern reader) made strong and persuasive arguments in favor of the original attribution of *Kinsmen*, and demonstrated Shakespeare's hand in the play beyond reasonable doubt. Given the evidence that Shakespeare and Fletcher also collaborated on a lost play called *Cardenio*, and that many scholars have found signs of Fletcher's hand in the canonically Shakespearean *Henry VIII*, the truth of Shakespeare's late phase of collaborative playwriting is rarely disputed.[5]

Rowley, like Fletcher, was a younger contemporary of Shakespeare; both Rowley and Fletcher, in fact, appear to have begun their literary careers around the same time, ca.

1607. Both men collaborated widely with many other dramatists—so that, from their viewpoints, there is nothing inherently unlikely in the idea of their having collaborated with Shakespeare. *The Birth of Merlin*, like *Kinsmen*, shows clear affinities with Shakespeare's final romances; I will argue that *Merlin* can be dated to the same period as *Kinsmen*, to the era during which we know Shakespeare was engaged in collaborative authorship. *Merlin*, I will attempt to show, possesses mixed Shakespearean and Rowleian characteristics, just as *Kinsmen* can be shown to possess mixed Shakespearean and Fletcherian characteristics—so that in both cases the internal evidence of the plays provides strong confirmation of the title-page attributions. If someone were to protest that Shakespeare couldn't have contributed to *Kinsmen* because the play simply isn't good enough, the objection would not be taken very seriously; *Kinsmen* is certainly a lesser work than Shakespeare's solo plays—but that is only logical, in that it is a collaboration and not a solo work. We do not hold *Kinsmen* to the standard of *Hamlet* or *King Lear* or *The Tempest* when evaluating it as a partially Shakespearean work; we should treat *Merlin* the same way, for the same reason.

While I see *Merlin* and *Kinsmen* as comparable plays, I do not regard them as undifferentiable; to the contrary, there are distinctions between the plays that help to explain why Shakespeare's hand in *Merlin* has been overlooked for so long. In the case of *Kinsmen*, we have a collaboration between the greatest literary artist of the English language and the most idiosyncratic and mannered stylist of the Jacobean age—two writers with literary voices that are readily distinguishable. Rowley, however, has a style that is much less distinctive than Fletcher's, a style more typical of the minor dramatists of his era. While Rowley possesses his own mannerisms and stylistic traits, these tend to be less blatant and noticeable than Fletcher's, and appear less consistently through his work. Rowley's participation in a collaborative effort, then, can have a levelling effect upon the more distinctive style of his collaborator. In *Kinsmen*, there are portions of the play in which Shakespeare's style is highly noticeable, sections that seem to be mostly or wholly Shakespearean in authorship; concentrations of obviously Shakespearean elements in these portions of *Kinsmen* make Shakespeare's partial authorship of the play hard to reject. In *Merlin*, Shakespeare's contribution seems less concentrated in any specific sections of the play; it is more thoroughly blended with Rowley's, and thus more effectively masked by Rowley's share. I would say that Shakespeare's is the minority share in *Merlin*, insofar as such an estimation can be made; his contribution to this play is more limited than in the case of either *Kinsmen* or *Henry VIII*. While Shakespeare's hand in *Merlin* is significant, I judge that Rowley's hand predominates. (If we were to think of the play, very roughly, as about four parts Shakespeare diluted with five or six parts Rowley, we might not be too far wrong.)

This, I believe, is the key point to be made about *Merlin*: the internal evidence reveals the play to be an intimate collaboration between its authors, in which their respective shares are merged together to such a degree that the result approaches a homogenization and hybridization of their individual styles. In past generations, many scholars of English Renaissance drama who have specialized in authorship and attribution study have tended to take a schematic and mechanical approach to collaborative plays, almost, at times, chopping the plays into bits and pieces and assigning the fragments to different authors—Collaborator A wrote scene I,i, Collaborator B wrote I,ii, etc. While this fragmenting strategy has some usefulness in some cases, it obviously neglects some essential aspects of writing plays (planning before composition, revision afterward), and imposes a crude and reductive interpretation on what is, of necessity, a far more flexible process—the creation of a unified, functional, actable dramatic work. Many modern critics recognize this; consider, as one example, Anthony

Harris' view of the authorship of another of Rowley's collaborations, *The Witch of Edmonton*. "The quarto states that the
work was composed 'by divers well-esteemed Poets; William
Rowley, Thomas Dekker, John Ford, etc.' Modern scholars ignore the 'etcetera' and are generally agreed in assigning the
Mother Sawyer scenes to Dekker, the Cuddy Banks episodes
to Rowley, and in giving overall responsibility for the Frank
Thorney/Winnifride/Susan plot to Ford (with help from
Dekker). Such arbitrary divisions are, of course, a gross oversimplification. From what we know of Jacobean collaborative
techniques, such clear-cut divisions are most unlikely, particularly where the plots overlap within single scenes . . ."[6]

Other plays from Rowley's canon could be cited to show
the limitations of a schematic approach; and I argue that
Shakespeare's late collaborations with Fletcher also display a
good deal of intimate collaboration (Appendix I). In the case
of *Merlin*, I believe that we have a play characterized by intimate collaboration between Rowley and Shakespeare—precisely the type of play that the traditional and outdated
schematic approach can deal with least effectively. C.F. Tucker
Brooke, the editor of the text of *Merlin* reproduced in this volume, once wrote that "There is not a single poetic passage in
The Birth of Merlin which will justify for an instant the hypothesis of Shakespeare's authorship"[7]—and if one insists on looking for "pure Shakespeare," his judgment is sound. But *Merlin*
is not a play that is this-part-Shakespeare, and that-part-Row-
ley; it is, overall, Shakespare-and-Rowley. The difference is
basic and crucial. Gold ore is not pure gold, but it does contain
gold; any gold miner who neglects this fact will place extreme
limits on his chances of success. This study will attempt to
show that *Merlin* contains some of Shakespeare's writing in
the same way. (A skeptic might wonder about the possibility
of our confusing fool's gold with the real thing; that is precisely the distinction that the ensuing chapters will elucidate.)

This essay, then, is an attempt at an attribution-of-authorship study. The past two centuries have produced a long series of such studies in English Renaissance drama—some successful and persuasive, others not; many lessons, both cautionary and emulatory, can be learned from them. Perhaps the best guide to this critical literature is Samuel Schoenbaum's classic *Internal Evidence and Elizabethan Dramatic Authorship: An Essay in Literary History and Method*. After a detailed review of the errors and excesses that have been perpetrated in attempts to use internal evidence to resolve questions of disputed authorship, Professor Schoenbaum proposes a list of eight guidelines for any further endeavors in attribution study.[8] I have tried to follow these guidelines in this book—or to deviate from them only for specific and legitimate reasons. It will be useful to consider Schoenbaum's eight rules individually, since they touch upon all the major areas of concern for an attribution-of-authorship survey.

1. *External evidence cannot be ignored, no matter how inconvenient such evidence may be for the theories of the investigator.*
The point is obvious and incontrovertible; for the study of the provenance of any work of art, as for any other historical inquiry, the facts of the documentary record are the essential starting point. This is not to say that all historical documents must be taken at face value—the implications of any such evidence can be disputed or even disproved if the countervailing evidence is sufficiently strong. But *evidence* is the requisite; mere doubt won't do.

In the present instance, my hypothesis about the authorship of *The Birth of Merlin* is drawn directly from the external evidence. There are three pieces of such evidence in the case of *Merlin*, three seventeenth-century ascriptions of authorship, all of which assign the play to Shakespeare and Rowley. In chronological order, they are: first, the play's entry in Francis Kirkman's play list of 1661 (repeated in his second list of ten

years later); second, the title page of the 1662 quarto, the first
and only publication of the play before the nineteenth century;
and third, the section on Rowley in Gerard Langbaine's *An
Account of the English Dramatick Poets* (1691), in which
Langbaine states that Rowley "was not only beloved by those
Great Men, Shakespear, Fletcher, and Jonson, but likewise
writ, with the former, *The Birth of Merlin*."[9]

Superficially, this seems a strong evidentiary record; some
unquestioned attributions of Jacobean plays are supported by
only a single piece of external evidence. Yet there is a complicating factor: all three of these *Merlin* attributions are thought
to derive from the same source, Francis Kirkman. The 1662
quarto was printed by "Tho. Johnson for Francis Kirkman,
and Henry Marsh." Also, Kirkman was Langbaine's principal
source of information—there appears to have been a personal
relationship between the two, and Langbaine questions
Kirkman's attributions only in rare instances. (It might be argued that Langbaine's positive statement about Rowley and
The Birth of Merlin goes far beyond a mere repetition of the
play's attribution—Langbaine appears to be recapitulating
more personal, circumstantial information from an independ-
ent source. This impression, though, is somewhat subjective,
and some commentators may dispute its usefulness.)

We are faced, therefore, with the question of Kirkman's reli-
ability as a source of information; and his reputation in that
respect is very low. The accuracy rate for the authorial attributions in Kirkman's play lists has been calculated at roughly 50
percent. While the lists do contain some valid attributions, a
mere even chance of being either right or wrong has hardly
impressed later scholars. It is true that some of the more egregious errors in Kirkman's lists were present in his sources;[10]
yet it is also true that Kirkman added some howlers of his
own.[11] Among the attributions of previously anonymous plays
made by Kirkman in his lists, the accuracy rate is again only
about 50 percent;[12] his more striking hits (the ascription of

Tamburlaine to Marlowe in the 1671 list, for example) cannot wholly outweigh his misses. Such limited dependability has sometimes provoked commentators to harsh words; verdicts like "Kirkman's word is valueless as evidence"[13] are not unknown in the relevant critical literature.

There are necessary distinctions to be drawn between forms of external evidence. Title-page attributions tend to be much more reliable than play-list entries, for instance; one can calculate an accuracy rate for title-page attributions at 80 percent or higher, depending on the approach used. Yet here again, Kirkman's performance falls well below the first level of accuracy, as we can see by looking at the plays he published around the time of *Merlin*. In 1661, his first year in business, Kirkman issued *A Cure for a Cuckold* and *The Thracian Wonder*, both as the work of Webster and Rowley; in 1662, the year of *Merlin*, he published *Anything for a Quiet Life* as the work of Middleton. Modern scholars generally accept *Cure for a Cuckold* as Webster's and Rowley's on the basis of internal evidence—but reject *Thracian Wonder* on the same basis.[14] *Anything for a Quiet Life* is widely attributed to Middleton and Webster rather than to Middleton alone.[15] It can seem that any one of Kirkman's attributions has an equal chance of being correct, or incorrect, or partially correct; it is not a reassuring situation.

This presents us with an interesting conundrum: to fulfill Schoenbaum's first guideline, we must depend upon "valueless" evidence. Fortunately, there is a simple way of resolving this difficulty. The *Merlin* attribution cannot be dismissed as worthless, since it is at least half right. I know of no one who disputes Rowley's connection with the play, so that the external evidence is sound with respect to one of the two parties mentioned; a piece of historical documentary evidence (several pieces, in fact) cannot be both "half right" and "valueless" simultaneously. The Rowleian connection stated in the external evidence is confirmed by clear and unambiguous internal evidence of various types; *Merlin*, in many respects, is like Row-

ley's known works in the ways that Rowley's works are like
each other as testimony to their common authorship. When
we find external evidence confirmed by internal evidence, we
have a strong prima facie case for authorship. The standard of
evidence that allows us to affirm Rowley's presence in *Merlin*,
and his and Webster's presences in *Cure for a Cuckold*, also allows us to make a determination concerning Shakespeare's
presence in the former play. I will attempt to show that *Merlin*
reveals abundant internal evidence to validate the external attribution in both its aspects—that Shakespeare is as readily de-
tectable as Rowley. Without the confirmation of internal
evidence, the external evidence would have very limited
worth; but with that confirmation, it cannot be lightly passed
over.

(The erroneous attribution of *Thracian Wonder* to Webster
and Rowley is interesting in another respect: its chronological
coincidence with *Cure for a Cuckold* suggests mere print-shop
confusion rather than any attempt to defraud. In Chapter II
we will discuss a similar error—*The Spanish Gypsy* having been
misattributed to Middleton and Rowley by the stationer who
issued *The Changeling* the year before. Most erroneous attributions in the relevant period are clearly the result of such confusion rather than overt deceit; stationers had nothing to gain
by making false attributions to men like Webster or Middleton
or Rowley, since their names could not reasonably have been
expected to attract much interest among the book-buying
public. Kirkman has sometimes been accused of having delib-
erately made a false attribution of *Merlin* to Shakespeare in order to increase his sales; but there is little justification for such
a charge. We know that during the Restoration period, the
plays of Beaumont and Fletcher were performed twice as often
as Shakespeare's, indicating their substantially greater popu-
larity.[16] Unscrupulous publishers would have had even
stronger motives for making false ascriptions to Beaumont and
Fletcher than to Shakespeare; Kirkman, in 1662, would have

done better for himself if he had issued *Merlin* under Beaumont's and Fletcher's names—if he were indeed dishonest. Yet false title-page attributions to Beaumont and Fletcher do not appear during the Restoration period.[17] Critics of the eighteenth and nineteenth centuries tended to assume that the laissez-faire conditions of their own eras applied equally well to the sixteenth and seventeenth centuries; we can see now that this was an anachronistic error, and that the stationers of the earlier periods functioned in a more hierarchic and authoritarian society with strong censorship controls, in which deliberate misattribution of authorship for commercial gain was much less likely to have occurred.[18] Fraud is a serious charge— at least, in my opinion, it should be taken seriously. In the absence of supporting evidence of fraudulent intent, we should recall the maxim "innocent until proven guilty." Even some of the cases of misattribution that seem blatant to us could easily have been the result of error or wishful thinking rather than fraud—the publisher involved may have thought that he had justification for his attribution that we cannot now perceive or recover.)

External evidence might not resolve an authorship question in an absolute or final sense—but it is the logical starting point for any such study. The matter can be summed up quite simply, in the end: for *The Birth of Merlin*, all the external evidence from seventeenth-century sources assigns the play to Shakespeare and Rowley. And, as Professor Schoenbaum has written, such evidence cannot be ignored.

2. *If stylistic criteria are to have any meaning, the play must be written in a style.*
The warning is against the use of stylistic judgments when the writer or writers under examination lack distinction enough to rise above the level of the commonplace, the general mediocre average of their time. Such a classification, I think, is obviously inapplicable to *Merlin*—inaccurate for Rowley, and absurd for

Shakespeare. Our survey of *Merlin* will show that the play combines the identifiable styles of its two authors into an often-homogeneous compound.

Once observed, this intimate blending of Shakespeare's style with Rowley's goes a long way toward explaining how most previous commentators overlooked the signs of Shakespeare's contribution. Rarely have scholars recognized the degree to which a work of Shakespearean collaboration might constitute a different kind of play from one of Shakespeare's undivided authorship; when forced to confront the possibility of Shakespeare's having written with a partner, scholars have hardly ever entertained the possibility of intimate collaboration, preferring instead the schematic and mechanical approach described earlier.

Merlin, however, reveals ample signs of being precisely such an intimate collaboration between Shakespeare and Rowley; their contributions, on the whole, are inseparably intertwined. The resulting mixture is odd and idiosyncratic. In a specific and limited sense, the style of *Merlin* can be called unique—in that we do not find this particular blending of Shakespeare's and Rowley's styles anywhere else in Elizabethan drama. This lack of an immediately available standard for comparison has proved a major obstacle.

3. *The investigator must always work with the most reliable texts, preferably directly with early prints or manuscripts.*
4. *Textual analysis logically precedes stylistic analysis.*
Since these two points are closely linked, they can be dealt with effectively together. The use of reliable texts is always a desideratum, but it is crucial when textual analysis is being conducted. Professor Schoenbaum offers a number of examples of investigators who have come to grief through reliance on poorly edited or heavily modernized texts for close study of an author's spelling, punctuation, speech prefixes, contractional forms, expletives, and other linguistic peculiarities that

were not accurately reflected in the texts. The best-known example, perhaps, is A.H. Thorndike's 1901 attempt to exploit the contractional form "'em" as a Fletcher-Massinger discriminator—while using an edition of Massinger's works in which all instances of "'em" had been silently expanded to "them."[19] I have chosen to use Tucker Brooke's 1908 text of *Merlin*; I feel it balances strong fidelity to the 1662 quarto with some of the advantages of a modern edition. (In the quarto, all the verse except the rhymed couplets was printed as prose. Modern editors, beginning with Henry Tyrrell in 1851, have realigned the verse.) Having had opportunities to compare Tucker Brooke's editions of several plays with the original editions, I find him highly reliable in reproducing the original textual features. (His revision and addition of punctuation does not impinge upon our study of *Merlin*.)

I think that a rational and informed dissent from Schoenbaum's fourth point is possible, especially where stylists as distinctive as Shakespeare are concerned. In some cases, stylistic evidence provides valid information that textual evidence does not (the instances of *A Match at Midnight* and *The Spanish Gypsy*, noted in the next chapter, are examples of this). For the purposes of this study, however, I have complied with Schoenbaum's guidelines: the first of the four chapters in this book directly concerned with the detailed features of *Merlin* discusses the textual evidence (see Chapter III). It will be my contention that the textual evidence in *Merlin* supports the attribution of the external evidence.

5. *Plays of which all the early printed or manuscript texts are continuously defective offer no fit quarries for evidence and are no fit subject for canonical investigation.*

None of the plays involved in this study—neither *Merlin*, the plays of the Shakespeare and Rowley canons, nor the plays of other Jacobean dramatists used for comparison—falls into this category of continuously defective texts.

6. *For any author proposed, a reasonable amount of unchallenged dramatic writing, apart from collaborations, must be extant.*

For Rowley, there are three plays that the critical consensus accepts as solo works: *All's Lost by Lust*, *A Shoemaker a Gentleman*, and *A New Wonder, a Woman Never Vexed*. Also, there is a clear general agreement in the scholarly literature as to the nature and the basic characteristics of Rowley's dramatic writing, evolved and accumulated over the past century, extending from the early work of Pauline Wiggin to modern work by D.M. Robb, Samuel Schoenbaum, and David Lake. This scholarly consensus is an indispensible advantage in the determination of Rowley's share in *The Birth of Merlin*. (A fuller consideration of Rowley's works and his style follows in Chapter II.)

As for Shakespeare: I have relied upon *The Riverside Shakespeare*[20] in preparing this work—a tremendously useful edition, given that the priceless *Harvard Concordance to Shakespeare*[21] is keyed to its line enumeration. The Riverside edition is particularly useful in that, in addition to the thirty-seven plays of the traditional canon (the thirty-six of the First Folio plus *Pericles*) it includes *The Two Noble Kinsmen* and the portions of *Sir Thomas More* mostly widely attributed to Shakespeare. I would assert that the same general standard of evidence that has been applied to *Pericles*, *Kinsmen*, and *More*, and which has led to the acknowledgment of Shakespeare's hand in those plays, can yield a similar conclusion when applied to *Merlin*.

The inclusion of all or part of thirty-nine plays in the Riverside edition can serve to remind us that not every play in which Shakespeare was involved as playwright was contained in the First Folio. It would seem that John Heminges and Henry Condell, in making their selections for the First Folio, tried to include all those plays they knew to be the work of Shakespeare alone, and to exclude those that they knew to be various forms of collaboration. This is not to say that every word in the First Folio is authentically Shakespearean; there are some minor cases of mixed authorship. The Folio text of *MacBeth*, our only source for that play, contains interpolations from Middleton's *The Witch*—the Hecate material and the witches' songs in III,v and IV,i are Middletonian and not Shakespearean in authorship,[22] though this does not have much effect on our acceptance of *MacBeth* as a Shakespearean work. It is also generally accepted that Fletcher is present in the text of *Henry VIII*; I heartily agree, though I think his contribution is far more limited than is often supposed, and that Heminges and Condell were essentially well justified in selecting *Henry VIII* for the Folio while omitting *Kinsmen* as a true collaboration (see Appendix I). Also, there is *Timon of Athens*: the theory that *Timon* is a mixed Shakespeare-Middleton text has some significant evidence behind it, I believe, and I tend to favor it.[23] We need to be aware, though, that Heminges and Condell did not originally intend to have *Timon* in the Folio; it was inserted into the space left for *Troilus and Cressida* when it appeared that the latter play would be unavailable because of a conflict over the rights to it. Thus there is no inherent conflict in the view that *Timon* is a mixed-authorship work that was nonetheless included in the Folio; its status as an anomaly in that respect is recognized.

The creation of the First Folio was a complex phenomenon, and I do not want to oversimplify it. I do think, though, that this overall hypothesis, that Heminges and Condell intended to exclude Shakespeare's collaborative works, has a fair degree of validity in light of the known facts. My point is that the exclusion of *Merlin* from the First Folio does not constitute evidence against the hypothesis of partially Shakespearean authorship. The omission of *Merlin* is comparable to the omission of *Kinsmen* and *More* and *Pericles*, works that were left out of the Folio not because they are wholly un-Shakespearean, but because they are not wholly Shakespearean—a vital distinction.

7. Intuitions, convictions, and subjective judgments generally, carry no weight as evidence.

Another incontrovertible point—though it should be noted that this stricture works both ways. Much of the orthodox response to *Merlin*, as illustrated by the quotes at the start of this chapter, has been of this intuitive, subjective, impressionistic nature; a judgment of its deficiency is not as radical as one may at first suppose.

(This impressionistic tendency has carried over into the responses to this study of *Merlin* as well. After reading the first edition of this book, one scholar asserted that the play "has good lines here and there, but they strike me as 'post-Shakespearean' rather than authentic Shakespeare." One reviewer wrote about his "feeling that the Shakespearean dimension of *The Birth of Merlin* is limited to the possibility that its author may have read or seen *Cymbeline*." These types of feelings and impressions have no value as evidence, and should not be allowed to contravene the legitimate evidence of Shakespeare's contribution to the play.)

This point about the problematical nature of subjective judgments is not confined to English Renaissance drama or to literary studies; it pertains in any field in which attribution or provenance questions arise. Thus, in a recent article on the drawings of Michelangelo and Leonardo da Vinci, Charles Hope has observed that when attributing drawings to the artists, "quality is often an inappropriate and always an inadequate criterion, because the standards we apply will almost inevitably be anachronistic."[24] There are various fairly obvious reasons for a finished work by even a great artist falling short of the level of his or her highest achievement: the piece in question could be a very early work (or even a very late one, since many artists produce their best and most characteristic work in the broad middle range of their careers); it could be a collaborative work; or it could be a piece produced under special and atypical circumstances. For Shakespeare, *The Comedy of Errors*, *The Two Noble Kinsmen*, and the William Peter *Funeral Elegy* can be taken as illustrations of these factors. I believe I can cite ample evidence for the placement of *Merlin* in a comparable category as a very late Shakespearean collaboration, authentic despite its status as a minor member of the canon.

8. *Wherever possible, stylistic evidence should be supplemented by bibliographical evidence.*
Bibliography, however, is a specialized skill and a demanding discipline, and I make no pretense to be qualified to undertake it; I have therefore refrained from any attempt at a bibliographic analysis of the 1662 quarto of *Merlin*. I would be fascinated to see the results of such an analysis—though I have to confess a measure of skepticism as to whether bibliographic evidence can be a determining factor in authorship study. Schoenbaum cites Fredson Bowers' bibliographic study of the Dekker-Massinger collaboration *The Virgin Martyr*, noting that "Bowers effectively supplements the stylistic evidence for scene allocations" between the dramatists;[25] yet it remains true that Bowers' survey arrives "at results similar to those of previous scholars,"[26] and true too that the authorship of *The Virgin Martyr* has long been recognized and accepted.

Without wanting to appear dismissive of the achievements of specialists in bibliographic or textual studies (I believe I can make a sincere claim to being a strong admirer of such achievements), I do not think that the question of the authorship of *The Birth of Merlin* can be wholly, or even primarily, resolved by specialized techniques of textual or bibliographic analysis. To use Prof. Schoenbaum's term, those techniques provide useful supplements to (but not substitutes for) a balanced general overview of an authorship question.

Professor Schoenbaum concludes his list of guidelines with this note: "The eight principles I have outlined do not exhaust the possibilities for cautionary advice to canonical investigators. Other strictures, at least as wholesome, will no doubt occur to readers who have concerned themselves with authorship problems."[27] Indeed, the rules can be multiplied almost indefinitely; yet it is difficult to avoid the impression that any set of rules extensive and stringent enough to preclude misuse of internal evidence would also inhibit legitimate use of such evidence. Elsewhere in *Internal Evidence*, Schoenbaum quotes E.K. Chambers' formidable roster of objections to the employment of internal evidence—a stance so rigorous that it would require a hefty volume to be written in response.[28]

Fortunately, though, much of the groundwork for successful address of authorship questions has already been laid, especially in respect to Shakespeare; if we know a lot about how *not* to go about attempting to establish Shakespeare's hand in a play, we also know some things about how to do the job right. If we turn back for a moment to Schoenbaum's sixth guideline, I think it is fair to say that by "unchallenged dramatic writing," Schoenbaum means works not regarded as doubtful by orthodox scholars—because, of course, Shakespeare's claim to his own works has been challenged repeatedly and vigorously for over a century, and is still disputed by some people. My aim in bringing up the subject of the Baconians and Oxfordians and other anti-Stratfordians is not in any way to endorse their views, none of which I hold; rather, my point is that there is an established standard of reasoning and of evidence to apply to questions of Shakespearean authorship—it is the standard by which Shakespeare's title to his own works is defended. That defense logically begins with the abundant external evidence that testifies to Shakespeare's authorship of his plays and poems; it continues through the many types of internal evidence that unite his works, and concludes with an observation of the lack of substantive contradictory evidence and

CHAPTER I: METHOD   23

the unsoundness of the objections against Shakespeare's authorship of those works. Individual Shakespearean works of
the acknowledged canon all meet this standard; partially
Shakespearean works like *Kinsmen* and *Pericles* also meet it, to
the degree that they are Shakespearean in authorship (and they
diverge from that standard insofar as they are the work of others—which is simply sensible). *Merlin* should be held to the
same standard; in my judgment, it meets that standard to a
degree that is reasonable for a partially Shakespearean work.

Much of the evidence that I will cite as indicative of Shakespeare's presence in *Merlin* is stylistic in nature (though external and textual evidence are also important in this study).
Stylistic evidence can be problematical, and has been used
sloppily by some earlier practitioners. As a consequence, such
evidence is now often dismissed as "parallel hunting" and re-
fused serious consideration. This attitude, however, is a rejoin-
der to the secondary literature more than to the plays
themselves; the plays, experienced directly and without the
mediation of the critical literature, assure us of the value and
validity of stylistic evidence. Individual playwrights do have
individual styles, sometimes quite personal, distinctive, and idiosyncratic ones; and the differences in their styles have been
exploited by careful and discriminating critics in insightful,
useful ways. If Schoenbaum's second guideline warns us
against attempting stylistic treatment of mundane works, it also implies an applicability of such treatment when the stylistic
materials involved are truly distinctive—and Shakespeare certainly qualifies there. R.C. Bald has written this about the
Shakespearean additions to *Sir Thomas More*: "It was the evidence of style that originally drew attention to the play, and
had there been no resemblances with Shakespeare's acknowledged works there would have been no attempt to marshal
other evidence. The thought and expression of the Additions
are therefore of fundamental importance, and evidence of
handwriting and spelling must be secondary to literary consi-

derations."[29] This primacy of stylistic evidence that Bald recognizes in the case of *More* is entirely appropriate in my judgment, both in general and in the specific case of *Merlin*; I have written this book very much in its spirit.

Concomitantly, I have tried to remain mindful of the real difficulties inherent in successful use of stylistic evidence. It is incumbent upon any practitioner to recognize that apparent commonalities between texts can be the result of factors other than common authorship: influence and imitation, derivation from a shared source, and simple chance resemblance are possibilities that have to be considered. Yet these factors, while relevant, are not insurmountable barriers; the Shakespeare canon shows us the way to mediate between the alternatives. From the start of his career, Shakespeare employed identifiable dramatic and linguistic elements—from the largest-scale thematic materials, to particular strains of imagery, to the smallest nuances of phrasing and word usage—that recur as continuing, developing, evolving traits and tactics throughout his subsequent works. Thus, each work by Shakespeare, from the earliest to the latest, shows myriad connections and linkages with the rest of his oeuvre; each work participates in what we might call a pattern of Shakespearean self-reference. This pattern is extensive, essentially continuous: almost every line in Shakespeare's canonical plays and poems has some link, major or minor, to something else in his output. In each of his larger-scale works, his plays or narrative poems, there are hundreds and thousands of such connections with the rest of the canon, touching upon many consistent features of his style—using that term in its broadest sense.

In a work that is only partially Shakespearean, like *Kinsmen*, this pattern will be qualified and adulterated by the inclusion of non-Shakespearean materials; but it will still be identifiable if Shakespeare's contribution is real. The works of other dramatists and poets do not share in this pattern of Shakespearean self-reference; commonalities between any non-Shakespearean work and the canon will be fewer and farther between, and will lack the contextual and thematic relations that typify the authentic works. This can be demonstrated easily (though not briefly) by taking a sample from one of Shakespeare's acknowledged works and illustrating its varied interrelationships with the rest of the canon—and also by showing that equivalent samples of non-Shakespearean writing do not reveal the same concentration of Shakespearean features. I hope that such a belaboring of the obvious is not required here (though we shall deal with related demonstrations in Chapters IV and V); I think that a few examples will suffice for most readers.

If we return for a moment to *Kinsmen*, we can identify patterns of apparently Shakespearean and apparently Fletcherian elements that stand as legitimate confirmation of the external attribution. In the opening scene of *Kinsmen*, for instance, we find the phrase "Vengeance and revenge" (I,i,58), an unusual phrasing that also occurs in *Richard II*, IV,i,67. In the play's third scene, a somewhat less distinctive but still useful phrase, "sickly appetite" (I,iii,89), is worth noting, in that it also appears in the fourth line of Shakespeare's Sonnet 147. By themselves, these two phrasings tell us little about the authorship of *Kinsmen*—but the essential point, of course, is that they do not occur "by themselves"; they are parts of a general pattern of hundreds of other links to the acknowledged Shakespearean works.

For the similar pattern of Fletcherian elements in *Kinsmen*, let us settle for one example of a rather different type. The compound coinage "fair-ey'd" occurs three times in the play (II,ii,37, II,v,29, and IV,i,8); this word is not used at all in Shakespeare's recognized works, though it does appear in Fletcher's (*The Humorous Lieutenant*, I,i,240; *The Captain*, III,i,15). It is reasonable, then, to accept these three instances of "fair-ey'd" as indices of Fletcher's hand in the play rather than Shakespeare's. This is not to say that Shakespeare *could not* have used the term "fair-ey'd"—of course, he *might* have done so; neither is it necessary to demand that "fair-ey'd" must be unique to Fletcher—common sense suggests that if we look long enough and hard enough through the vast corpus of English Renaissance drama and verse, we will likely find other instances of "fair-ey'd." Yet even with these qualifications, we can still reasonably interpret these three uses of "fair-ey'd" in *Kinsmen* as pointers toward Fletcher rather than Shakespeare. In and of themselves, they do not "prove" anything about the play—but neither are they wholly irrelevant.

The approach delineated above is broader and more flexible than some scholars would allow; Donald Foster, for instance, has written that "verbal parallels ... are *altogether worthless* as evidence unless it can be shown that the examples cited are distinctive of a particular poet"[30] (emphasis added). Conversely, E.H.C. Oliphant once argued that the most distinctive features of a poet's style are the ones most likely to be imitated by other writers, and that we are better off looking for the "little tricks of expression that no one would think of copying."[31]

In my judgment, the plays themselves indicate the desirability of a broad view, balanced with cautious interpretation. Certainly, the most peculiar and distinctive features are the most telling—but more minor features (like "fair-ey'd" in *Kinsmen*) have potential too. It is too severe, I think, to discard any kind of evidence as "altogether worthless"; just as textual evidence is "relative," depending on the elements that individuals do or do not use (see Chapter III), so too can items of stylistic evidence have "relative" value. (If we insisted that textual features be "distinctive of a particular poet," the valid use of textual evidence would end.)

Upon examination, *Merlin* shows a range of features that are either employed by Rowley but not by Shakespeare, or employed by Shakespeare but not by Rowley; and clearly, such features have something to tell us, even if they are not actually unique to either dramatist. In the chapters that follow, I will cite these types of features and more: distinctive paral-

lels, "little tricks of expression," theme and plot elements, vocabulary and word usage, characterization, imagery, other elements of "style" in the widest sense, coupled with textual and
external evidence to demonstrate the status of *Merlin* as a
Shakespeare-Rowley collaboration.

CHAPTER II

William Rowley

Iᴛ ɪs a certainty that readers of this book will be much less familiar with William Rowley's canon than with Shakespeare's. Rowley is not one of the major voices in Jacobean drama. We can give this survey of *Merlin* some perspective, then, by pausing to consider Rowley's career and his style of drama.

Nothing whatever is known of William Rowley's birth, parentage, background, education, or early life. His date of birth is usually given as "ca. 1585," though this year is selected simply by reading backward from the known facts, and assuming that he probably began his public career when he was in his early twenties. It's a reasonable assumption, though not necessarily an accurate one: Middleton's first published poem was issued when he was only seventeen, while Fletcher began his work as a playwright when he was nearly thirty. Rowley enters the historical record in 1607, when his dramatic collaboration with John Day and George Wilkins, *The Travels of the Three English Brothers*, was printed. For nearly two decades after that date, Rowley was active as both an actor and a playwright. He began his career with the Queen's Men, though by 1609 he had switched to the Duke of York's (later Prince Charles') Men.

Most of his acting career was spent with the latter company; by 1616 he had become one of its leaders. Rowley was with the King's Men, Shakespeare's company, from 1623 to 1625. He died in 1626.

Rowley must have been a gifted comic actor, since he rose to be the leading clown in one of the leading companies of his time. He must also have been a rather large man, since he specialized in fat clown roles. He played Plumporridge in Middleton's *Inner Temple Masque*, the Fat Bishop in the same author's *A Game at Chess*, and Simplicity in the two men's collaboration *The World Tossed at Tennis*. Rowley also wrote fat clown roles for himself: Jaques in his *All's Lost by Lust* ("personated by the Poet," as the quarto tells us), and Bustopha in *The Maid in the Mill* (his collaboration with Fletcher). He most likely played Chough in *A Fair Quarrel*, still another of his collaborations with Middleton. Indeed, many of Rowley's plays contain clown parts that he could have played, and could have written or helped to write with that casting in mind. As we shall see, the part of the Clown in *Merlin* shows every sign of being another Rowleian fat-clown role.[1]

As a writer, Rowley was almost exclusively a playwright; the prose pamphlet *A Search for Money* (1609) is his only sustained non-dramatic work. And as a dramatist, Rowley's reputation has always been low, though in recent years he has received at least a partial and limited revaluation. Rowley's significance in the study of English Renaissance drama is rooted in his collaborations with Middleton, especially *The Changeling* and *A Fair Quarrel*. These two plays have long been accepted as masterpieces of their respective genres, tragedy and tragicomedy. Until recently, however, Rowley's share in these plays has been widely denigrated. If one agrees with Samuel Schoenbaum's 1955 verdict that Rowley's subplot in *The Changeling* is the play's "worst blemish . . . stupid and tedious, and . . . offensive to the modern reader,"[2] one will have a far lower opinion of Rowley's work than do those more recent

critics who consider the play to be an instance of successful
plot integration.[3] Similarly, if one accepts the view that the
ending of *A Fair Quarrel* is a "preposterous happy solution,"[4]
one will see Rowley as a lesser artist than do those who judge
that play to be another example of successful thematic union of
plot elements.[5]

The modern tendency to value *The Witch of Edmonton*, another Rowleian collaboration, as one of the most significant
plays of his era, has also helped to raise Rowley's standing in
our critical estimation. Thus, a few recent commentators have
found a few good things to say about Rowley: "Rowley was
essentially a man of the theatre who knew how to capture the
interest of a popular audience."[6] (It may be worthwhile to remember what it meant to be one of those men of the theater of
Shakespeare's age—to recall Alfred Harbage's dictum that
Shakespeare, as an actor-manager in the leading theatrical en-
terprise of his day, would have been a more remarkable man
than the Earl of Oxford even if he had never written a word.[7]
By the same token, William Rowley was an actor-manager
intimately involved with the most important theatrical companies of the Jacobean age, and who in a few instances contributed to the authorship of plays that are recognized as
masterpieces—hardly an inconsiderable achievement.)

Primarily because of his collaborations with Middleton,
Rowley's style has received a fair share of attention and study,
so that a reasonably unambiguous picture of its main features
can be drawn.[8] Rowley, in some senses, can be regarded as the
opposite of his most frequent collaborator, Middleton: Rowley is romantic and affirmative in his overall outlook, and his
viewpoint is that of the common people; his work tends to be
simple and unsophisticated, straightforward and vigorous. His
verse is often perfunctory and sometimes very weak, though it
can also be rather good at times, as at some points in *The
Changeling*; he is more than just a hack.

Rowley's characterizations are mainly black-and-white figures without much depth or subtlety—but their interaction can be very energetic: his people argue with, spit at, and beat each other with alacrity. He has a passion for puns, especially for puns on place names; puns on the names of flowers are also common. He has a penchant for references to Wales and Welshmen, not always in a derogatory manner. (Whether this reveals something about his background—that he was perhaps a West Country man like Shakespeare—is impossible to say.) His dialogue is not infrequently distinguished by "cue-catching," the practice of linking speeches in a scene by shared words or phrases so that the actors effectively cue each other along—a sign of his practical stage experience.

Like most of his contemporary dramatists, Rowley tended to re-use materials—themes and ideas, plot elements and situations, specific phrases and words—from one work to another; his writings have an internal consistency that can reveal his presence in works of uncertain authorship. He likes to use large words and sometimes to coin his own; "Paracelsian" may have originated with him.[9] Classical allusions recur in his works, and Latin tags are not unknown; but his classical references are often present merely to supply a pun—he is not Jonsonian in this respect. (There is no record of Rowley's attendance at either of the universities; most scholars judge him to have been largely self-educated, with perhaps a grammar-school grounding in fundamentals—like Shakespeare, or indeed Jonson too.)

It is unsurprising that only one of Rowley's extant solo plays is a tragedy, and that comedy dominates his output: his skills as an actor and his personality as a writer both appear to have led him in that direction. It is important to remember, though, that Rowley was not exclusively a comedian; when studying his collaborative works, we should not assume that his contribution was solely or even primarily in the comic subplots. As D.M. Robb has noted, "In *The Travels of the Three English Brothers* (1607) it was Day, not Rowley, who supplied

the comic interest: Rowley commenced dramatist as a romantic, not a comic, playwright."[10] Other of Rowley's collaborations also show that he did not restrict his hand to clown parts
and comic scenes.

Recalling Schoenbaum's dictum about the need for "unchallenged dramatic writing, apart from collaborations," for an
author to be a fit candidate for attribution study, we must note
that there are three plays currently accepted as solo works by
Rowley: *A Shoemaker a Gentleman* (written ca. 1607-9; published 1638), *A New Wonder, a Woman Never Vexed* (ca. 1610;
1632), and *All's Lost by Lust* (1619; 1633). Three other works that
might well have been plays written by Rowley alone have not
survived: *Hymen's Holidays or Cupid's Vagaries* (1612), and *A
Knave in Print* and *The Fool Without Book* (both 1613).

Of the three extant solo plays by Rowley, one in particular
has great importance for the hypothesis of this essay. For *A
Shoemaker a Gentleman*, Rowley drew upon the first two sto-
ries in Thomas Deloney's collection *The Gentle Craft, Part
One* (1598); he created a play that blends the popular trades-
men comedy of works like Dekker's *The Shoemakers' Holiday* or
Heywood's *The Four Prentices of London* with the Christian
hagiography and martyrology of a work like Dekker's and
Massinger's *The Virgin Martyr*.[11] Most significantly for our
purposes, however, *A Shoemaker* shares plot materials with
Shakespeare's *Cymbeline*, a play dating from the same era, ca.
1609. In both plays, we find two brothers, sons of an English
king of the Roman period, who live disguised in humble circumstances under assumed names, and who help lead the English army to a great victory in a battle that appeared lost before
their intervention. (It is an open question as to whether Rowley was influenced by Shakespeare's play, or vice versa; we
have no way at present of determining the relative priority between the two plays with any degree of certainty.) It is a piece
of marvelous luck that *Merlin* also contains some of the same
materials, so that the treatment of the common elements in

Merlin can be compared with Rowley's work in *A Shoemaker* on the one hand, and Shakespeare's in *Cymbeline* on the other. I hope to show that this comparison helps to demonstrate Shakespeare's hand in *Merlin*. Rowley's *A Shoemaker* is further useful in that it shares other materials with *Merlin*: the Winifred subplot in Rowley's play has clear affinities with the Modestia subplot in *Merlin*. Yet here again, I will argue that the treatment of the common material in *Merlin* shows Shakespearean aspects that are absent from Rowley's play, and that comprise solid evidence of Shakespeare's contribution.

When discussing Rowley's solo plays, there is one other work that demands examination. *A Match at Midnight* is thought to have been written ca. 1622; it was first printed in 1633 as the work of "W.R.," who was identified as Rowley in Edward Archer's play list of 1656. Nineteenth-century scholars generally accepted this attribution at face value; but Cyrus Hoy, in his textual analysis of the Fletcher canon and related plays, suggested that Rowley was not the sole author, since the play's textual profile differed substantially from the norm of Rowley's other plays, especially in its frequent use of "ye" for "you."[12] Later scholars have gone further than Hoy: Stephen Blase Young, in his 1980 edition of *A Match at Midnight*, uses the textual evidence to cast doubt on a wide range of potential candidates; he considers, and rejects, Rowley, Middleton, Fletcher, Field, Ford, Shirley, Sharpham, Dekker, Davenport, Marston, Munday, and Robert Armin, and concludes that "The question of authorship remains undetermined."[13]

I think that the case is not so severely occluded as this, however; textual analysis can be confusing and misleading when three or more writers combine in a single play, and this seems to be the case with *A Match at Midnight*. Rowley, I would say, is certainly present, most clearly in the character of Tim Bloodhound. Tim shows many signs of being a typical Rowleian clown; he is a fat clown, judging from his joke about breaking his girdle at I,i,126. (Falstaff, another writer's fat clown charac-

ter, makes the same joke in *1 Henry IV*, III,iii,151.) Much of the
material about Tim's eating and fasting (I,i,8-11 and 211-21, etc.)
makes sense for a fat-clown character. Tim and his servant Sim
have the same kind of relationship that Chough and Trimtram
have in *A Fair Quarrel*, and that Sancho and Soto have in *The
Spanish Gypsy*. Sim is eager to take advantage of any amorous
opportunity that comes through his place as a servant (I,i,120),
just as Trimtram is (*Fair Quarrel*, II,ii,110-11). Tim's father,
Old Bloodhound, has the same kind of relationship with Sim
as Alibius has with Lollio in Rowley's share of *The Changeling*.
(The wordplay on "Ancient Young" in *Match*, I,iii,76-9 is reminiscent of the "old Lollio" wordplay in *Changeling*, I,ii,19-20.)
There is a place-name pun on "Theeving lane" in *Match*,
I,iii,13; the same pun occurs in *Witch of Edmonton*, V,i,199, in
the part of Cuddy Banks, the clown character who shows
many Rowleian traits. "Here was Good Finne the fish-woman
fetcht home her Ring last night," in *Match*, I,i,12-13, echoes the
episode of finding the ring in the salmon in *New Wonder*,
I,ii,121-72; the courting banter between Moll Bloodhound and
Ancient Young in *Match*, I,iii,141-59 parallels that of Robert
Foster and Jane Bruyne in *New Wonder*, III,i,191-222 in
brusqueness and bawdiness.

For relevance to *Merlin*, we can note "If she be quick, shee's
with child, whosoever got it, you must father it" in *Match*,
I,iii,39-40; for the mentions of Sir Nicholas Nemo in *Match*,
IV,iii,45-6 and V,ii,28, "Nemo" being Latin for "nobody,"
compare the character of Sir Nichodemus Nothing in *Merlin*,
III,i.[14] Some of the textual features in *Match*, like "'snailes"
(I,i,37) or "the to'ther" (II,iii,99) among others, also suggest
Rowley. A full inquiry into all the evidence of Rowley's hand
in *Match at Midnight* would take us far away from the main
focus of this study; my point is simply that the play does indeed belong on a list of Rowley's collaborative works, though
it should not be grouped among his solo plays.

I agree, furthermore, with earlier commentators like Fleay

and Bullen who saw Middleton's hand in *Match*; there are significant links between *Match* and several of Middleton's plays, like *A Chaste Maid in Cheapside*, *Michaelmas Term*, and *The Puritan*, and a range of specific stylistic and textual features suggestive of his manner. Indeed, *Match* has many connections with *Wit at Several Weapons* and *The Old Law*, the plays that Middleton and Rowley are thought to have written with the involvement of third collaborators (Fletcher and Massinger, respectively). *Match* and *Wit* are almost alternative versions of the same plot: both plays focus on an old hellion father and a young hellion son (Old Bloodhound and Alexander; Sir Perfidious Oldcraft and Witty-pate), supplemented with a collection of more openly larcenous rogues (Captain Carvegut and Lieutenant Bottom; Sir Ruinous Gentry and company) and an array of clowns (Tim, Sim, and Randall; Mr. Credulous, Sir Gregory Fopp, and Pompey Doodle). The garish and extreme food-and-eating imagery that is such a striking element in *Wit* can be found in *Match*, II,iii,144-6.[15] Characters in *Match* calculate their ages down to the month and day (I,i,138-40; II,ii,55-6) just as characters in *The Old Law* do; all three plays are concerned with radically aggressive and competitive father-son relationships. Here again, the evidence for Middleton's participation in the authorship of *A Match at Midnight* could be pursued much further, but only through a long digression and a major detour from our primary subject; my goal here is merely to place *Match at Midnight* in some perspective in Rowley's canon. For the purposes of this study, I would classify *Match* as another play that Middleton and Rowley wrote with one or more other (as yet unidentified) collaborators.

This brief discussion of *A Match at Midnight* provides a good illustration of some of the difficulties inherent in the definition of Rowley's canon. Some other examples may be worth noting too. One of the plays from Rowley's era that is no longer extant, that has survived only as a title in the records, is *A Late Murder of the Son Upon the Mother, or Keep the Widow*

Waking. This play was licensed by the Master of the Revels in September of 1624 as "Written by Forde, and Webster," and such entries in the Revels accounts are normally regarded as solid evidence of authorship. In the case of *Keep the Widow Waking*, however, documents relating to a suit involving the play have been preserved in the Public Records Office, documents that include Thomas Dekker's testimony that the play was actually written by Dekker, Ford, Webster, and Rowley in a four-way collaboration.[16] It is entirely possible that other plays, extant works as well as lost ones, may have contributions from Rowley's pen that are not reflected in the external evidence.

One such play may be *Wit Without Money*, one of the works of the Beaumont-Fletcher canon traditionally assigned to Fletcher alone. Cyrus Hoy, after examining the play's textual profile, decided that the surviving text of *Wit Without Money* was another writer's revision of a Fletcherian original. This view has received some acceptance: Baldwin Maxwell dated the authorship of the original to 1614 and the revision to 1619.[17] To the best of my knowledge, no one has suggested Rowley as a candidate for the reviser of *Wit Without Money*—yet the play offers several hints of Rowley's presence, mostly, and appropriately, in the comedy materials involving the clown character Shorthose. In V,i,20-1, Shorthose says, "This morning-prayer has brought me into a consumption; / I have nothing left but flesh and bones about me." This is one of Rowley's standard fat-clown jokes; compare "I am even pin'd away with fretting, there's nothing but flesh and bones about me" in *Merlin*, III,i,188-90 (spoken, naturally, by the Clown).

There are other indications that Shorthose is a fat clown in the Rowleian mold: references to his sweating occur more than once. Consider his lines in IV,v,14-16: "Fie, how I sweat / Under this pile of beef! an elephant / Can do no more." Rowley's clowns also have a marked tendency to "bawl"—Bustopha in *The Maid in the Mill*, II,ii ("dost thou bawl? ... my

Sister bawls, and I bawl," etc.) being probably the extreme example. (Apparently, extravagant crying and exclaiming was a
not-insignificant part of Rowley's stage persona.) In *Wit
Without Money*, IV,iv,3-4, Lady Heartwell calls Shorthose "you
blown pudding, you bawling rogue," to which the clown replies, "I bawl as loud as I can." The lines in II,iii,53 and 66, "Do
not fright him . . . Cry not," also seem to indicate some "bawling" behavior on Shorthose's part. Some of the jokes of
Shorthose and his companions have parallels in Rowley's un-
doubted works; to cite only one example, Shorthose's "birds'
nests . . . bush-beard" joke in II,iv,87-8 is paralleled in both
New Wonder, IV,i,81-2 ("we have stood beating the Bush and
the bird's flowne away") and *Witch of Edmonton*, I,ii,74-5
("beats the bush . . . bird is flown")—all three usages being in
courting contexts. And in light of the preceding paragraph, it
is interesting to note the "Widow, I'll keep you waking" in
V,iv,51. Rowley may well have revised Fletcher's original in order to adapt the comic parts to his own special gifts. Are we
then justified in adding *Wit Without Money* to the roster of
Rowley's plays? I would say no; the Rowleian features, while
suggestive, are far from conclusive—and that is the point.

There are many plays in which individual scholars have seen
Rowley's hand, plays that have been assigned to him on
stronger or weaker grounds—Robb puts the count at over fif-
ty. In all probability, it will be permanently impossible to ar-
rive at a full tally of Rowley's dramatic output. The plays on
the list that follows are those that are most generally and least
ambiguously assigned to him, likely comprising only a small
portion of his total canon—and critical opinion is far from
unanimous even on these works, so that choices must be
made. My ascription of *Merlin* to Shakespeare and Rowley
may be premature at this point, though I hope to justify it in
ensuing chapters.

Another open case occurs with *The Spanish Gypsy*: this play
was first printed in 1653 as a Middleton-Rowley collaboration,

but its problematical style has led modern scholars to dispute the original attribution in favor of the claims of Dekker and Ford. David Lake, in his survey of the Middleton canon, argues strongly for Dekker and Ford, and deduces the absence of both Middleton and Rowley on the basis of the play's textual evidence.[18] While the verdict concerning the absence of Middleton appears well justified, there is, as Norman Brittin has observed, significant stylistic evidence of a Rowleian contribution in the clown parts.[19] Sancho and Soto in *Spanish Gypsy* are pale reiterations of Chough and Trimtram from *Fair Quarrel* (note Sancho's "Trim, tram, hang master, hang man" in IV,iii,74), and possess many common features with other Rowleian clowns (Soto is even called "Lollio" in IV,ii,80-6). *The Spanish Gypsy* was written in 1623, during a period when Dekker, Ford, and Rowley are known to have worked together: they wrote *The Witch of Edmonton* in 1621, and combined with Webster on *Keep the Widow Waking* in 1624. The critical consensus recognizes a Rowleian contribution to *Witch*, most prominently in the part of the clown character Cuddy Banks; yet the textual evidence for Rowley's presence in that play is slim—Lake sums it up as "two instances of *Tush* and one *'um* for *'em*."[20] The absence of such evidence from *Spanish Gypsy* is not weighty enough, I don't think, to counter the external and the stylistic evidence of Rowley's presence. On that basis, I have included *Spanish Gypsy* among Rowley's known works.

What we might call the core canon of Rowley's dramatic career, then, can be listed this way (dates of authorship are often approximations; dates of first publication follow in parentheses):

1. *The Travels of the Three English Brothers*, with Day and Wilkins, 1607 (1607).
2. *Fortune by Land and Sea*, with Heywood, 1608 (1655).
3. *A Shoemaker a Gentleman*, 1608 (1638).
4. *A New Wonder, a Woman Never Vexed*, 1610 (1632).

5. *Wit at Several Weapons*, with Middleton and Fletcher, 1613 (1647).
6. *The Birth of Merlin*, with Shakespeare, 1613-15 (1662).
7. *The Old Law*, with Middleton and Massinger, 1614-18 (1656).
8. *A Fair Quarrel*, with Middleton, 1616 (1617).
9. *All's Lost by Lust*, 1619 (1633).
10. *The World Tossed at Tennis*, with Middleton, 1620 (1620).
11. *The Witch of Edmonton*, with Dekker and Ford, "&c.," 1621 (1658).[21]
12. *The Changeling*, with Middleton, 1622 (1653).
13. *A Match at Midnight*, with Middleton and one or more others?, 1622 (1633).
14. *The Maid in the Mill*, with Fletcher, 1623 (1647).
15. *The Spanish Gypsy*, with Dekker and Ford, 1623 (1653).
16. *A Cure for a Cuckold*, with Webster, 1625 (1661).

As mentioned earlier, there are caveats to be made even to such a conservative list as this. Most crucially, some scholars have argued that Heywood is present in the later scenes of *New Wonder* (IV,i and after).[22] If true—and the evidence is significant—this would further limit the extent of Rowley's unassisted dramatic work. Many critics have found it difficult to find signs of Fletcher's hand in *Wit at Several Weapons*, or Massinger's in *The Old Law*, and have tended to interpret these plays simply as two more Middleton-Rowley collaborations.[23] I think it is wise to be cautious about such judgments; when three or more playwrights combine in a single work, the result is almost guaranteed to be complex and deceptive (as in *A Match at Midnight*).

It is hard to generalize about Rowley as a collaborator. He wrote significant portions of the main plots of *The Changeling*, *The Maid in the Mill*, and *A Fair Quarrel*. In the first two of these plays Rowley is responsible for roughly half of the final whole, while in the third he produced almost two-thirds of the play. In these three plays, the textual evidence reveals a fairly clear dichotomy between the shares of Rowley and his co-worker; in *Fortune by Land and Sea*, in contrast, the shares of Rowley and Heywood are difficult to disentangle—that play may be another intimate collaboration. In a few other cases, scholars have cut up a play between collaborators in schemes that are not entirely convincing.

The above list appears to show an alternation between periods of intenser dramatic composition (1623, for example) with relatively fallow periods (say, 1617-18)—though this is likely an illusion founded in the uneven survival of his works. Like other men who wrote to supply the popular companies' constant need for new material (Dekker, Heywood, Fletcher, Munday, Chettle, many others), he was probably a frequent and regular author, especially in collaborative efforts.

We should note that Rowley did not necessarily restrict his activity as a playwright to the company with which he was acting at any given time: in 1624 he was a member of the King's Men, and in August of that year was playing the Fat Bishop in their sensational Globe production of Middleton's *A Game at Chess*—yet in the same year he joined with Dekker and company to write *Keep the Widow Waking* for the Red Bull Theatre. This has obvious relevance to the case of *Merlin*: the fact that Shakespeare and Rowley were connected with rival companies during the overlapping period in their careers does not, in and of itself, mean that they wouldn't have, couldn't have collaborated together.

The rich variety of collaborative effort in Rowley's canon can be tremendously helpful to us in understanding the authorship of *Merlin*. One clear lesson it teaches is that writers with distinctive individual styles tend to work in those styles even in collaboration. In *The Changeling*, for instance, we find both Middleton's and Rowley's styles; we do not bother to wonder if Rowley might have written the play alone, imitating Middleton's style in the main plot—or, conversely, if Middleton might have written the play alone, imitating Rowley in the Rowleian portions. Rather, we accept the self-evident conclusion that the play is precisely what the external attribution says it is, a Middleton-Rowley collaboration. The observation that Middleton's style is not manifested in *The Spanish Gypsy*, but that Dekker's and Ford's styles are, tells us much about the authorship of that play. We can note too that Middleton and Rowley collaborated at least five times over a decade, but that neither man's style nor approach to drama "rubbed off" on the other to any perceptible degree. We see, in short, strong stylistic consistencies.

This is not to imply that there are no traces of influence in Rowley's work—of course there are. In *All's Lost by Lust*, for example, the character Fydella probably owes something to the precedent of Zanche in Webster's *White Devil* (1612)— both are Moorish servingmaids who help their mistresses commit murders. The ghostly procession seen by Roderick in V,ii of Rowley's tragedy resembles the spectral procession in IV,i of *MacBeth*. In comparing *Merlin* both to Shakespeare's works and to Rowley's, we do get a sense that the act of collaboration brought some slight Shakespearean influences into Rowley's work, that Rowley in effect picked up a few things from Shakespeare through the experience of working with him. Yet these few features are not enough to negate the overall stylistic consistency of Rowley's work. When we survey *Merlin* in detail, we naturally do find many points of commonality with Rowley's style as displayed in his other works; these Rowleian features are blatant confirmation of Rowley's authorial contribution to the play. Simultaneously, we find many features that are quite unlike anything in Rowley's works, but strongly suggestive of Shakespeare; and by the same standard of evidence and reasoning, these Shakespearean elements constitute legitimate signs of Shakespeare's authorial contribution.

In the chapters that follow, I do not intend to exhaust the internal evidence of Rowley's contribution to *Merlin*; I plan

only to cite enough Rowleian features to show how Rowley's
share in the play intermingles and blends with Shakespeare's.
The reason for this choice should be obvious: Rowley's participation in the play's composition is not in doubt. Yet suppose
for a moment that someone were to dispute Rowley's hand in
Merlin; it would be easy to demonstrate the truth of Rowley's
part-authorship, by citing the abundant internal evidence in
Merlin that confirms the external attribution to him. The same
would be true if this hypothetical rejection of Rowley's claim
were not the mistake of an individual, but rather an expression
of consensus opinion; the evidence of the play would still
stand as valid. All this may seem to be too obvious to merit
mention—yet these same points are as sound when applied to
Shakespeare as to Rowley. Along with its Rowleian features,
The Birth of Merlin reveals many specific, detailed, subtle, complex, distinctive Shakespearean elements, far beyond anything
that can be explained away as influence or imitation—as we
shall see.[24]

CHAPTER III

Textual Evidence

BEFORE TURNING our attention to *The Birth of Merlin* as a literary work in the traditional sense—before considering its form, subject, style, plot or characters or themes—it will be well to follow Schoenbaum's fourth guideline for attribution studies, and address the play as a "text" that contains textual evidence of its authorship. Twentieth-century scholars have welcomed the development of textual analysis as an unambiguous, quantifiable alternative to the uncertainties and inevitable subjectivities of stylistic evidence. While an author's style is largely conscious and overt, and susceptible to alteration via influence and imitation and various other factors, the same author's "accidentals"—his preferences in orthographic and contractional forms, in linguistic choices such as "has/hath," "does/doth," etc., in expletives and oaths and similar parts of speech—are seen as largely unconscious and habitual, immune to deliberate alteration, and constant over time.

It is indisputably true that textual analysis has proven extremely useful in the study of English Renaissance dramatic authorship; it is also true, though, that textual analysis has limitations and can be used unsuccessfully—it is not quite the skeleton key to unlock the secrets of Elizabethan drama that some of its practitioners have hoped for. Textual analyses have been most valuable in cases where two writers with readily distinguishable textual habits (Middleton and Rowley, for example) join in collaborative works, or where a single writer possesses a textual profile so individual that it sets him apart from all of his contemporaries (John Fletcher being the extreme case in this respect). Conversely, when the writers involved do not have distinctly different textual preferences, when the amount of evidence is limited, or when three or more writers combine in a single project, textual analysis becomes much more problematical. Proving the absence of a writer through textual analysis can be particularly risky; as noted in the previous chapter, I find that attempts to deny Rowley's hand in *The Spanish Gypsy* and *A Match at Midnight* purely on textual grounds are contradicted by the totality of the evidence in these cases.

The potential problems and limitations involved in the use of textual evidence have been recognized by some leading advocates of the technique. As Cyrus Hoy has written, "The value to be attached to any body of linguistic criteria is, in the end, completely relative: all depends upon the degree of divergence between the linguistic patterns that are to be distinguished."[1] In the case of *Merlin*, the external evidence involves two dramatists whose textual patterns show relatively little divergence, which complicates the application of textual analysis to this play. To quote Hoy once again, "Shakespeare uses no language forms which, either in themselves or by virtue of their rate of occurrence, can serve to point immediately and unmistakably to his presence in a play of doubtful authorship."[2]

The same point can be made about Rowley; neither man compares with Fletcher in the distinctiveness of his textual habits. The canons of both men show that we need to be cautious when assuming that their textual preferences are reliably consistent. In two of Rowley's three solo plays, *All's Lost by Lust* and *A New Wonder, a Woman Never Vexed*, the contractional form "y'are" is used to the exclusion of the alternative "you're"; in the third, *A Shoemaker a Gentleman*, "you're" is used to the exclusion of "y'are." If Rowley's three lost solo plays had survived, what other divergences of this type might they show?

There are points in the Middleton-Rowley collaborations where scenes that are usually assigned to Rowley display un-Rowleian textual features; to cite one example, there are two instances of the oath "'slid," atypical of Rowley, in the scenes in *Wit at Several Weapons* that Lake ascribes to Rowley. Does this show that Middleton had some input in Rowley's scenes—or does it show that Rowley could vary his "normal" preferences, as Lake suggests?[3] In a canon like Rowley's, in which solo works are vastly outnumbered by collaborative efforts, we have to wonder how accurate a textual profile we can define.

A writer's textual preferences can also change over time. Throughout his works, Shakespeare shows a consistent preference for "doth" over "does"—until, that is, we reach his final works. In *The Winter's Tale*, instances of "does" outnumber those of "doth" by twenty-three to seven, as they do in *The Tempest*, fifteen to thirteen. The late collaborations with Fletcher show similar proportions; even when we rely on the most conservative estimations of Shakespeare's hand in *Henry VIII* and *The Two Noble Kinsmen*, we find this same atypical preference for "does" over "doth."

There are some textual features relevant to the study of *Merlin*, elements like "'slid" and "pish," that almost never occur in Shakespeare's works—except on those rare occasions when they *do* appear. This touches upon a key problem in textual analysis: textual features have meaning as evidence only when they accumulate in meaningful patterns; single features can always be anomalous usages by any writer.

Indeed, it is possible to question the appropriateness of *any* textual study of *Merlin*. Samuel Schoenbaum has objected that tests of textual evidence "are of no use at all when the several writers have pooled their talents in intimate collaboration."[4] I argue that the stylistic evidence of the play shows that *Merlin* is precisely this kind of intimate collaboration. Nonetheless, I think that a textual survey can serve some purpose in the case of *Merlin*—it can have a supportive, if not a determinative, function. Some commentators have suggested Middleton and Beaumont and Fletcher as possible collaborators in the play; others simply assign the play to Rowley alone. I will argue that the textual indices in *Merlin* point away from all of these possibilities. If they do not offer strong evidence of Shakespeare's hand in the play, they do tend to support rather than contradict the attribution of the external evidence.

Shakespeare's linguistic and textual preferences are well known, and easily determined, checked, and confirmed with the aid of a concordance. Rowley's preferences coincide with Shakespeare's in many respects.[5] Both men use "I am" rather than "I'm," "'tis" rather than "it's," "i'th'" rather than "i'the," and "y'are" rather than "you're"; both men use "ye" and "'em" relatively rarely in comparison with some of their contemporaries. All of these preferences are reflected in *Merlin*, as the following table shows.

There are thirty-three instances of "I am" in the play, against none of "I'm"; there are forty-two instances of "'tis," against none of "it's"; there are 290 uses of "you" but only sixteen of "ye," and twenty-one of "them" but only three of "'em." (Rowley's occasional use of the spelling of "'um" for "'em" has been useful in delineating his hand in some of his collaborative efforts; but since "'um" is wholly absent from two of his three solo plays, its similar absence from *Merlin* tells us nothing.)

The proportion of "yes" to "ay" ("I") in the play, twenty-seven to eleven, is surprising at first, since both Shakespeare and Rowley generally favor "ay" over "yes"; yet in one of Rowley's plays, *All's Lost*, instances of "yes" outnumber those of "ay" ten to nine, as they do in one of Shakespeare's, *Much Ado About Nothing*, six to one. So it can be said that the "yes/ay" ratio in *Merlin* is within the observable range of usage of both playwrights. (And this is another reminder of the variability of textual preferences.) There are two uses of "y'are" in *Merlin* (III,vi,132 and V,ii,37) but none of "you're," which is what we would expect from either man. There are eleven instances of "i'th'" in the play, and five of "on't,"[6] comparable to the normal usage patterns of both playwrights. The domi-

Textual Analysis of The Birth of Merlin, *by scenes*

	HAS/HATH	DOES/DOTH	THEM/'EM	I AM	'TIS	"I"/YES	YOU/YE
I,i	3/0		2/0	1	2	1/0	13/0
I,ii	0/2	0/1	4/0	2	6	0/1	16/0
II,i	4/2		1/1	10	2	1/2	37/3
II,ii	2/0	1/0	1/0			0/1	16/1
II,iii	4/2	0/1	1/0	1	13	1/4	13/1
III,i	3/0		1/2	6		2/2	28/0
III,ii	0/1			3	2		28/2
III,iii			1/0				4/0
III,iv	2/0	1/0		1		0/4	27/1
III,v	0/2						
III,vi	1/0	2/0	3/0	1	6	1/1	30/0
IV,1	1/1	0/1	1/0	3	5	3/7	43/8
IV,ii				1			2/0
IV,iii						0/1	
IV,iv			2/0				
IV,v	1/3	2/0		1	2	0/2	9/0
V,i				3		0/1	12/0
V,ii	1/1	1/0	4/0	1	3	2/1	12/0
Totals	22/14	7/3	21/3	33	42	11/27	290/16

nance of "does" over "doth" is typical of Rowley, and would be logical in a late Shakespearean work as well.

There are particulars in which Rowley's textual habits do differ from Shakespeare's; and *Merlin* shows us some interesting things concerning them. The preference for "has" over "hath" is typical of Rowley, and reflected in each of his solo plays; Shakespeare's preference for "hath" is consistent throughout his works. The words "Th'art" (I,ii,199, II,iii,227, III,v,29, and IV,i,105) and "'sfoot" (I,i,67, II,i,35 and 199 and 205) occur in frequencies that suggest Rowley rather than Shakespeare; the word "Th'ast" (III,ii,16) also points to Rowley—Rowley uses it repeatedly, Shakespeare never does. Conversely, the exclamations employed in *Merlin* lie beyond Rowley's normal range: the play contains one use of "tush" (III,i,41), two of "pish" (I,ii,94 and IV,i,222), and one of "push" (III,i,136). Rowley, in his solo works and in the best-authenticated parts of his collaborations, uses "tush" and "tut" exclusively. Shakespeare also prefers "tush" and "tut," though he will occasionally use "pish" (twice each in *Henry V* and *Othello*), or "pah" (once in *Hamlet*, twice in *Lear*), or "puh" (once only, in *Hamlet*). There is also an instance of "push" in *Timon*; this may be a nonce use by Shakespeare, or it may be a sign of Middleton's hand in that play—again, the interpretation of single textual elements is intrinsically doubtful. (*Merlin* also contains a "phu" at IV,v,84, which might be a misprint for "puh," or else a variant spelling for Rowley's "phew" or Shakespeare's "foh.") Overall, it seems unlikely that Rowley alone would have generated this pattern of exclamations.

There is a scattering of other oaths, exclamations, and contractions in the play that tell us little. There is one use of "'sdeath" in I,ii,90, a word that is found once in Rowley's solo plays and once in Shakespeare's too. The instance of "t'other" in V,ii,6 might point toward Rowley; Shakespeare prefers "th'other," while Rowley uses both forms. The play contains two instances of "th'infernal" (III,iii,23 and V,i,47), a word that also appears in *2 Henry IV*, II,iv,157 and in *Titus Androni-cus*, V,ii,30. It has been observed that "Shakespeare frequently uses a verb in *-s* with a noun that is plural in form"[7]—as in "Virtue's steely bones / Looks bleak i'th' cold wind" in *All's Well That Ends Well*, I,i,103-4, or as in "As knots . . . Infects the sound pine" in *Troilus and Cressida*, I,iii,7-8. *Merlin* reveals an ample supply of these plurals: "All crosses feeds both his spleen and his impatience," II,ii,18; "temperate minds / Covets that health," II,iii,18-19; "burning Tapers makes false Ware seem right," III,ii,90, etc. Yet we must also note that such plurals are common in Rowley's works too: "good faces as faces goes now a dayes" and "Why weepes those boyes?" in *A Shoemaker*, I,ii,72-3 and 132, etc. Many other features in the play are also common to both men, and to other writers of the era as well.

The textual profile of *Merlin* certainly does not "prove" that the play is a Shakespeare-Rowley collaboration—but it does tend to support rather than refute that attribution. It is also important to realize that the textual evidence in the play tends to contradict hypotheses of other playwrights' participation in the play's authorship, hypotheses that have been advanced by previous commentators. Beaumont and Fletcher have been connected with the play, primarily through the common mate-rials shared by *Merlin* and their play *Cupid's Revenge*. These common materials will be considered in Chapter VI; for the moment, we should note that the paucity of the primary Fletcherian discriminators "ye" and "'em" and the lack of Fletcher's distinctive prosody in *Merlin* make it extremely un-likely for his hand to be present.

A stronger case has been made for Middleton. Middleton was first connected with *Merlin* by P.A. Daniel in 1884;[8] early critics like F.G. Fleay and F.A. Howe accepted the idea of the play as a Middleton-Rowley work, though the attribution nev-er won general currency through a lack of sound evidence. (David Lake does not bother to consider *Merlin* in his survey of attribution problems in the Middleton canon.) Recently, though, Donald Foster has raised the possibility of Middleton's hand in the play once again; he cites the following features in *Merlin* as possible Middletonisms:

> ... the interjections "'slid," "law," and "push"; the phrases "spake on" (for "spoke of") and "talkt on" (for "gossip'd about"); "who's" for "who is it" and "'cause" for "because"; sentences ending in a rhetorical "tro?" (= "think you?"); and a marked preference for "has" over "hath." All these features are unusual or unknown in Shakespeare's works, and rare also in Rowley, but characteristic of Middleton.[9]

A good deal of qualification is necessary here, however. Rowley consistently prefers "has" over "hath" in his solo works, as David Lake has shown and as we have previously noted. (Interestingly, he evinces a preference for "hath" in some of his collaborations with Middleton—which yet again reminds us that a given author's textual habits are not always stable and predictable.) On other points, I think that Prof. Foster over-interprets some very minor features. Consider: the contraction "'cause" occurs three times in Rowley's *Shoemaker* (II,iii,73 and 80, and IV,i,100), and once in *All's Lost* (V,v,73), as well as eleven times in Shakespeare's acknowledged works. The word "law" occurs as an exclamation in *Fair Quarrel*, I,i,182 and V,i,190 (Rowley's portion), and in *Love's Labor's Lost*, V,ii,414, *Pericles*, IV,i,76, *2 Henry IV*, II,iv,26, and *Henry V*, III,ii,88 and 92 and 113, and IV,vii,143. A use of "troe" occurs at the end of a sentence in *Shoemaker*, IV,i,172, with a "troe yee" in IV,i,234 of the same play. The use of "who's" in *Merlin* appears in the line "who's that talks so?" (III,i,211); this phrase can be interpreted reasonably as meaning "who is that who talks so?"—and similar elisions of "who" and "that" and "which" are common in *Merlin* ("What's that we did conclude," I,ii,93, etc.), in Rowley's works, and in Jacobean English generally. (Also, we can observe that instances of "law," "tro," and "'slid" occur in the scenes in *Wit at Several Weapons* that Lake assigns to Rowley.)

The best argument against the idea that the features cited by Prof. Foster are evidence for Middleton is that they occur in the comedy subplot, especially in the speeches of the Clown. The Clown speaks all four instances of "'slid" (III,i,7 and 156 and 211, and III,iv,59), plus the single instances of "Law, law" (II,i,87), "spake on" (II,i,124), "'cause" (III,i,67), "who's" (III,i,211), and "talkt on" (III,iv,124), and both instances of "tro" (II,i,219 and III,i,181). Sir Nichodemus Nothing, another character in the comic subplot, has the single use of "push" (III,i,136). In Middleton's and Rowley's collaborative plays,

ERRATUM

Page 50, line 21:
for "eleven times" read "twice"

writes the comedy materials;[10] the distri- posedly Middletonian textual features is f what we could logically expect in a lay. We shall see in the following chapter eches are rich in Rowleian traits, as we o be. Middleton's characteristic pattern of "I've," "y'ad," "y'ave," "we're," "w'are," c.) is totally absent from the play, as are s," "snigs," "lin," etc.) that Lake identifies the larger scale of the play's subject mat- racterizations, etc., there is similarly little ; it is not surprising that *Merlin* is omit- -ranging study of attribution problems in

 a response to authorship questions has ad and well-accepted that some current nally neglect the basic, necessary cautions ted earlier, Shakespeare departs from his normal preferences for "tut" and "tush" in a few of his plays, to employ alternatives like "pish" and "puh." Both of these words are far more common with Middleton than Shake-speare; should we, then, suppose that Middleton had a hand in *Henry V* and *Othello* and *Hamlet* and *Lear*? Most people, I think, can see the error in placing too much emphasis on a few unrepresentative textual elements. Reading Middleton into *Merlin* on the basis of the textual features listed by Prof. Foster is like reading Rowley out of *A Match at Midnight* and *The Spanish Gypsy*: too sweeping a conclusion is drawn from too limited a sampling of the evidence.

Before leaving the subject of Middleton (for the present), we should consider the relationship between *Merlin* and *Hengist, King of Kent, or The Mayor of Queenborough*. Commonalities between these two plays were cited in a 1906 study by F.A. Howe as evidence that Middleton helped write *Merlin*.[11] While a few of these links are worth noting (and will be so noted in Chapter IV), most of the connections pointed out by Howe are, in my judgment, insubstantial and ephemeral. To say, for instance, that Amselme the Hermit in *Merlin* and Constantius in *Hengist* resemble each other "in many respects," as Howe does, is to make a very strained comparison. Anselme is consistently portrayed as an entirely admirable character, a man of genuine and serious spiritual attainment, while Constantius is a superstitious weakling, the butt of Vortiger's political manipulations. The differences between the two characters are far more substantive than the similarities.

Other of Howe's linkages have the same liability: to say that in *Hengist* "Raynulph acts as Chorus to hasten the action" while in *Merlin* "Merlin serves that purpose, by means of his supernatural knowledge revealing distant events" is to draw a wholly artificial parallel (Merlin is not a Chorus; Raynulph is neither a magician nor in any other way like Merlin). The relationship that does exist between the two plays is best explained as an act of imitation on Middleton's part. *Hengist*, written ca. 1616-20, followed *Merlin* by a few years; if *Merlin* was written in 1615 as I suspect (see Chapter VI), and *Hengist* in 1616, the connection of chronology and influence could be very close.

How can we differentiate between connections based on

imitation and those based on authorship? There are elements in *Merlin* that link it to *Hengist*, but not to Middleton's canon as a whole; and such linkages between specific individual plays are best explained as imitation or influence or other derivative relationships. We shall see another example of this phenomenon when we consider the common features in *Merlin* and *Cupid's Revenge* in Chapter VI. Authorial connections, conversely, tend to unite a play with the whole of the author's output. This is the pattern that the Rowleian elements in *Merlin* display: while the commonalities with *A Shoemaker a Gentleman* are notably strong and frequent, the play also shows relationships with the entire range of Rowley's dramatic composition. The Shakespearean elements in *Merlin* show the same broad pattern: while the commonalities with the late romances are especially noticeable, they are accompanied by connections that extend throughout the acknowledged Shakespearean canon. This contrast, of interrelationships with the entire canons of Rowley and Shakespeare on the one hand and with single plays by Middleton and by Beaumont and Fletcher on the other, is, I think, plain and self-evident; I argue that the former are indicative of common authorship while the latter are due to other derivative forms of connection. (Of course, this view is in consonance with much of consensus scholarship and criticism; the hypotheses that *Merlin* is either a Middleton-Rowley play or a Beaumont-Fletcher-Rowley play have not won general acceptance. To the best of my knowledge, no one has gone to the extreme of suggesting that *Merlin* might have been written by Beaumont, Fletcher, Middleton, and Rowley altogether; yet a failure to distinguish between authorial and non-authorial commonalities could easily lead to that extreme.)

CHAPTER IV

Stylistic Evidence

W HEN WE compare *The Birth of Merlin* to the works of both Rowley and Shakespeare, we find the kinds of resemblances and shared elements that indicate common authorship. The comedy materials in *Merlin* are particularly reminiscent of Rowley's work, and the play as a whole bears significant commonalities with his *A Shoemaker a Gentleman*. For Shakespeare, connections with *King Lear* and the late romances are most immediately apparent. (Such connections can interact in interesting ways, as we shall see when we consider the relationship between *Merlin*, *Shoemaker*, and *Cymbeline*.)

The presence in *Merlin* of a Duke of Gloster who has a son named Edwin, and the inclusion of a courtier named Oswold, inevitably remind us of the Gloucester, Edgar, Edmund, and Oswald in *Lear*. Such common names cannot, needless to say, stand as strong evidence of common authorship—though they do comprise one kind of feature that normally unites the works of a given author, as some critics have recognized.[1] (Fletcher re-uses names like Chilax and Leucippe, among others, in his plays; Shirley re-uses Fabio, Alphonso, Contarini, Depazzi, etc. For Shakespeare, there are Juliets in *Romeo and Juliet* and *Measure for Measure*, Claudios in *Measure for Measure* and *Much Ado About Nothing*, Rosalines, or -linds, in *As You Like It* and *Love's Labor's Lost* and *Romeo and Juliet*, etc., etc. Many examples from the works of other playwrights could be added.)

Donobert's rages at his daughters when they refuse to marry echo Lear's toward Goneril and Regan. Both *Merlin* and *Cymbeline* begin their action at the British Court, then shift to portray military combat in Wales, and return to England for their conclusions; in both plays the kingdom is threatened with invasion while members of the royal family are missing (in *Cymbeline*, the king's children; in *Merlin*, the king's brother). The king's wife is the principle villain in both. Both Anselme and Merlin are versions of the virtuous-magician figure that Shakespeare employs in his late plays, Cerimon in *Pericles* and most notably Prospero in *The Tempest*; the similarities between Merlin and Prospero are quite striking.[2]

Merlin utilizes the masque-like dramatic techniques that are a prominent feature in the late Shakespearean plays: the appearance of the Roman goddess Lucina and the Fates and the dance of spirits in III,iii of *Merlin* recall the appearance of Diana in *Pericles*, V,i; the masque of the ghosts and Jupiter in *Cymbeline*, V,iv; the masque of Juno, Ceres, and Iris in *Tempest*, IV,i; and the dance of spirits in *Henry VIII*, IV,ii.

The prophesying of Archbishop Cranmer on the glories of the coming reign in *Henry VIII* is similar to Merlin's in IV,v and V,ii. The sumptuous displays of theatrical pomp in *Merlin* (the processions in II,ii and III,ii; the contest of magic in II,iii; Merlin's fighting dragons in IV,i; his confrontation with his devil father in V,i; and the pageantry in V,ii) compare well with what we find in Shakespeare's final works (in *Tempest*, Prospero's magic, especially the banquet illusion in III,ii and the masque in IV,ii; in *Henry VIII*, the shepherd masquers in I,iv and the processions in II,i and iv, IV,i, and V,iv).

Clearly, these plays are expressions of the same lavishly visual style of theater production. And naturally there is more

than a question of style involved; the company for which
Merlin was written would have to have possessed the resources
to mount such a production—which points squarely to the
King's Men. Rowley's solo plays, written for companies of
more limited means, are correspondingly stingier with pomp:
Shoemaker offers the angel at Winifred's Well (I,iii), *All's Lost*
the spectral procession in the enchanted castle (V,ii)—and
little else.

A similar point can be made about the "special effects," if we
can use the term, that are required in *Merlin*, most notably the
prophetic meteor in IV,v. The Globe Theatre was famous for
its shooting-star effect, and the presence of this stage spectacle
in a play has sometimes been taken as evidence that the play in
question (*The Revenger's Tragedy* is a good example) was written for the King's Men.[3] Even if we accept the idea that *Merlin*
was intended for Shakespeare's company, it would not necessarily mean that Shakespeare helped to write it; yet these factors do have clear relevance for our comprehension of the play.

Merlin has other interesting features too. Structurally, the
play is a three-level hierarchy of the type analyzed so deftly by
Richard Levin in his *The Multiple Plot in English Renaissance
Drama*. On the first level, the characters of the main plot are
royal, and their concerns are those of statecraft and national
welfare; on the second level, the characters are aristocratic, and
their concerns are those of personal, emotional, or spiritual
fulfillment; and on the third level, the comic subplot, the characters are common and their concerns are largely sensual. Yet
Merlin has some interesting variants on the usual three-level
formula; it is in some ways a surprisingly innovative play. In a
typical three-level plot, the comic subplot is the least important; Levin uses the term "two-and-one-half-plot" plays to
refer to works in which characters "of the clownish sort" are
featured "in more or less isolated episodes rather than in a se-
quential line of action . . . it would be more accurate to speak
of it not as another plot, or fraction thereof, but as another

level of emotional tone or sensibility."[4] The reverse is true in *Merlin*, in which the third-level plot attains so much importance that it blends into the first-level plot toward the play's end. Merlin is a key character on the first level as well as the third. This integration of the most and least serious levels is original and innovative; the presence of extra-human characters, Merlin and his devil-father, frame the three levels of human experience with intimations of divine and infernal realms beyond.

A surprising fecundity and subtlety in the structure of *Merlin* is shown in its exploitation of triadic progressions of plot elements. There are three contests of magic in the play, arranged in an order of ascending intensity: in II,iii there is the confrontation between Anselme and the Saxon magician Proximus, who, at this point in the play, embody the cosmic opposites of good and evil; in IV,i Merlin meets and kills Proximus; and in V,i Merlin defeats his devil-father and confines him to the underworld. Interspersed with these contests of magic are three pastoral episodes: firstly, Uter's wandering in the forest and his encounter with the Clown and Joan Go-too't; secondly, Joan's retirement to the forest for Merlin's birth in III,iii-iv; and thirdly, the journey to Wales that occupies all of Act IV. Each of these "pastoral oases," to use David Young's phrase, fulfills to some miniature degree the pastoral sequence of "extrusion, sojourn, and return"; and the "normal curve of the pastoral, with the ceremonious defeat of the bad brother and the good brother's restoration to society,"[5] is realized through the conflict between Aurelius and Uter.

The blend of pastoral and spiritual elements in *Merlin* recalls the similar blending in *Cymbeline*, *Winter's Tale*, and *Tempest*, as well as in earlier plays like *A Midsummer Night's Dream* and *As You Like It* (the latter being the most blatantly pastoral of Shakespeare's pre-romance works, and the only one that includes the kind of theophany that characterizes the romances).[6] *Merlin* is neither a "pure" pastoral nor a particularly profound experiment in the genre; still, it makes something of the same kind of application of pastoral elements to political and social themes that we find in *Lear*. It may also be worth noting that William Empson, in his classic study *Some Versions of Pastoral*, considers *Henry IV* such a version, in that the contrasting worlds of Prince Hal's experience embody the essential court-country dichotomy of the pastoral form. Here again we see pastoral elements combining with magical-spiritual ones: in *1 Henry IV*, as in *Cymbeline* and *Merlin*, a journey to Wales means an encounter with the other-worldly and the occult.

It can be argued that such large-scale elements in *Merlin* are simply too general to count for much as evidence of authorship; and I certainly concede that much more is required to make a convincing case for Shakespeare's participation in the composition of *Merlin*. We should note, however, that the relationship between this play and Shakespeare's later works is unusually extensive and multifarious. There are not many Jacobean or Caroline plays that reveal clear and substantive debts to the late romances, and those that do—*Philaster*, let's say, with its links to *Cymbeline*, or *The Sea Voyage*, with its borrowing from *The Tempest*[7]—fail to show the range and multiplicity of connections with the late plays that *Merlin* possesses. Beyond these cited links to Shakespeare's final plays, *Merlin* contains a vast supply of subtler connections with the whole of Shakespeare's canon; that pattern of Shakespearean self-reference that distinguishes work from Shakespeare's pen is abundantly present. We can trace the relevant patterns of Rowley's and Shakespeare's hands through a scene-by-scene survey of the play.

Act I, Scene i

The opening scene of the play, in addition to setting up the main plot through second-hand report, introduces the characters of the Modestia subplot. As mentioned in Chapter II, the Modestia material in *Merlin* has many links with the Winifred plot in *A Shoemaker a Gentleman*. In III,i,56-60 of Rowley's play we find these lines spoken between Winifred and her suitor, Sir Hugh:

> *Winifred:* Be this the finall answer to your suite;
> If ever mortall man have attribute
> Of Winifreds Husband, 't shall be Sir Hugh,
> If it be debt to any 'tis your due.
> *Hugh:* A desperate debt, hopelesse of recovery.

Compare Modestia's "a desperate Game, indeed, this Marriage" in line 99 of the opening scene in *Merlin*, plus her words in lines 107-10:

> . . .let this mild Reply
> Give answer to your suit: for here I vow,
> If e're I change my Virgin name, by you
> It gains or looses.

Other, more minor parallels between the two scenes also exist: both suitors, Hugh and Edwin, speak of "my duty" (*Shoemaker*, III,i,40; *Merlin*, I,i,105); both women ask their suitors to cease their suits (*Shoemaker*, 63-8; *Merlin*, 111-12), and both men then exit. Such parallel scenes are often found in the works of a given dramatist, and are wholly unsurprising in plays credited to the same man by external evidence.

Similarly, there is an important structural and thematic link between this opening scene in *Merlin* and the second scene of *The Witch of Edmonton*. Both scenes portray two old men, one the father of a son, the other of two daughters; both daughters are being courted by young men, one of whom is the son of the first father. One daughter is content with her suitor, the other is not. Compare the characters from *Merlin*, I,i with those from *Witch*, I,ii:

Gloster / Old Thorney
Edwin / Frank Thorney
Donobert / Old Carter
Modestia / Susan
Constantia / Katherine
Cador / Somerton

The parallels are not exact, of course—the father's son is rejected as a suitor in *Merlin*, accepted in *Witch*; Susan prefers another man for a husband, not Modestia's commitment to spiritual chastity—but the commonalities are nonetheless quite striking. Both Old Carter and Donobert specify that their consent is conditional upon their daughters' likings (*Witch*, I,ii,38; *Merlin*, I,i,8-9, 43-4). *Witch* is the later play chronologically; it seems clear, then, that when Rowley and his collaborators sketched the plot of *Witch*, Rowley recalled and was influenced by a play he'd helped to write some years before.

Rowley's style is not as rich in distinctive phraseology as Shakespeare's; yet some of the more commonplace usages here in I,i share interesting contextual similarities with usages in Rowley's plays. Donobert, in a speech to his daughter's suitor, uses the phrase "Let it suffice" (43); Alderman Bruyne uses the same phrase while speaking to his daughter's suitors in *New Wonder*, III,i,2. Both fathers use the phrase to make the same point, that the suitors have the father's blessing so long as they can win the daughters' goodwill. (The laissez-faire attitudes of Rowleian fathers toward their daughters' marriages are very different from the attitudes of Shakespearean fathers.) For "My lord, you are a soldier" (30), compare "you are a soldier, sir" in *All's Lost*, I,ii,45, in a comparable love vs. war context. Various other small consistencies with Rowley's works can be found in this opening scene in *Merlin*; since Rowley's contribution to the play is not in dispute, my purpose is merely to illustrate his presence in this scene.

Yet if this initial scene in *Merlin* has the predictable common features with Rowley's plays, it also possesses elements that point away from Rowley and toward Shakespeare. If Modestia and Winifred share similarities, their differences are also noteworthy. Winifred, significantly, has no family, while Modestia has a father and a sister. They become involved in a constellation of intense emotions concerning the identities of daughters and fathers, and suitors and sons-in-law, that typifies Shakespearean drama—*The Taming of the Shrew* and *A Midsummer Night's Dream*, *Much Ado About Nothing* and *As You Like It*, and *Lear* and the romances, among other of his works, all partake of this dominating pattern.

Such general considerations are reinforced with specific parallels. Cador, in his ultimately unsuccessful pursuit of Constantia, employs the phrase "Debt of Love" (2); Orsino uses the same phrase in his similarly unsuccessful pursuit of Olivia in *Twelfth Night*, I,i,33. For "youthful Lord" (6), we find the same phrase applied to yet another unsuccessful suitor, the Count Paris, in *Romeo*, IV,ii,25. The phrase "in game" (93) occurs in *Dream*, I,i,240, in a relevant courting context; for "difficult obtaining" (104), compare "desperate of obtaining" in *The Two Gentlemen of Verona*, III,ii,5, again in a relevant courting context (and recall the "desperate game" in line 99).

These parallels are typical of Shakespeare—individual features in his pattern of consistent style. There are various others in I,i. The phrase "duty and observance" (105) occurs in *As You Like It*, V,ii,96, "life, and being" (118) in *Othello*, I,ii,21; the unusual usage "much rather" (29) is found in *Love's Labor's Lost*, II,i,146. For "You teach me language" (1), compare "You taught me language" in *Tempest*, I,ii,363; for "faith and credence" (112), compare "love and credence" in *All's Well That Ends Well*, III,iii,2; "Great natures wisdom" (121) resembles "great nature's second course" in *MacBeth*, II,ii,36, and "wise nature's end" in *Cymbeline*, V,v,367; "to fly from goodness" (126) compares with "to fly from God" in *Henry V*, IV,i,168, with ten more "fly from . . ." usages elsewhere in Shakespeare's acknowledged works. None of these phrases has a comparably close parallel in Rowley's solo plays.

Phrasings and items of imagery suggestive of or consistent with Shakespeare's style are frequent through the scene. We have already mentioned the use of the phrase "in game"; Cador asserts that Edwin and Modestia "are in game, / And all their wits at stake to win the Set" (93-4). Compare "a game play'd home, the rich stake drawn" in *Winter's Tale*, I,ii,248, in a relevant sexual context. Modestia says that marriage is "a desperate game ... / Where there's no winning without loss to either" (99-100); her meaning becomes clearer when we compare Juliet's "learn me how to lose a winning match, / Play'd for a pair of stainless maidenhoods" in *Romeo*, III,ii,12-13. The phrase "gains or looses" (110) occurs in *Cymbeline*, II,iv,59, in the context of Posthumus' and Iachimo's wager on Imogen's chastity. For "You are a cunning Gamester, Madam" (98), compare "You are a merry gamester, / My Lord Sands" in *Henry VIII*, I,iv,45-6, again in a relevant sexual context. Note too another use of "gamester" in a sexual context in *All's Well*, V,iii,188.

In fact, the imagery in I,i—love/marriage-as-game/wager imagery, love/sex-as-food imagery (37-40)—is strongly typical of Shakespeare. I want to be cautious about exploiting it as evidence of authorship, however, since other dramatists of the age, including Rowley, use similar kinds of imagery. I think it is most productive to concentrate on those Shakespearean features that are least like anything in Rowley, and so I intend to pass over some otherwise interesting and relevant items in the text. I ask the reader to remember that in this sense we are looking at a sampling of the Shakespearean features only, and not a complete analysis. In instances in which the imagery is distinctive enough, in my judgment, I will note it; for Donobert's line to Modestia, "thou shalt quicken him" (41), for example, compare "Quicken with kissing" in *Antony*, IV,xv,39.

In lines 44-5, Donobert speaks a couplet with the closing line, "She is a woman, sir, and will be won." Three times in his recognized works, Shakespeare uses similar lines: "She is a woman, therefore may be won" in *Titus Andronicus*, II,i,83, "She is a woman, therefore to be won" in *1 Henry VI*, V,iii,79, and "Was ever woman in this humor won" in *Richard III*, I,ii,228. The common element in these lines is proverbial in origin, so that some readers may question this feature's usefulness as evidence of Shakespeare's hand in *Merlin*; yet Rowley's habitual use of the cant phrase "Far fetched and dear bought for ladies" is regularly and sensibly cited as evidence of his hand (see *Merlin*, III,iv, 117-18). If non-original material can help to identify Rowley, the same should be true for Shakespeare. (Other playwrights also use proverbial material in distinctive ways; think of Middleton's uses of "in dock, out nettle" in *More Dissemblers Besides Women*, IV,i,233 and *The Inner Temple Masque*, 226.)

In the same spirit, compare "for ought that I can see" (82) with "for aught that I can tell" in *Dream*, III,ii,76, and note that "for aught I see" occurs three times in Shakespeare's acknowledged works, along with variants like "for aught I know" and "for aught that I have ever read." The phrase "in the trial" (16) appears three times in the collected works, "my honor'd Lords" (47) five times, plus variants; "Trust me" (80) is used as a mild oath, as here in *Merlin*, fifteen times in the acknowledged works. For "fair Success" (4), we can note five Shakespearean uses of "good success"; for "long suit" (5), compare "long and vehement suit" in *John*, I,i,254. Such minor features can provide context for the more striking Shakespearean elements when they indicate real differences between Shakespeare's and Rowley's stylistic habits.

In lines 74-6 we have a description of how Anselme the hermit brought victory to the Britons in their recent battle with the Saxons; Toclio says that the hermit:

> Not onely saved our army,
> But without aid of man o'rethrew
> The pagan Host . . .

There are twenty-two such "not only this, but that" phrasings in Shakespeare's acknowledged works. It is curious that in three instances in the later plays, Shakespeare begins successive verse lines with "Not only" and "But"; see *Lear*, I,iv,201-2, *Winter's Tale*, V,i,166-7, and *Tempest*, I,ii,98-9. It is tempting to see lines 74-5 in this opening scene of *Merlin* as another such instance—though a large measure of caution is necessary here. We need to remember that the verse of the play (except for the rhymed couplets) was printed as prose in the 1662 quarto, and that this verse was later re-aligned by modern editors (in the case of our text, by C.F. Tucker Brooke). Much of this relineation is fairly obvious, as in Cador's opening speech in I,i, or in Modestia's closing soliloquy; but there are rough patches and points of doubt as well—as with the lines quoted above, which are irregular and short.

Upon inspection, Tucker Brooke's lineation reveals many points of commonality with Shakespeare's manner; verse lines tend to begin and end in the same ways they do in Shakespeare's acknowledged works. It would be very risky to try to make something out of this as evidence of authorship, and I don't intend to do so; still, it is a curious aspect of the text, worth a passing mention.

We can extend this discussion down to the level of single words, to show that the scene contains applications of specific words typical of Shakespeare. Consider Modestia's statement that Edwin has lately been "employ'd in blood and ruine" (33); compare "employ those soldiers" in *Hamlet*, II,ii,74, "famine, sword, and fire / Crouch for employment" in *Henry V*, Pr.,7-8, and "employ'd in danger" in *John*, IV,ii,226. Modestia's use of the word "inequality" in line 125, in an allusion to the differences between men and beasts, is interesting; the word occurs only once in the collected works, in *Measure*, V,i,65, where it is used by a similar character, Isabella, in a similar sense/reason context. Modestia's use of "imperfect" and "speech" in lines 123-4 is worth noting, in that Shakespeare repeatedly uses the former word in speech/reason references—"imperfect speakers" in *MacBeth*, I,iii,70, and "judgement maim'd, and most imperfect" in *Othello*, I,iii,99; in *Lear*, IV,vi,5-8, Edgar tells Gloucester that "your other senses grow imperfect" when Gloucester says, "Methinks thy voice is alter'd." Other examples from this scene are possible; we will have more to say about vocabulary in Chapter V.

The scene's closing couplet in lines 130-1 merits some attention:

> . . . To him alone
> That made me thus, may I whence truly know,
> I'le pay to him, not man, the love I owe.

Compare "To pay that duty which you truly owe" in *John*, II,i,247, and "To give obedience where 'tis truly ow'd" in *Macbeth*, V,ii,26; note too that "truly know" occurs in *1 Henry IV*, I,ii,5, that "truly know" and "truly knows" are found in *Othello*, IV,ii,38-9, and that "truly known" appears in *Henry VIII*, V,iv,36. This couplet ends the closing soliloquy in I,i, in which Modestia expresses her preference for the religious life over marriage. The mere existence of this soliloquy is interesting: Trudi Laura Darby has observed that "Rowley uses few soliloquies, preferring to give the audience the information it needs through a dialogue with a 'confessor' figure."[8] Winifred, Modestia's counterpart in Rowley's *Shoemaker*, speaks no soliloquies, expressing her similar commitment in conversation with her religious preceptor Amphiabell.

The soliloquizing tendency in *Merlin*, especially embodied in Uter, the play's hero (see II,i,69-111 and II,iii,183-205 and 247-61), is quite beyond Rowley's usual mode of dramatic composition. In her soliloquy in I,i,114-31, Modestia exploits ideas and expressions that remind us of well-known Shakespearean speeches, especially Hamlet's "What a piece of work is man" and Isabella's "But man, proud man"; she also reaches levels of idealistic ideation, of introspection and intellection, that are not found in Rowley's other works. (To put it bluntly, Modestia is smarter than Rowley's characters, and speaks with more fluency and eloquence.)

To forestall misunderstanding, I want to be clear about what I think the stylistic patterns manifested in I,i signify. I certainly do recognize and admit that some common features in Jacobean plays are merely chance resemblances grounded in shared dramatic and poetic idioms. Examples are easy to find; if we turn to the opening scene of Rowley's *Shoemaker*, we find phrases like "assur'd destruction" (4) and "unhappy day" (24) and "grim death" (47) and "distressed queen" (49), among others, that are also to be found in Shakespeare's acknowledged works. Obviously, such occasional, random, trivial features do not constitute evidence that Shakespeare helped write *Shoemaker*. The Shakespearean elements in I,i of *Merlin*, however, rise above this level of the trivial, the random, and the occasional; they are more consistent, more contextual, and more substantive than mere chance resemblances; they join together to form a version of that pattern of self-reference that distinguishes a work of Shakespearean authorship. That pattern is not as blatant in the opening scene of *Merlin* as it is in works of the acknowledged canon—but the scene itself tells us why this is so: the presence of many Rowleian characteristics assures us that the scene is one of mixed authorship. The evidence for Shakespeare's hand in I,i is at least as good as the evidence for Rowley's; if I were to assert that the Rowleian features in I,i were only chance resemblances that told us nothing about the authorship of the scene, I could be accused, quite legitimately, of engaging in obfuscation and obscurantism. I have to suggest that the same common-sense standard we apply to Rowley should also be applied to Shakespeare.

Before leaving I,i, there is a final point to consider. Twice in this scene, in lines 28 and 38, we find fairly standard (if not wholly regular) pentameter verse lines with a sixth stressed syllable, "sir," tacked on to the end (if, that is, we accept Tucker Brooke's lineation). Shakespeare never indulges in this habit; among other Jacobean playwrights, this sixth stressed syllable is most common in Fletcher (see Appendix I), though other contemporaries, including Rowley, also employ this trick of versification. We can cite various examples from Rowley's works, including *New Wonder*, IV,i,66 and 95 ("And put a stone in't worth a thousand pounde, Sir"), and *All's Lost*, I,iii,100, II,ii,28, and V,v,46 ("Oh spare my child! Entreat for me? forbeare, sir"), among others. Indeed, the general roughness of the versification in I,i is entirely in keeping with Rowley's method, and shows the continuity of his presence in the scene—moreso, perhaps, than do the specific traces of his style. The general impression I get from this scene is that it is fairly equally the work of both men. Obviously, a scene that is about 50 percent Shakespeare (to make a crude arithmetical estimate of proportion) will be a lesser thing than a scene that is 100 percent Shakespeare; this is a key point that I press the reader to keep in mind.

Act I, Scene ii

The action shifts to the royal court of Britain in this next scene, where circumstances narrated in I,i are depicted firsthand. Here again, we find clear signs of Rowley's presence. Late in the scene (lines 220-58), Modestia and Anselme have a conversation about religious faith that reinforces the parallels with Winifred in *Shoemaker*; for Anselme's "look up, / Behold yon firmament: there sits a power, / Whose foot-stool is this earth" (250-2) and Modestia's "on Heaven I fix my love" (255), compare Winifred's "Within yon house of starres the Bridegroome sits" and "My love is fixt" in *Shoemaker*, III,i,44 and

51. (The Middletonian parallel for this passage cited by Howe, from *Hengist*, I,ii,149ff., "stars / To kiss the pavements" etc., is, I think, less close and substantive.)

In an earlier portion of I,ii, Aurelius and Donobert have some curious exchanges: Donobert takes an aggressive tone toward Artesia and the Saxons, and is repeatedly rebuked by the king (93-105, 130-4). The same pattern occurs in *Shoemaker*, IV,i,160ff., where the Shoemaker's Wife reproves Crispinus and the Shoemaker in turn attacks her with belittling words. The "ageism" of Aurelius' responses to Donobert (88-9, 131-3) is also suggestive of Rowley; Rowley's clowns (Bustopha in *Maid in the Mill*, Cuddy Banks in *Witch of Edmonton*) tend to talk this way about their own fathers. Much of the verse in this scene has the relative simplicity and irregularity that is typical of Rowley, and the impression of his presence is supported by some specific parallels in phrasing; for "gilded pill" (87), for instance, the closest parallel in either Rowley's or Shakespeare's works is "gilded poyson" in *Shoemaker*, III,i,69, used in a relevant context of erotic desire.

At the same time, we can note abundant signs of a Shakespearean contribution to I,ii. What I consider the most important of these occurs early in the scene, in Aurelius' description of the recent victory of the Britons over the Saxons (17-25):

> Our Army being in rout, nay, quite o'rethrown,
> As Chester writes, even then this holy man,
> Arm'd with his cross and staff, went smiling on,
> and boldly fronts the foe; at sight of whom
> The Saxons stood amaz'd: for, to their seeming,
> Above the Hermit's head appear'd such brightness,
> Such clear and glorious beams, as if our men
> March't all in fire; wherewith the Pagans fled,
> And by our troops were all to death pursu'd.

In *Cymbeline*, V,iii, a similar circumstance occurs. The Britons have just won a battle over the invading Romans, in which the tide of battle was turned from apparent defeat to victory by the intervention of Posthumus Leonatus and of Belarius, Guiderius, and Arviragus. In regard to the latter three, the First Captain says to the Second, "'Tis thought the old man and his sons were angels" (V,iii,85). In both *Merlin* and *Cymbeline*, the Britons are facing defeat at the hands of an invader, when disaster is turned into triumph with the aid brought by an old man; in *Cymbeline* that aid appears divine to witnesses, while in *Merlin* the aid is divine in fact.

The close correspondence between the two plays can be illuminated by contrasting them with *Shoemaker*, which utilizes similar material in markedly dissimilar ways. In Act III of Rowley's play, it is the royal brother Crispianus who has the hero's part in the battle with the Vandals and Goths; he rescues Diocletian as Posthumus and the brothers rescue Cymbeline in their play. Roderick, king of the defeated Vandals, expresses himself this way in III,v,1-4:

> This Brittaines are all Divells,
> And amongst them there's one master Divell,
> That bears the face of a base Common souldier;
> Yet on his hornes he tosseth up our Vandals.

All three of these plays, then, exploit common materials; yet there are particulars that are shared by *Cymbeline* and *Merlin* that are missing from *Shoemaker*. In the first two plays, the battle is on British soil against an invader, so that the fate of the nation is at issue; the battle in Rowley's play takes place in France. There is no old-man figure in *Shoemaker*, and the rescue is seen not in angelic terms but demonic, as the quote above shows. The nationalistic and providential implications of the victory are stressed in *Merlin* and *Cymbeline*, but are absent from Rowley's play; among the three, *Merlin* and *Cymbeline* share the important thematic elements that *Shoemaker* lacks.

Shoemaker is usually dated to ca. 1608, and *Cymbeline* to ca. 1609, so that it may seem that Rowley's play has chronological priority; yet these dates are "soft" and need to be treated with caution. In some ways, *Shoemaker* gives the impression of being the derivative work. As noted above, Posthumus, Belarius, Guiderius, and Arviragus rescue Cymbeline when the king is captured by the Romans in battle (*Cymbeline*, V,ii,10-15); Crispianus rescues Diocletian not once but twice (*Shoemaker*, III,iv,15-20 and 37-54). The double rescue, while allowing Crispianus to defeat both barbarian kings (Roderick of the Vandals and Huldricke of the Goths), has little point in the larger narrative; one gets the sense that Rowley the imitator is merely expanding upon his source. The overall treatment of the common material in *Shoemaker* seems weaker, looser, more diffuse, and less meaningful than in the other two plays—certainly than in *Cymbeline*. To be sure, such impressions are "soft" too, and cannot support firm conclusions; yet it is at least possible that in *Cymbeline* we have the original Shakespearean treatment of the common material, and in *Shoemaker* the imitation of a lesser writer. If so, then it is striking to see that *Merlin* has much more in common with the Shakespearean original than the non-Shakespearean imitation has with either; *Merlin* reproduces, and enlarges upon, the context and the meaning of the materials from *Cymbeline* in ways that *Shoemaker* does not.

This viewpoint is supported by the specific Shakespearean features to be found in lines 17-25 of I,ii. For Aurelius' description of how Anselme "went *smiling* on, / And boldly *fronts* the foe" (19-20), compare "both our powers, with *smiling fronts* encountering" in *Coriolanus*, I,vi,8, in a relevant context of divine influence upon the outcome of a battle; note too that Antony comes "smiling" from battle in *Antony*, IV,viii,17. And for "boldly fronts the foe," compare "boldly stand and front him" in *2 Henry VI*, V,i,86, with similar phrasings elsewhere in Shakespeare. Other usages in Aurelius' speech have closer parallels in Shakespeare's works than in Rowley's: for "stood amaz'd" (21), compare "stand amaz'd" in *Twelfth Night*, III,iv,337, and "stand not amaz'd" in both *Othello*, IV,ii,239 and *The Merry Wives of Windsor*, V,v,231; for "to their seeming" (also 21), compare "to thy false seeming" in *Measure*, II,iv,15; for "wherewith the Pagans fled" (24), compare "wherewith we fly" in *2 Henry VI*, IV,vii,74 (in a "heaven" context).

The Shakespearean features in I,ii are not confined to this single speech; rather, they are spread throughout the scene. For "No tiding of our brother yet?" (1), compare "No tidings of him?" in *Cymbeline*, V,v,10, in an identical context, protagonist missing after victorious battle. (The peculiar relationship between these two plays continues to manifest itself.) Before the Saxon ambassadors are called into the presence, Aurelius uses the phrase "We are resolv'd" (65); compare Henry's use of "Now are we well resolv'd," just before the French ambassadors are allowed in, in *Henry V*, I,ii,222. Both kings use similar phraseology to express the firmness of their prepared stance toward foreign emissaries.

For "give order, / The Embassadors being come to take our answer, / They have admittance" (33-5), compare "Give first admittance to th'embassadors" in *Hamlet*, II,ii,51. Aurelius is "mild and vertuous" (120) in the words of his future queen; another queen applies the same phrase to her king in *Richard III*, I,ii,104—and note "The Duke is virtuous, mild" in *2 Henry VI*, III,i,72. For Artesia's "breed dislike" (206), addressed to Aurelius, compare Katherine's "kindle your dislike," addressed to Henry, in *Henry VIII*, II,iv,25. The phrase "all submission" (32) occurs in both *John*, V,vii,103 and *2 Henry VI*, V,i,58, while "terms of love" (75) is found in *1 Henry IV*, V,v,3, "on equal terms" (139) in *Richard II*, IV,i,22, "hellish charms" (186) in *Richard III*, III,iv,62, "earthly man" (199) in *Pericles*, II,i,2, "tie you to your word" (208) in *Kinsmen*, III,vi,236, and "fair advantage" (61) and "to hasten on" (213) in *Two Gentlemen*, II,iv,68 and I,iii,77 respectively; "worthy praise" (121) is used in both *1 Henry VI*, V,v,11 and *2 Henry VI*, III,i,68. For "Powerful and pithie" (43), we might compare "pith and piussance" in *Henry V*, III,Pr.,21.

"Fair'st of creatures" (95) compares with similar usages in Shakespeare—though it is perhaps more interesting to note that the contractional form "fair'st" occurs in both *Winter's Tale*, IV,iv,112 and *Troilus and Cressida*, I,iii,265. For "send some messenger" (102), note that there are five such "send some" usages in the collected works—compare "send some better messenger" in *Two Gentlemen*, I,i,151, and "send some other messenger" in *The Comedy of Errors*, II,i,77. For "we . . . never use to sue, / But force our wishes" (115-17), compare "We were not born to sue, but to command" in *Richard II*, I,i,196. For "to be seduc't / By smoothing flattery or oyly words" (127-8), compare "To be seduced by thy flattery" in *Two Gentlemen*, IV,ii,97; note too that Shakespeare's canonical uses of the word "smoothing" appear in relevant contexts—"smoothing word(s)" in *2 Henry VI*, I,i,156 and *Richard III*, I,ii,168, and "smoothing titles" in *Lucrece*, 892. And, for "oyly words," compare "that glib and oily art / To speak and purpose not" in *Lear*, I,i,224-5. For "loud fame" (120), compare "loud infamy" in *Kinsmen*, I,ii,76.

For lines 140-1, "let a perpetual League / Seal our united bloods," compare "united vessel of their blood" in *2 Henry IV*, IV,iv,44 and "united league" in *Richard III*, II,i,2, along with Shakespearean usages like "perpetual peace," "perpetual amity," "perpetual honor," etc. For "The infinite sum of my felicity" (165), we can cite Shakespearean phrasings like "the very sum of my confession," "the grand sum of his sins," and "the sum of my disgrace." "Warm not a serpent in your naked bosom" (189) echoes "you but warm the starved snake, / Who, cherish'd in your breast, will sting your heart" in *2 Henry VI*, III,i,343-4. For "Proud earth and dust" (223), compare "valiant dust" in *Much Ado*, II,i,61, and note that "earth and dust" is found in *3 Henry VI*, V,ii,27. (Rowley's closest parallel is less close: "earth and clay" in *Shoemaker*, IV,ii,127.) For "learn and utter" (234), we might cite "utter learned things" in *Kinsmen*, III,v,14; for "your prayers / Are the same Orizons which I will number" (236-7), compare "Numb'ring our Ave-Maries with our beads" in *3 Henry VI*, II,i,162. Many other usages in I,ii have more significant parallels in Shakespeare than in Rowley—"peace and health to great Aurelius" (76), "The fairest present e're mine eyes were blest with" (79), "unto your State and Person" (83), "embrace the Princely Offers of a friend" (107), "oppose our will" (155), etc.

For "in seeking peace" (115), note that there are five similar "in seeking" phrasings in the collected works; for "came of purpose to conclude the Match" (154), note comparable "of purpose to" usages in *Timon*, III,i,25 and *1 Henry VI*, V,iv,22. For "I can scarce keep patience" (184), note that there are eight "can scarce" or "scarce can" usages in Shakespeare's acknowledged works. The phrase "heavenly power" (68) may be a commonplace—but it seems worth noting that Shakespeare's two uses of the phrase occur in very late works, in *Tempest*, V,i,105 and *Kinsmen*, V,iii,139. "Till when" (216) appears four times in Shakespeare, in *Tempest*, *Pericles*, *Coriolanus*, and *Troilus*. Indeed, this scene is full of rather commonplace phrasings that nonetheless occur repeatedly in Shakespeare but not in Rowley: "What's here" (71), "dearest Love" (145), "without offence" (225), many others; to list them all would likely give the impression of trivializing the argument, though it remains true that such usages can have a place in delineating the extent to which the writing in I,ii is like Shakespeare's style and unlike Rowley's.

The medical metaphors employed in I,ii are worth a mention; both Shakespeare and Rowley use such metaphors in their works, and the "gilded pill" image in line 87 is most likely Rowley's, as noted above. Two other medical metaphors, however, suggest Shakespeare. Donobert's imagery in 44-8 is one such: his use of the word "receipts" in the sense of medications or prescriptions (45) is prefigured in *All's Well*, II,i,105, while "being appli'd" (46) compares with "being so applied" in *Lucrece*, 531, also in a phramacological metaphor. Aurelius' imagery in lines 191-3 resembles a passage in *Lucrece*, 244-7: both touch upon ideas of disputing about desire for a woman, opposites of freezing and burning, and a cautionary old-man figure.

In discussing I,i, we noted the difficulties involved in any attempt to use features of prosody as evidence, due to the fact that the verse of the play was printed as prose in the 1662 quarto; yet this consideration does not apply to the rhymed couplets, which were printed as the verse they are. The couplet in lines 108-9 rhymes "merit" with "inherit," while the couplet in 135-6 rhymes "neither" and "together"; both sets of rhymes are found in *Love's Labor's Lost*, in IV,i,20-1 and IV,iii,189-90 respectively. In 41-2 we find a couplet ending with the line "Mischiefs not ended are but then begun"; compare "To mourn a mischief that is past and gone / Is the next way to draw new mischief on" in *Othello*, I,iii,204-5. The point about putting "mischiefs" behind oneself in order to prevent further misfortune is made in both.

Some points of word usage in I,ii are also worth noting. For Artesia's use of the phrase "my sex" (118), note that Shakespeare's women have a tendency to talk about their "sex"—see *Tempest*, III,i,49, *Winter's Tale*, II,i,108, *As You Like It*, IV,i,201, *Julius Caesar*, II,i,296, etc.; Rowley's women do not share this habit. The use of "linck" (177) in a love/marriage context, and the use of "doom" (202) in the sense of "sentence," have recurrent parallels in Shakespeare; for "possess" (240) in the sense of "inform," see *Much Ado*, V,i,281. Here as in I,i, various other examples of word usages typical of Shakespeare rather than Rowley could be given; I think, though, that enough has been said to define the basic nature of the writing in I,ii.

Like the play's first scene, this second scene reveals abundant evidence of a Shakespearean contribution. The intermingling of Rowleian and Shakespearean features again suggests an intimate collaboration. Consider the line "Th'art immortal and no earthly man" (199); this line would be a regular verse line if the initial contraction had been left in its uncontracted form, as "Thou art." Comparable lines can be found in Rowley's solo plays; from *New Wonder*, compare "Th'art a beame in't, and I'le teare it out" in III,iii,139, and "Th'art no brother, and I'le be no man" in V,i,180. All three of these lines would be standard pentameter verse lines if "Th'art" had been left as "Thou art." Indeed, this habit of "irregularizing" verse lines with contractions is common in Rowley's works; "You'r my Sonnes, I charge you to obey me" and "Plac'd by Saturne, and great Iupiter" in *Shoemaker*, I,i,137 and 159 are only two of many possible examples. Shakespeare tends to employ contractions to the opposite end, to make his verse more regular. Yet we have also cited the phrase "earthly man" in line 199 as common to *Pericles*, II,i,2; if we accept Tucker Brooke's lineation of the verse in *Merlin*, we can observe further that both uses of "earthly man" fall at the end of verse lines. Some readers will complain that line 199 cannot be the work of Rowley and Shakespeare simultaneously; but the intermixture of elements in the scenes of Act I of *Merlin* reveals the play to be the kind of intimate collaboration that could in fact produce such hybridization.

Act II, Scene i

The first scene of Act II introduces the characters of the comic subplot, the otherwise-unnamed Clown and his sister, Joan Go-too't. The Clown, in this and subsequent scenes, exhibits many of the traits typical of Rowley's clowns. His relationship with his sister, centering on her sexual and marital affairs, is typical of Rowley's comedy; Jaques in *All's Lost* and Bustopha in *Maid in the Mill* provide obvious parallels. The Clown in our play is sexually inexperienced, but still bawdy—"I am her

elder, but she has been at it before me" (II,i,126-7)—again typical of Rowley's clowns (like Tim Bloodhound in *Match at
Midnight*). The basic idea of a man being found to father an
illegitimate child is a regular element in Rowley's works,
sometimes winning expression in surprising forms and contexts; in his dedication of *Fair Quarrel* to Robert Gray, Rowley writes, "this child of the Muses is yours; whoever begat it,
'tis laid to your charge, and (for aught I know) you must father and keep it too." The bawdy humor of the Clown, with its
strong emphasis on the male genitalia, is a hallmark of Rowley's style. Trudi Laura Darby, in her edition of *New Wonder*,
points out a specific parallel of this type between II,i,227 of
that play and II,i,25-6 of *Merlin*,[9] and various other examples of
this kind of humor in Rowley's works could be cited. Other
specifics link this scene with Rowley's comedy; while looking
for a husband for his sister, the Clown calls out "So ho, boy, so
ho, so ho" (61), just as Bustopha calls out "Soh hoh" while
looking for his father in V,ii of his play.

It is important to recognize, too, that the signs of Rowley's
presence in II,i are not restricted to the comic characters. At
mid-scene Prince Uter enters; he haunts the forest where he
first caught sight of the woman he loves. Compare the opening of *The Changeling*, where Alsemero returns to the church
where he first saw Beatrice-Joanna; both men have fallen in
love at first sight with strange (and sinister) women, and both
linger at the sight of that first encounter. The pile-up of mythological references in 'lines 95-100 (Marius' soldiers, the
gorgon, and Pygmalion, all crowded into five lines) is suggestive of Rowley; Robb identifies this habit as one of Rowley's
telltale traits. Oswold, expressing sympathy with Joan, begins
one of his speeches with "Would I could" (184); similar
"Would I could" speeches occur in *New Wonder*, I,ii,231 and in
Maid in the Mill, II,ii. The verse in II,i shows much of the
roughness of Rowley's manner, lines 93, 107, and 109 being
good examples.

Simultaneously, we must note the many indices of a Shake-spearean contribution to II,i. It is interesting that there are no substantive signs of Shakespeare's hand in the first sixty-eight lines of the scene, the portion preceding Uter's entrance. It would appear that this opening section of II,i is mostly, per-haps wholly, the work of Rowley. This is only reasonable, giv-en the strongly Rowleian nature of the comic materials. (We do find some Shakespearean elements in the Clown's speeches later in the scene, and in subsequent scenes too; the collabora-tors may have begun with an assumption that Rowley would handle the Clown part, and then modified this division of labor as the project evolved.)

This opening portion of the scene provides us with at least a limited form of negative check on our hypothesis: if the appar-ently Shakespearean features we've been noting were merely chance resemblances or other non-authorial elements, they should be evenly distributed through the play—yet they are absent from a segment of the play that is strongly Rowleian in character. This opening dialogue between the Clown and Joan also provides an intriguing example of Rowley's stage-writing technique, in that the Clown addresses three questions to Joan in their first six exchanges; in effect, the adult actor playing the Clown could cue the boy actor playing the woman's role through the first part of their scene. It's an excellent demon-stration of practical stage experience reflected in dramatic composition.

After Uter's entrance at line 69, Shakespearean elements are frequent through the rest of the scene. Perhaps the strongest single sign of Shakespeare's hand occurs in Uter's speech in lines 89-102; to understand its significance, we must turn to Caroline Spurgeon's classic *Shakespeare's Imagery*. Spurgeon identified a peculiar brand of animal imagery in Shakespeare's plays and poems—imagery that shows vivid sympathy with animals as sentient beings, with the limed bird and the bated bear, with the animal in pain or the prey of the hunt, with humble creatures like insects and snails and worms; a kind of imagery that is generally absent from the rest of the writing of his age.[10] It is not necessary to suppose that this type of imagery tells us something about Shakespeare as an individual, as Spurgeon tends to do; the focus of our interest is on this sympathetic animal imagery as a distinctive characteristic of Shakespeare's style.[11] Shakespeare's application of his characteristic animal imagery to hunting is noteworthy; to cite only one of many possible examples, consider Orsino's lines in *Twelfth Night*, I,i,20-22:

> That instant was I turn'd into a hart,
> And my desires, like fell and cruel hounds,
> E'er since pursue me.

The allusion, of course, is to the story of Actaeon; yet Orsino's identification with the hart, and the stigma placed on the "fell and cruel hounds," is entirely typical of Shakespeare. In this light, consider Uter's lines in II,i,89-94:

> For having overtook her;
> As I have seen a forward blood-hound strip
> The swifter of the cry, ready to seize
> His wished hopes, upon the sudden view,
> Struck with astonishment, at his arriv'd prey,
> Instead of seizure stands at fearful bay . . .

At least twice in the acknowledged works, we find similar pictures of dogs in the hunt. In *1 Henry VI*, IV,ii,50-2, Talbot tells his soldiers to be like

> . . . desperate stags,
> Turn on the bloody hounds with heads of steel
> And make the cowards stand aloof at bay;

and in *Henry V*, II,iv,69-71 the Dauphin observes that

... coward dogs
Most spend their mouths when what they seem to threaten
Runs far before them.

Conversely, the closest usage in Rowley's plays does not in-
volve hunting at all; in *New Wonder*, III,i,183-6, we find, "I
have seene for all the world, a couple of cowardly Curs quarrell
in that fashion, as t'one turnes his head, the other snaps behind; and as he turnes, his Mouth recoyles againe." Clearly,
the passage in *Merlin* is much more in Shakespeare's manner
than Rowley's; its similarity to the quoted lines in *1 Henry VI*
("stands at fearful bay" and "stand aloof at bay") seems especially noteworthy to me. (This does not mean, though, that we
must suppose the lines in *Merlin* to be "pure" Shakespeare; as
mentioned earlier, the roughness of the versification suggests
Rowley is present also.)

In addition to this striking animal imagery, Uter has more
to tell us. At this point in the play he is wandering alone in the
forest, lovesick after having caught sight of Artesia. He con-
fesses his feelings in a long speech (69-111) overheard by the
Clown and Joan, and punctuated by the Clown's comic remarks. At the end of Uter's speech, the Clown says, "had I
been a woman, these kinde words would have won me" (114-
15). In *Othello*, I,iii, we find a parallel situation: Othello, like
Uter, is divulging his romantic situation, and gives his famous
speech, "Her father lov'd me, oft invited me, / Still question'd
me the story of my life" (128-70)—at the end of which the
Duke of Venice says, "I think this tale would win my daughter
too" (171). This strong parallel, coupled as it is with Shakespeare's animal imagery, yields a plain indication of Shakespeare's presence.

The pattern of verbal commonalities that normally distinguishes Shakespeare's work is amply in evidence here in II,i.
For "my power, / Whose cloud aspir'd the Sun, dissolv'd a
shower" (97-8), compare "That gallant spirit hath aspir'd the

clouds" in *Romeo*, III,i,117, and "Dissolve, thick cloud, and rain" in *Antony*, V,ii,299. (This phrasing occurs in the midst of that cluster of mythological references already associated with Rowley; yet again, elements of both men's styles jumble together in the same lines.) For "winged with sweet desire" (226), compare "winged with desire" in *3 Henry VI*, I,i,267. In lines 139-40 we find "hell, and mischief" and "Witch"; a comparable two-line passage in *1 Henry VI*, III,ii,38-9 offers "witch" and "hellish mischief." "Here did I see her first, here view her beauty" (78) conforms to a pattern of double "here" lines in Shakespeare; see *Lucrece*, 1485-6, *Julius Caesar*, II,i,101, and *Titus*, I,i,153-4 for some examples. For "past imagination" (101), compare "beyond imagination" in both *Errors*, V,i,201 and *Kinsmen*, II,iii,5, and "beyond the imagination" in *Winter's Tale*, IV,ii,39; for "saw and felt" (102), compare "feel nor see" in *Kinsmen*, I,i,120. For Uter's oath, "Lightning consume me" (150), we can cite "a plague consume you" in *Timon*, V,iv,71; "how fare you" (161) appears only once in the collected works, in *Timon*, III,vi,26; for "cast away your self" (210), compare "cast away thyself" in *Timon*, IV,iii,220.

"Lend me one word with you" (176) compares with "lend your prosperous ear" in *Othello*, I,iii,244 (that key scene again), and "lend thy serious hearing / To what I shall unfold" in *Hamlet*, I,v,5-6. For "My rage o'reflowes my blood, all patience flies me" (151), we find a similar connection in "rage and stern impatience" in *1 Henry VI*, IV,vii,8; note too that "all patience" occurs four times in the collected works. The phrase "perpetuall thrall" (106) is interesting, in that Shakespeare rhymes the two words in lines 10 and 12 of Sonnet 154. For "curse your selves" (147), compare "curse myself" in *Two Gentlemen*, III,i,148. "Oh fate" (104) appears in both *Much Ado*, IV,i,115 and *Henry VIII*, II,iii,85, "have a fling at" (196) in *1 Henry VI*, III,i,64, "A womans fault" (127-8 and 187) and "two-leg'd creature" (231) in *1 Henry IV*, III,i,240 and II,iv,188 respectively.

We can note an interesting situational parallel between this scene and *As You Like It*, II,iv. Here in *Merlin*, Joan is wandering through the forest, pregnant and abandoned by the father of her expected child, accompanied only by the Clown; toward the end of the scene she faints when she thinks she has found the man she's looking for, because "too much joy / Opprest my loving thoughts" (212-13). In II,iv of *As You Like It*, Rosalind and Celia are wandering through the Forest of Arden, accompanied by Touchstone; they meet Corin, to whom Rosalind says that her companion is "with travel much oppress'd / And faints for succor" (74-5). Young women, disadvantaged and vulnerable, wandering through forests, accompanied only by fools, faint and "oppress'd"; *Merlin* and *As You Like It* have a good deal in common in this respect. (In light of this commonality, we might note another, more distant one: the Clown's lines here in II,i,50-2, "Ile make Proclamation; if these Woods and Trees, as you say, will bear any witness, let them answer," give a faint echo of Orlando's habit of hanging his verse on the trees of the Forest of Arden. In III,ii,1 of his play, Orlando describes his verses as "in witness of my love.") Finally, before leaving II,i, we can note the presence of usages like "fair advantage" (166) and "Trust me" (181) that were cited in discussion of previous scenes.

Act II, Scene ii

II,ii is a key scene in the authorship equation, in that it contains the most substantive of the play's interpolations from Beaumont and Fletcher's *Cupid's Revenge*. These interpolations, and their importance for the determination of the authorship of *Merlin*, will be discussed in Chapter VI; for the present, we can say that the Beaumont-Fletcher materials in II,ii appear in a scene that is rich in Shakespearean elements.

Earlier, I asserted that non-authorial connections between plays tend to lack the grounding in common themes and subject matter that authorial connections often display. II,ii provides excellent examples of the latter. The scene's opening line contains the phrase "hasty marriage," a phrase that also occurs once in Shakespeare's acknowledged works, in *3 Henry VI*, IV,i,18. This certainly seems to be a trivial point—until we compare the two scenes in which the common phrase appears. This scene in *Merlin* begins with a procession in which the newly married Aurelius is accompanied by Artesia, his new queen; then comes an emotional confrontation among the British courtiers over the inappropriateness of the king's marriage; after predictions of dire consequences, a key nobleman announces his withdrawal from court. This is very much the same as what we find in IV,i of *3 Henry VI*: a similar procession occurs, with an English king (Edward IV) and his new queen (Lady Jane Grey), a surprise choice to the members of his court; courtiers are similarly disturbed and disruptive over the consequences of the match, with one of the king's key supporters announcing his withdrawal of that support. The two scenes present alternative versions of the same basic situation; and this is the kind of parallel in structure and subject that often unites scenes in Shakespeare's works. For contrast, note that Rowley's closest verbal parallel, "hastie matching" in *New Wonder*, III,ii,48, occurs in a scene that reveals nothing of this common relationship.

Consider another aspect of II,ii: Edoll, Earl of Chester, the British commander in the recent battle with the Saxons, is vocal in his outrage over the marriage of Aurelius and Artesia. Announcing his withdrawal from court, he says, "Prepare my horses" (34). Donobert, trying to calm the situation, says, "Preserve your patience, Sir" (40). That counsel is unavailing, for Edoll continues his vigorous expression of his feelings. In *Lear*, I,iv, similar conditions prevail: Lear is incensed at his treatment by Goneril, and announces his intention to depart with the identical phrase, "Prepare my horses" (258). Albany counsels patience—"Pray, sir, be patient" (261)—with as little effect as Donobert to Edoll.

Consider the discussion of the politico-military circumstances in II,ii: Donobert says that Edoll had "full Commission to dispose the war" (62), while Edwin mentions "the Peace, and all Conditions" (68) negotiated by Artesia. In *2 Henry IV*, IV,i, Prince John also has "full commission" (160) to deal with the enemy, who later talk about the "conditions of our peace" (182). Similarly, Othello is "in full commission" in *Othello*, II,i,29. In reference to line 68 of II,ii, we can cite "conditions of a friendly peace" in *1 Henry VI*, V,i,38, with related usages elsewhere in Shakespeare. This web of connections between II,ii and scenes in Shakespeare's canonical plays is typical of Shakespeare's work, and strongly indicative of his hand in this scene in *Merlin*.

Edoll is described this way before his entrance (18-21):

> All crosses feeds both his spleen and his impatience;
> Those affections are in him like powder,
> Apt to inflame with every little spark,
> And blow up all his reason.

Compare Friar Lawrence's words in *Romeo*, III,iii,130-4:

> Thy wit, that ornament to shape and love,
> Misshapen in the conduct of them both,
> Like powder in a skilless soldier's flask,
> Is set afire by thine own ignorance,
> And thou dismemb'red with thine own defense.

Impatience and ignorance overriding wit and reason with the volatility of exploding gunpowder: the two passages express similar ideas in similar words. During his tirade, Edoll is so overwrought that he hardly recognizes the courtiers who salute him: "I scarcely know you" (33). Compare a similarly overwrought Othello's "I scarce did know you," addressed to Gratiano in V,ii,201 of his play.

Many other Shakespearean features occur in II,ii. For "take

the advantage, whilst 'twas offer'd" (7), compare "take when
once 'tis offer'd" in *Antony*, II,vii,83; both scenes concern
political leaders who yield a strategic advantage to their "competitors"—*Merlin*, II,ii,58, *Antony*, II,vii,70. The unusual construction "even already made victorious" (45) is paralleled by
another "even already" construction in *Troilus*, III,iii,138. For
Edoll's "laid before his tender youth" (53), referring to Aurelius and the counsel he should have been given, compare "Our
reasons laid before him" in *Henry VIII*, V,i,50, the "him" being
another English king. The phrase "want of wisdom" (52) is
found in *Henry VIII*, V,ii,48, in a similar context.

The phrase "too credulous" (8) occurs in *Venus*, 986, "commanded home" (10) in *Othello*, IV,i,258, "never fail" (57) in
Cymbeline, III,iv,178, "for wisdoms sake" (103) in *Love's Labor's
Lost*, IV,iii,354; "Lawful Kings" (55), a phrase which recurs in
later scenes of the play, appears ten times in singular form in
the collected works. For "quickly wooed and won" (2), we can
cite "quickly wooed" in *1 Henry IV*, V,i,56 and "quickly won"
in *Romeo*, II,ii,95, while "quick speed" (5) is a kind of redundancy that Shakespeare sometimes perpetrates, as in "quick ce-
lerity" in *Measure*, IV,ii,110 or "speedy and quick" in *1 Henry VI*, V,iii,8.

The phrase "airy words" (92) occurs in singular form in *Romeo*, I,i,89, with "airy tongue" in II,ii,162 of the same play. "Oh
the good Gods!" (64) appears in *Antony*, V,ii,221, with many
variants elsewhere in Shakespeare: "O the gods!" in *Troilus*,
IV,ii,84, "Good gods!" in *Kinsmen*, II,iii,13, etc. (The speaker
of this line, Edoll, is supposedly a Christian like the rest of the
Britons. Rowley does not share Shakespeare's habit of giving
his Christian characters pagan oaths.) The phrase "perswade
his patience" (15) is almost identical to the "persuade me patience" in *3 Henry VI*, III,iii,176; for "the League confirm'd? /
The Marriage ratifi'd?" (28-9), compare "confirm'd, sign'd, rat-
ified" in *Merchant*, III,ii,148.

For "dulls my senses" (33), compare "dull the sense" in

Cymbeline, I,v,37; for "Preserve your Honors" (41), compare "preserve mine honor" in *Pericles*, II,ii,16; for the continuation of the passage, "Your Lives and Lands" (42), compare "Lives, honors, lands" in *1 Henry VI*, IV,iii,53, and "Our lands, our lives" in *Richard II*, III,ii,151, both in relevant contexts of "life and land" being threatened in a politico-military conflict. "Lend ear to parly with the weakned foe" (63) resembles "To sound a parley to his heartless foe" in *Lucrece*, 471; for "Lend ear," recall the Shakespearean usages cited in connection with II,i,176. For "nor they nor you" (88), we can cite many comparable doubled "nor" usages in the collected works: "nor me nor you" in Sonnet 72,12, "nor his, nor hers" in *Lear*, II,ii,91, "Nor thou, nor he," "Nor her, nor thee," and "Nor thou, nor these" in *Titus*, I,i,294, 300, and 344, etc.

For "all our whole Kingdom" (111), compare "All our whole city" in *Romeo*, IV,ii,32, plus other Shakespearean phrasings like "all the whole world," "all the whole army," etc. For "Which Ile prevent, or perish" (112), we find a similar "or perish" usage in *Cymbeline*, III,v,101; for "his rage transports him" (113), compare "transported by my jealousies" in *Winter's Tale*, III,ii,158; for "These passions set apart" (114), compare "all reverence set apart" in *John*, III,i,159. For "a braver soldier / Breathes not i'th' world this day" (114-15), compare "A nobler man, a braver warrior, / Lives not this day within the city walls" in *Titus*, I,i,25-6, and "A braver soldier never couched lance" in *1 Henry VI*, III,ii,134. Edoll's "thou liest beneath thy lungs" (99) resembles "the lie i'th' throat / As deep as to the lungs" in *Hamlet*, II,ii,574-5 (and see also *Henry V*, II,i,49). For the redundant "servile slavery" (108), compare "slavish weeds and servile thoughts" in *Titus*, II,i,18.

Edoll's speech in lines 82-6 is striking in that it follows immediately upon one of the interpolations from *Cupid's Revenge*, yet clearly conforms to Shakespeare's style:

Never was man so palpably abus'd,

So basely marted, bought and sold to scorn.
My Honor, Fame, and hopeful Victories,
The loss of Time, Expences, Blood, and Fortunes,
All vanisht into nothing.

For the first line quoted, compare "there was never man so notoriously abus'd" in *Twelfth Night*, IV,ii,88, plus usages like "rankly abus'd" and "mightily abus'd" elsewhere in Shakespeare. The usage of "bought and sold" (83) is also striking: while the phrase is a commonplace, note that Shakespeare tends to apply it not in commercial or financial senses but as a metaphor for military betrayal. Four out of Shakespeare's five canonical uses of "bought and sold" occur in this sense: see *John*, V,iv,10 ("Fly, noble English, you are bought and sold!"), *1 Henry VI*, IV,iv,13 ("bought and sold Lord Talbot"), *Richard III*, V,iii,305 ("Dickon thy master is bought and sold"), and *Troilus*, II,i,46 ("thou art here but to thrash Troyans, and thou art bought and sold"). And obviously, it is in a very similar sense that the phrase is used here in *Merlin*. Also, for "bought and sold to scorn," we might compare "scorn is bought with groans" in *Two Gentlemen*, I,i,29. For "Honor . . . loss of Time, Expences, Blood, and Fortunes" (84-5), compare "honor, loss of time, travail, expense, / Wounds, friends" in *Troilus*, II,ii,4-5, with similar usages elsewhere in Shakespeare. (Rowley's closest usage, "odds and losse of blood" in *Shoemaker*, III,ii,187, is less close.) Even the commonplace phrase "vanisht into nothing" (86) is worth a glance, since Shakespeare uses similar phrases like "vanish into air" and "vanish'd out of sight," while Rowley doesn't. We can see, therefore, that the borrowing from Beaumont and Fletcher in lines 72-81 of II,ii is ensconced within material that is clearly Shakespearean in style. (The interpolations themselves, moreover, tend to be rephrased in ways suggestive of Shakespeare's hand, as we shall see in Chapter VI.)

There are various other, more minor features in II,ii that

could be noted; to take a single example, the phrase "by the Rood" (23) occurs, verbatim or in close variants, five times in Shakespeare's plays, but never in Rowley's. I do not find any plain indications of Rowley's presence in this scene—though I would be cautious about forming any assumption of his absence; the style and versification are generally continuous with what we see in the earlier scenes of the play. Shakespeare does seem to be very strongly present in II,ii, with almost every line yielding some parallel or commonality with his acknowledged works. This is not surprising, given the subject matter of the scene: a serious consideration of dynastic conflict and the resulting political and military effects is much more in Shakespeare's vein than Rowley's. Repeatedly in *Merlin* we find this kind of consistency, of subject matter that is characteristic of one of the writers being written in that writer's style—which is only logical in a collaborative work.

Act II, Scene iii

This next scene gives a good illustration of the point made above, that subject matter typical of one member of the collaboration tends to be written in that writer's style. The confrontation between Anselme and the Saxons in II,iii, especially in lines 12-40, with its vigorous, assertive, perhaps even chauvinistic advocacy of Christianity, is quite unlike Shakespeare, but is strongly reminiscent of passages in Rowley's *Shoemaker*; see II,ii,46-77 and IV,ii,1ff. Unsurprisingly, Shakespearean features are sparsely distributed in this part of the scene. In the speeches of the Saxons in lines 29-36, there are no signs of Shakespeare's hand that I can see. (On Rowley's side, we might note that the phrase "Christian slave" in line 30 is found in plural form in *Shoemaker*, IV,ii,26.[12])

Elsewhere in II,iii, however, we do find many signs of a Shakespearean contribution. In the speeches that follow Uter's entrance at line 128, we get a strong expression of the romantic and erotic triangle involving Aurelius, Artesia, and Uter; and

this triangle, of king, queen, and king's brother, is a version of
the triangle of Hamlet senior, Gertrude, and Claudius in
Hamlet, a commonality that provides the thematic rationale
for several links between this scene and *Hamlet*. (I say "a version" of the triangle, because of course the plots and characters
in question also display major differences that I do not mean
to slight. Yet the basic similarity of the situations seems to
have been evident to Shakespeare on some level, given the echoes of *Hamlet* that have found their way into this scene.) In
lines 214-15, Artesia's Waiting-Gentlewoman gives Uter a jewel
as a token from her mistress:

> *Gentlewoman:* It is an artificial crab, Sir.
> *Uter:* A creature that goes backward.[13]

A more famous crab that goes backward appears in *Hamlet*:
"yourself, sir, shall grow old as I am, if like a crab you could go
backward," II,ii,202-4. (The subtext of another erotic and incestuous triangle, Hamlet, Ophelia, Laertes, is also worth noting.) In this scene in *Merlin*, spirits are conjured by the Saxon
magician Proximus; for Proximus' "The center of the Earth,
the Sea, the Air, / The region of the fire, nay, hell it self" (75-6),
compare "in sea or fire, in earth or air," in a similar spiritualis-
tic context, in *Hamlet*, I,i,153. For "hell it self" (76), note that
two of Shakespeare's three canonical uses of the phrase fall in
Hamlet, in I,ii,244 and in IV,v,188 (the third being in *Romeo*,
III,iii,18). Proximus' demons are greeted with the phrase "The
apparition comes" (89), a phrase that also occurs in *Hamlet*,
I,ii,211 (and note "this apparition come" in I,i,28). Taken individually, the connections are rather minor or general; taken together, they seem more suggestive.

In addition to the connection with *Hamlet*, this scene reveals the pattern of Shakespearean elements observed in earlier
scenes. The phrase "argument of Love" (15) occurs in *Twelfth
Night*, III,ii,11, with variants in *Love's Labor's Lost*, V,ii,747 and

John, I,i,36; "death or sickness" (25) is found in *Dream*, I,i,142, "time and fortune" (155) in *Timon*, III,v,10, "hard lesson" (238) in *Much Ado*, I,i,293, and "betray my life" (250) in *Lucrece*, 233. For "brave Hector, our great Ancestor" (81), compare "Aeneas, our great ancestor" in *Julius Caesar*, I,ii,112, and note that "brave Hector" occurs three times in the collected works. For "My Princely Brother, all my Kingdoms hope" (133), compare "my brother, nay, my kingdom's heir" in *Richard II*, I,i,116, and note that princely brothers receive mention in *Richard III*, III,i,34 and *Troilus*, IV,v,174. "Bar'd me from all society of men" (143) resembles "abjure / For ever the society of men" in *Dream*, I,i,65-6; for "with so strange and fixt an eye" (159), compare "With so eternal and so fix'd a soul" in *Troilus*, V,ii,166.

For "Oh, you immortal powers" (162), compare "O you immortal gods" in *Troilus*, IV,ii,94, "O ye immortal gods" in *Julius Caesar*, IV,iii,157, and "O immortal gods" in *Shrew*, V,i,66. The last usage reminds us of Shakespeare's habit of giving his Christian characters pagan oaths—"By Janus" in *Othello*, I,ii,33, "by two-headed Janus" in *Merchant*, I,i,50, etc. Uter's oath here in II,iii,162 partakes of this tendency. As noted in reference to II,ii,64, Rowley does not share in this habit; as we might expect from the author of *A Shoemaker a Gentleman*, his Christianity is too self-conscious to allow it. The Christian characters in *Merlin* talk like Shakespeare's characters in this respect, not like Rowley's.

The phrase "stuck full of objects" (3) compares with "stuck full of eyes" in *1 Henry IV*, V,ii,8, while "mirth and triumphs" in the same line recalls the "triumphs, mirth" in *Two Gentlemen*, V,iv,161. For "this old frame or these cras'd limbes" (24), we might cite "crazy age" in *1 Henry VI*, III,ii,89; for "recreant bosoms" (45), the "recreant limbs" in *John*, III,i,129-33 and 199 may be worth noting. For "sawcy impudence" (72), compare "impudent sauciness" in *2 Henry IV*, II,i,112 and 123; for "double damnation" (101), compare "double damn'd" in *Othello*,

IV,ii,37; for "mis-believing Pagan" (108), compare "misbeliev-ing Moor" in *Titus*, V,iii,143. In lines 112-13 we find "spirits rais'd from the low Abyss / Of hells unbottom'd depths"; com-pare "bottom in th'uncomprehensive depth" in *Troilus*, III,iii,198, in a relevant Achilles-Hector context. Note too that "low Abyss" is a redundancy, a feature that Shakespeare em-ploys surprisingly frequently in his works; in the same spirit, compare "the Joys / Of my high Bliss" (171-2) with "bliss and joy" in *3 Henry VI*, I,ii,31.

For "more pleasing sports" (119), compare "more pleasing stuff" in *Shrew*, In.,ii,139, and "more pleasing sound" in Son-net 130,10; "To mock the reason" (149) resembles "to mock the mind" in *Lucrece*, 1414; for "thy Traitors thoughts" (190), com-pare "thy traitor's speech" in *2 Henry VI*, I,iii,194. "Commend-ing her affection in this Jewel" (210) echoes "this jewel, pledge of my affection" in *1 Henry VI*, V,i,47; "She binds my service to her" (211) compares with "you bind me to your highness' service" in *3 Henry VI*, III,ii,43, plus the "bind me to her" us-age in *Kinsmen*, I,i,37. For "a deeper reach" (254), compare "reach deep" in *Timon*, III,iv,15.

Connections with the later Shakespearean plays are frequent in II,iii, as they are throughout *Merlin*. The phrase "humane shapes" (48) occurs in singular form in *Tempest*, I,ii,284, with "this satisfaction" (58) in *Winter's Tale*, I,ii,31, "now I think on't" (175) in *Henry VIII*, III,i,21; like these other phrases, "most prais'd" (173) occurs only once in the acknowledged works, in *Cymbeline*, I,i,47. In line 131 Aurelius calls Uter "my second Comfort," his first being Artesia; in *Winter's Tale*, III,ii,96, Hermione calls Mamilius "my second joy," her first being Leontes. "For sorrow to creep in" (164) might be com-pared with "harm / Is creeping toward me" in I,ii,403-4 of the same play. "Prithee, tell me" (223) occurs verbatim only once in the collected works, in *Pericles*, IV,vi,156 ("I prithee, tell me" appears five times in various plays). For "Our charms are all dissolv'd" (97), compare "the charm dissolves" in *Tempest*,

V,i,64; for "wish a greater happiness" (57), the closest Shake-spearean usages are "wish thee happiness" in *Pericles*, I,i,60, and "wishes you all happiness" in *Cymbeline*, III,ii,45.

The word pair "Love / And Duty" (15-16) is used twice in *Othello* and twice in *Henry VIII*; for "Disgrace and mischief" (111), compare Shakespearean usages like "disgrace and hor-ror," "disgrace and downfall," "disgrace and dishonor," "mis-chief and despair," and "hurt and mischief." For "quake or tremble" (104), the nearly identical "quake and tremble" ap-pears three times in the collected works. For "all the whole Court" (9), note that six "all the whole . . ." phrasings occur in the acknowledged works—"all the whole world," "all the whole time," etc. (Recall the "all our whole Kingdom" in line 111 of the preceding scene, II,ii.) For "Oh, say, I was born deaf" (166), we can cite similar "Oh, say" usages in *Twelfth Night*, IV,i,65, *Titus*, III,i,87, and *Hamlet*, III,iv,109, with an "O, never say" in Sonnet 109,1. Here in II,iii as in earlier scenes, specific word usages in *Merlin* echo Shakespearean us-ages. One example: in line 163 Uter asks rhetorically why a hu-man being has so many "entrances" for sorrow; compare "No penetrable entrance to her plaining" in *Lucrece*, 559. Again, many similar examples could be given.

(It may be possible, on occasion, to distinguish between Shakespeare's and Rowley's uses of a single word. In the open-ing lines of II,iii, Aurelius refers to "each room / And *angle* of our Palace"; compare *All's Lost*, III,i,153, where Roderick com-mands that "every *angle*" of his castle be searched for the miss-ing Jacinta. Both lines give us the same indoor, structural application of the word "angle." Conversely, for "any *angle* underneath the Moon" in II,iii,74, compare "an odd angle of the isle" in *Tempest*, I,ii,223, both of which apply the word "an-gle" to exterior landscape and terrain. The first use of "angle" in this scene suggests Rowley, the second Shakespeare. Per-haps this involves drawing too fine a distinction between mi-nor details; yet the hands and styles of the two men do seem to be manifested in this text in all sorts of ways, from the largest to the smallest.)

I concentrate on specific phrasings and word usages to display Shakespeare's hand in *Merlin* because I find these features to be unambiguous and self-evident components in his pattern of stylistic self-reference. Yet there are various other elements that could also be examined. Consider Aurelius' speech in line 50-2:

> There is a law that tells us words want force
> To make deeds void; examples must be shown
> By instances alike, e're I believe it.

For "words want force / To make deeds void," we could cite "words are no deeds" in *Henry VIII*, III,ii,154, among similar Shakespearean usages. It may be more interesting, though, to observe that Shakespeare's characters have a habit of looking for "example(s)" and "instance(s)" for their thoughts, words, and actions. *As You Like It*, III,ii,52-69 provides the most extreme installment of this habit, but there are several others; a comparable linkage of "examples" and "instance" occurs in *2 Henry IV*, IV,i,82-3. This habit is not equally common with Rowley; for a rare Rowleian usage of this type, see *Shoemaker*, III,i,22.

Consider the uses of anthropomorphic imagery in this scene. "His presence speaks my truth" (128), "Envy speaks no such words" (178)—abstractions "speak" in this way quite commonly in Shakespeare: "th'occasion speaks thee," "your desert speaks loud," "report speaks goldenly," etc., etc. For "happiness attends me" (127), note that abstractions "attend" like human servants regularly in Shakespeare: "Fair thoughts and happy hours attend on you" in *Merchant*, III,iv,41, "illness should attend" and "our just censures / Attend" in *MacBeth*, I,v,20 and V,iv,14-15, etc.

Or consider what might be called statements of self-reference, people speaking of or acting upon themselves rather than others: the phrases "Betray thy self" (191) and "accuse themselves" (226) have close parallels in Shakespeare's collected works, and participate in a larger pattern of such phrasings in this play ("assure themselves" in II,ii,56, etc.). This is far more typical of Shakespeare than Rowley. Characters in *Merlin* not only talk, but think and feel in ways Shakespearean characters normally do; they show levels of conceptual sophistication and complexity that suggest Shakespeare more than Rowley. Obviously, such factors are difficult to quantify; they are less certain than the specific phrase that either does or does not occur in a given writer's works. Nonetheless, they represent aspects of the play that merit some attention.

Act III, Scene i

In this scene the Clown and Joan return for the first time since II,i, and add to the strongly Rowleian impression in the comic subplot of the play. Two references in this scene specify that the Clown is a typically Rowleian fat clown: in lines 79-80 he describes himself and his pregnant sister as "A couple of Great Brittains you may see by our bellies," and in 188-90 he says, "I am even pin'd away with fretting, there's nothing but flesh and bones about me." (For the Clown's assertion that he has "pin'd away," we might compare Julio's concern that Bustopha will "pine away" in *Maid in the Mill*, II,ii.) The Clown's speech in 83-6 deserves special attention for a rural image for Joan's predicament:

> There's one of your Courtiers Hunting Nags has made a Gap through another mans Inclosure. Now, sir, here's the question, who should be at charge of a Fur-bush to stop it?

Rowley uses very similar metaphors in other of his works. The most extreme example is in *A Cure for a Cuckold*, IV,i,176-81, where the clown character Compass draws upon the same kind of illustration to stake his claim to his wife's bastard son:

> Suppose this is my ground: I keep a sow upon it, as it might
> be my wife; you keep a boar, as it might be my adversary
> here; your boar comes foaming into my ground, jumbles
> with my sow, and wallows in her mire; my sow cries
> "Weke," as if she had pigs in her belly:—who shall keep
> these pigs? he the boar, or she the sow?

Two comparable usages, in related sexual contexts, are
found in *The Spanish Gypsy*, both spoken by the Rowleian
clown character Soto. The first is in III,ii,141-4:

> Through a gap in your ground thence late have been stole
> A very fine ass and a very fine foal;
> Take heed, for I speak not by habs and by nabs,
> Ere long you'll be horribly troubled with scabs.

The second occurs in IV,iii,28-30:

> ... no such sheep has broken through their hedge; no such
> calf as your son sucks or bleats in their ground.

Finally, we can note the exchange between Isabella and Lollio in Rowley's portion of *The Changeling*, III,iii,7-10:

> *Isabella:* Is it your master's pleasure or your own
> To keep me in this pinfold?
> *Lollio:* 'Tis for my master's pleasure, lest being taken in an-
> other man's corn, you might be pounded in another place.

Rowley consistently exploits this parallel between illicit human sexuality and the violation of farmers' property rights to
their domesticated animals and their land. The cited passage in
Merlin, III,i,83-6 conforms to this tendency in Rowley's work.

As for other Rowleian features in III,i, we can note the
presence of the character Sir Nichodemus Nothing; the con-

nection with Sir Nicholas Nemo from *Match at Midnight* was cited in Chapter II. Also, we can mention a feature that points both to Shakespeare and to Rowley in different ways—"Use your best skill" (42). The phrase "best skill" occurs in *Kinsmen*, I,iv,47, and also fits a pattern of related uses in Shakespeare's solo plays, "good skill," "better skill," "sufficient skill," "skill infinite," etc. "Use your best skill" also appears in a later Rowleian play, *Witch of Edmonton*, II,i,58, in the part of the Rowleian clown character Cuddy Banks. From the chronology of the works, one can get the impression (and it is only that) that the "best skill" in *Merlin* originated with Shakespeare, and that Rowley later reproduced it in one of his own works. There are several small features in *Merlin* that conform to this pattern, and give the same impression.

Clearly Shakespearean elements are also present in III,i. They are most common in the speeches of Joan, the Devil, and the courtiers, though Shakespeare appears to have added some touches to the Clown's part too. "See, see" (26) occurs eleven times in Shakespeare's acknowledged works. ("See, see" recurs in later scenes of *Merlin*, in III,ii,52 and 57 and V,ii,17. I do not find comparable instances of the phrase in Rowley.) "Oh, beast" (33) compares with "O you beast" in *Measure*, III,i,135, and "O monstrous beast" in *Shrew*, In.,i,34; "Oh brave!" (215) occurs in *2 Henry VI*, IV,vii,129. For "Ile have another bout with him" (71-2), note that variants of "have a bout with you" occur three times in the collected works, in *Twelfth Night*, III,iv,306 and in *1 Henry VI*, I,v,4 and III,ii,56; for "thus the matter stands" (82), compare "how stands the matter" in *Two Gentlemen*, II,v,20, and "as the matter now stands" in *Measure*, III,i,196. For "you say wisely" (105), we may compare "wisely I say" in *Julius Caesar*, III,iii,16, with many similar usages elsewhere in Shakespeare; for "worshipful old man" (148), compare "worshipful old master" in *Shrew*, V,i,54. "You think we jest" (151) fits with phrasings like "Think'st thou I jest" in *Errors*, II,ii,23, and "Do we jest now, think you" in *Measure*,

IV,iii,49. And in the Clown's closing line, we might compare "at all adventure" with "at adventure" in *Kinsmen*, I,iii,75. In all of these particulars, the Clown's speeches resemble Shakespeare's work more than Rowley's. While the Clown's part is strongly Rowleian in authorship, it also betrays some indications of a Shakespearean contribution—more testimony to the close collaborative effort that generated this play.

Elsewhere in III,i: for "Be but content a while" (12), compare "Content thyself a while" in *Othello*, II,iii,378; for "what else is needful" (48), compare "what needful else" in *MacBeth*, V,ix,37; for "pity my distress" (202), compare "pity his distress" in *All's Well*, V,ii,24 and "in pity of my hard distress" in *1 Henry VI*, II,v,87. For "heaven and goodness" (203), we might cite "Bliss and goodness" in *Measure*, III,ii,215, and for "in spight of fear and death" (214), "in spite of death" in *Venus*, 173. Donobert, in urging Edwin to pursue his suit to Modestia, says, "haste, haste about it" (43), and Edwin replies, "I am gone" (44). Similar exchanges recur in Shakespeare: "Away!" ... "I am gone" in *Cymbeline*, I,i,127-30, "Away with her!" ... "we are gone" in *Winter's Tale*, II,iii,124-30, and "I prithee be gone" ... "I am gone" in *Twelfth Night*, IV,ii,119-20 (with another "I am gone" in *Timon*, II,ii,87). Such phrasings are generally absent from Rowley's work—though one does occur in *New Wonder*, V,i,252-3, in that part of that play that shows signs of Heywood's presence.

The phrase "out of my element" (87) can be classed with "beyond our element" in *Merry Wives*, IV,ii,178, and "not of your element" in *Twelfth Night*, III,iv,124. "The fatal fruit thou bear'st within thy womb" (209) echoes "Murther not then the fruit within my womb" in *1 Henry VI*, V,iv,63; note too that Tamora's bastard is called "the base fruit of her burning lust" in *Titus*, V,i,43. "Ile be thy Advocate" (122-3) compares with "I will be known your advocate" in *Cymbeline*, I,i,76—both statements are hypocritical, made by characters who have no intention of fulfilling them. The rhymed couplet in lines 173-4 merits some notice: if we ignore Tucker Brooke's emendation of "ended" to "defended," we can observe that the same "amended/ended" rhyme appears in *Lucrece*, 578-9, with similar rhymes elsewhere in Shakespeare—"amends/depends" in Sonnet 101,1-3, and "offended/amended" in *All's Well*, III,iv,5-7.

Act III, Scene ii

This scene is devoted exclusively to the Modestia subplot—the only scene in the play that is. The strong commonalities with the Winifred materials in *Shoemaker* continue to appear, with corresponding characters speaking similar lines; thus, Anselme and Amphiabell, the two holy men, both make the point that there is nothing inherently wrong with marriage, though they regard it as inferior to a spiritual commitment to chastity— compare Amphiabell's "For Wedlocke is an ordinance from Heaven" in I,iii,70 of his play with Anselme's "Marriage was blest, I know, with heavens own hand" here in *Merlin*, III,ii,24. The aphoristic couplets of Modestia and Constantia (83-94, 102-10, 119-25, 142-3) are reminiscent of passages in Rowley's play. Predictably, these portions of III,ii show relatively few Shakespearean features (though a scattering of Shakespearean traces can be found in the lines in question).

But if Modestia's subplot has many shared characteristics with Winifred's, it also has a key difference. Modestia, as noted earlier, has a sister and a father, unlike the solitary woman in Rowley's play; and the opposition of these relatives to Modestia's religious vocation arouses Shakespearean reverberations. Once Modestia converts Constantia to the religious life, Donobert's anger reaches a peak; and a father raging at his two daughters quickly reminds us of *King Lear*. Consider lines 144-7 here in III,ii:

> Bewitched Girls, tempt not an old mans fury,
> That hath no strength to uphold his feeble age,

But what your sights give life to: oh, beware,
And do not make me curse you.

The echo of *Lear* is obvious. In other respects, too, this
scene touches upon the canonical play. When Donobert orders
Modestia "Out o' my sight!" (99), he echoes Lear again; compare "Out of my sight!" in *Lear*, I,i,157 (Lear to Kent), "Out,
varlet, from my sight!" in II,iv,187 (Lear to Oswald), and
"Hence, and avoid my sight!" in I,i,124 (Lear to Cordelia).
Such usages are not unique to *Lear*, of course; both Shakespeare's and Rowley's characters use similar lines in other
plays. Yet the *Lear* connection seems striking enough to merit
mention. When Constantia tries to calm her father with,
"Good sir, forbear" (101), we can compare "Dear sir, forbear"
in *Lear*, I,i,162, in precisely the same context. In lines 99-100,
Donobert expresses his disappointment in Modestia by saying, "sure, I was half asleep / Or drunk, when I begot thee";
Edgar makes a similar point about inferior-quality children
"Got 'tween sleep and wake" in *Lear*, I,ii,15.
Constantia's conversion by Modestia here in III,ii will seem
precipitous and unrealistic to many modern readers. We
should note, however, that a similar conversion under a similar
influence occurs at least once in Shakespeare's acknowledged
works. In *1 Henry VI*, III,iii, Joan of Arc convinces the Duke
of Burgundy to switch sides from the English to the French,
through an appeal to his idealism and patriotism; Burgundy
wonders if Joan has "bewitch'd me with her words" (58). Similarly, Constantia's conversion under Modestia's arguments is
seen in terms of bewitchment (113, 144).
More generally, III,ii shows the same Shakespearean stylistic pattern that characterizes earlier scenes. The phrase "pale
and bloodless" (30) occurs three times in the collected works,
"good success" (55) five times; "a sad passage / To a dread
Judgement-Seat" (39-40) compares with "dreadful judgment
day" in *1 Henry VI*, I,i,29, and "seat of judgment" in *2 Hen-*

ry IV, V,ii,80, plus the hyphenated "judgment-place" in *Romeo*, I,i,102. The phrases "On afore" (59) and "half asleep" (99) appear in *Othello*, V,i,128 and IV,ii,97 respectively, with "burning Tapers" (90) in *Titus*, IV,ii,89, "So many miseries" (107) in *Richard III*, IV,iv,17, "all goodness" (114) in both *Pericles*, V,i,70 and *Henry VIII*, III,ii,282, "borrowed robes" (117) in *MacBeth*, I,iii,109, "strange alteration" (130) in *Coriolanus*, IV,v,148. While "eternal happiness" (127) is a commonplace, it may be worth noting that Shakespeare's single canonical use of the phrase occurs in a late collaboration, *Henry VIII*, IV,ii,90. The phrase "careful Father" (159) appears in *Romeo*, III,v,107, in a similar context of a father trying to force an unwanted husband on his daughter.

The phrase "beauteous sister" (47) occurs in plural in *Romeo*, I,ii,65, in a curious phrase, "County Anselme and his beauteous sisters"—Anselme being the name of the hermit in *Merlin*. The phrase "craved your company" (3) is almost identical to "crave my company" in *2 Henry IV*, II,iii,68; "To part with willingly" (9) resembles "To give up willingly" in *Henry VIII*, III,i,140, and "willingly part withal" in *Hamlet*, II,ii,216. For "low despised life" (77), compare "low despise" in *Pericles*, II,iii,26.[14] The phrase "desire instruction" (80) occurs as "desires instruction" in *Antony*, V,i,54; "stand at gaze" (131) appears as "stands at gaze" in *Lucrece*, 1149. For "Your words are air" (142), recall the "airy words" in II,ii,92 of this play, with its Shakespearean parallels. For "sad departure" (18), compare "dire departure" in *1 Henry VI*, IV,ii,41; for "drown'd a sisters name" (67), compare "My drown'd queen's name" in *Pericles*, V,i,205. The phrase "good assurance" (10) resembles Shakespearean usages like "better assurance" and "great assurance"; "love and merit" (11) compares with "love's merit" in *Kinsmen*, V,i,128, and "my love, or thy dear merit" in Sonnet 108,4.

"Cover me with night" (50) resembles "cover'd with the night's black mantle" in *3 Henry VI*, IV,ii,22, among similar Shakespearean phrasings; for "without much grief" (103), we can note two "without much ..." usages in the collected works, in *Winter's Tale*, V,iii,11 and *Henry V*, I,ii,25. "To seek eternal happiness in heaven, / Which all this world affords not" (127-8) compares with "this earth affords no joy" in *3 Henry VI*, III,ii,165, plus "The world affords no law" in *Romeo*, V,i,73, and "The sweet desires that this brief world affords" in *Timon*, IV,iii,253. For "trouble me no further" (130), we can cite close variants in *Coriolanus*, II,iii,109, *Timon*, V,i,213, *Othello*, IV,iii,1, and *Antony*, II,iv,1. "Grief and amazement strive which Sense of mine / Shall loose her being first" (139-40) can be compared with canonical Shakespearean personifications of amazement: "Distraction, frenzy, and amazement, / Like witless antics, one another meet" in *Troilus*, V,iii,85-6; "trouble, torment, wonder, and amazement / Inhabits here" in *Tempest*, V,i,104-5; and "wild amazement hurries up and down" in *John*, V,i,35.

Also, as in earlier scenes, there are other more minor consistencies with Shakespeare's works in III,ii, features that have some usefulness in delineating Shakespeare's contribution vis-à-vis Rowley's—features that Shakespeare uses but Rowley doesn't. For "waste and spend the time" (118), note that "waste the time" occurs in both *Merchant*, III,iv,12 and *Pericles*, II,iii,93, that "spend the time" is found in both *3 Henry VI*, V,vii,42 and *Coriolanus*, II,ii,129, and that both phrases have many variants in Shakespeare's works. (In fact, this idea of wasting time seems to have been something of a standing preoccupation with Shakespeare, something I do not find true of Rowley.) For the "reacht / At" phrasing in 1-2, we could cite several comparable usages in Shakespeare. For "pray, stay" (62), note that Shakespeare has a fondness for this alliterative effect, using variants of it—"I pray you stay," "I pray thee stay," "I pray you stay not," etc.—repeatedly in his works.

While discussing earlier scenes, we noted Shakespeare's habit of giving his Christian characters pagan oaths and expressions. An excellent example of this tendency occurs in

III,ii,132, where Cador—speaking to two bishops, no less!—
uses the phrase "be equal to the Gods." This consistent "pa-
ganizing" tendency in *Merlin* has its most extreme expression
in the following scene.

Act III, Scene iii

This brief, masque-like scene depicts the birth of the magician,
with an accompanying appearance by the Fates and by Lucina,
the Roman goddess of childbirth, and a dance of spirits. (It is
interesting to note that Shakespeare's three canonical references to Lucina all fall in the late romances, specifically in *Pericles* and *Cymbeline*.) The similarity of the masque-like effects
here in III,iii to those in Shakespeare's final plays has already
been mentioned; a further comparison with the appearance of
the angel in *Shoemaker*, I,iii,102-19 is also revealing. Shakespeare's theophanies are never overtly Christian in nature. In
plays like *Pericles* and *Cymbeline*, with their settings in the pagan ancient world, appearances of deities like Diana and Jupiter are simply apropos; yet even in a play with an unquestionably Christian setting such as *Henry VIII*, Queen Katherine's dream-vision in IV,ii does not include angels or any other
identifiably Christian figures, but rather "personages" (IV,ii,82
s.d.), "spirits of peace" (83). Despite the strongly Christian
plot and atmosphere of *Merlin*, here again the spiritual manifestations lack overtly Christian traits. In II,iii Proximus makes
infernal spirits appear in the guises of Hector and Achilles,
while Anselme merely forces those spirits away without calling
forth any in response; and the ensuing magical confrontations
in IV,i and V,i conform to this precedent. Here in III,iii, in the
play's most dramatic episode of spiritual intervention in the
mundane world, the presences—Lucina, the Fates, the dancing "Anticks"—are pagan or neutral rather than Christian.
The contrast with Rowley's Christian angel in *Shoemaker* is
quite clear. The treatment of spiritual elements in *Merlin* is far
more symptomatic of Shakespeare than Rowley.

The invocation of Hecate and other pagan deities (Lucina, Proserpine, Erichtho) by Merlin's devil father (lines 1-14) touches upon apocalyptic and infernal strains in Shakespeare's art. It is reminiscent, in general terms, of Lear's rages in the storm, of MacBeth's summoning of the witches. As for specific features: for "earth and heaven dissolve" (1), compare "the great globe itself / . . . shall dissolve" in *Tempest*, IV,i,153-4, in the masque scene in that play; for "turn to Chaos" (2), compare "Chaos is come again" in *Othello*, III,iii,92, and "chaos comes again" in *Venus*, 1020. Erictho is called "midnight Incubus" in line 13, while the unborn Merlin is "this mixture of infernal seed" in 18; we find a similar conjunction of terms in *Hamlet*, III,ii,257-8, where the actor playing Lucianus in the play-within-the-play personifies his poison as:

> Thou *mixture* rank, of *midnight* weeds collected,
> With *Hecat's* ban thrice-blasted . . .

For Merlin as "infernal seed," we might note Caliban as "hag-seed" in *Tempest*, I,ii,365. (Other connections between the two characters will be examined in Chapter V.)

The phrase "abortive birth" (5) appears in *Love's Labor's Lost*, I,i,104 (though note the "abortive propagations" in *Fair Quarrel*, I,i,96); "birth prodigious" (14) occurs as "prodigious birth" in *Romeo*, I,v,140. The phrase "quick dispatch" (17) is found in *Love's Labor's Lost*, II,i,31, while usages like "swift dispatch" and "quickly dispatch" occur elsewhere in Shakespeare; "infernal deeps" (12) appears in singular form in *2 Henry IV*, II,iv,157; "inhabit here" (36) occurs in *Errors*, III,ii,156 and IV,iii,11, and in *Kinsmen*, II,ii,45, with close variants in *Tempest*, V,i,105 and *Two Gentlemen*, IV,ii,48. "Even from this minute" (30) compares with "Even in a minute" in *Twelfth Night*, I,i,14; "in a moment" (10) occurs eight times in the collected works. For "assisting powers" (25), compare "assisted / By

wicked powers" in *Winter's Tale*, V,iii,90-1 (in the demi-
theophany in that play, the famous statue scene); for "th'in-
fernal King" (23), compare "th'infernal kingdom" in *Titus*,
V,ii,30. The compound word "all-admiring" (27) appears in
Henry V, I,i,39, while "Manlike" (31) is found in *Antony*, I,iv,5.
The personifications of envy and mischief in lines 37-8 have
precedents in Shakespeare: see *Romeo*, V,i,35, *Julius Caesar*,
III,ii,260, *Troilus*, II,iii,21, *Pericles*, IV,Ch.,12, etc.

The speeches of Lucina and the Devil in 23-39 are written in
pairs of couplets with unrhymed lines interspersed, in an a-a-
b-b-c scheme. Rhyme is also used extensively in the miniature
masques of the late romances; the verse spoken by Diana in
Pericles, V,i, and by the ghosts and Jupiter in *Cymbeline*, V,iv,
reveals some of the same irregularity found here in *Merlin*.
Many of the rhymes employed in III,iii have precedents in
Shakespeare's acknowledged works; "hither/together" (10-11)
occurs in *Kinsmen*, III,v,119-20, with "thither/together" in
Diana's speech in *Pericles*, V,i,240-2. The "Arts/parts" rhyme
(25-6) can be compared with "art/part" rhymes in *All's Well*,
II,i,132-3, *Lover's Complaint*, 144-5, and Sonnet 48,10-12, while
"stand/land" (28-9) is used in Sonnet 44,5-7; "appears/years"
(30-1) occurs as "year/appear" in Sonnet 53,9-11. The "live/
give" rhyme (35-6) is a favorite of Shakespeare's, used in *Lucrece*, 986-7 and 1051-3, and in six separate Sonnets—13,2-4;
31,9-11; 37,10-12; 39,5-7; 54,2-4; and 79,10-12. The "wings/sings"
rhyme (38-9) is used in *Venus*, 305-6. I find only the most common of these rhymes, "live/give," in Rowley; see *Shoemaker*,
I,ii,154-5.

Act III, Scene iv

The Clown returns in III,iv, and his speeches provide some of
the most blatant indices of Rowley's hand that appear in this
play. There is a cluster of place-name puns in one of the
Clown's speeches; see lines 124-31:

> By your Mothers side, cousin, you come of the Go-too'ts,
> Suffolk bred, but our standing house is at *Hocklye i'th' Hole*,
> and *Layton-buzzard*. For your father ... I think his Ances-
> tors came first from *Hell-bree* in Wales, cousin.

Puns on place names are one of the hallmarks of Rowley's style; indeed, one of the ones used here is paralleled elsewhere in his work—see "Hockey Hole in Somersetshire" in *Fair Quarrel*, V,i,171. The addition of a Welsh reference in line 131 accentuates the Rowleian impression, as does the "far fetcht and dear bought" in lines 117-18.

As in earlier comedy scenes, the Clown's part appears to have been written mainly by Rowley, but with some input from Shakespeare. For "rid him out of your company" (45), we may compare "Rid me these villains from your companies" in *Timon*, V,i,101; for "a witch or a conjurer" (46), compare "with witches and with conjurers" in *2 Henry VI*, II,i,168. "O brave!" (18) recurs here, after the Clown's initial use of the phrase in III,i,215; "Do not Uncle me" (81) resembles "uncle me no uncle" in *Richard II*, II,iii,87. In line 64 the Clown calls Merlin a "Moncky," and in 82-3 suggests that "some Baboon begot thee"; compare "The strain of man's bred out / Into ba-boon and monkey" in *Timon*, I,i,250-1. The phrase "many a weary step" (116) occurs in *As You Like It*, II,vii,130; for "do you juggle with me" (98), compare "I'll not be juggled with" in *Hamlet*, IV,v,131.

The speeches of the other three characters in the scene, Joan, Merlin, and the Devil, also show Shakespearean features. The phrase "to sound the depth" (23) appears in *Shrew*, V,i,137, with "sounded all the depths" in *Henry VIII*, III,ii,436; "more strange" (31) occurs four times in Shakespeare; "by the same token" (40) appears in *Troilus*, I,ii,281, with similar usages else-where. For "my dear, dear son" (25), compare "My dear dear lord" and "this dear dear land" in *Richard II*, I,i,176 and II,i,57, and "my dear dear love" in *Julius Caesar*, II,ii,102, with another "dear dear" in *Lucrece*, 1602. The "common births" in line 71 fits with the "common sons" and "common mothers," among similar phrases, in Shakespeare; "liberal hand" (108) is found in *Othello*, III,iv,46, with usages like "liberal tongue," "liberal eye," and "liberal heart" elsewhere. For "supply your wants" (113), compare "supply the ripe wants of a friend" and "Supply your present wants" in *Merchant*, I,iii,63 and 140; "lack nothing" (also 113) occurs in *2 Henry IV*, V,iii,69.

In lines 74-7 the Clown and Merlin have an interesting exchange: when the Clown asks Merlin about his father's "profession," the magician replies, "He keeps a Hot-house i'th' Low Countries." At first this sounds like more of Rowley's wordplay and place-name punning; note, however, that Mistress Overdone "professes a hot-house" in *Measure*, II,i,65-6. Once more, we have a single line in *Merlin* that resembles the work of both Rowley and Shakespeare in different respects— another indication, I believe, of the very close collaborative effort that produced this play.

Joan's reference to Merlin as "the happy fruit" of her pregnancy (52) is typical of Shakespeare's habit of applying this term to human progeny; my favorite example is his "orphans and unfathered fruit" (!) in Sonnet 97,10, though various other instances could be cited (some of which were quoted in connection with III,i,209). For "whence we do derive our name" (132), compare "whence 'tis deriv'd" in *Measure*, V,i,247, and "whence thou cam'st, of whom deriv'd" in *3 Henry VI*, I,iv,119. For "practise Treason" (139), we might compare "practic'd dangerously against your state" in *2 Henry VI*, II,i,167. The "years/appears" rhyme from III,iii,30-1 is repeated in III, iv,30-1.

Act III, Scene v

This scene is brief and functional, with little embellishment: thirty-three lines of verse, the longest speech being a mere eight lines. The scene does not yield a great deal of stylistic evidence, though it does show Shakespearean features that are consistent with previous scenes. The phrase "winged speed" (2) occurs verbatim in Sonnet 51,8 (though "wings of speed" in *All's Lost*, V,iv,1 is close); "be vigilant" (13) is found in *1 Henry VI*, II,i,1; "at an instant" (20) appears three times in Shakespeare's works. "Hye thee to Wales" (3) can be compared to "Hie thee to France" in *Richard II*, V,i,22, among similar Shakespearean usages; for "these our Letters" (4), compare "these your letters" in *Hamlet*, IV,vi,32; "surpriz'd and taken" (21) occurs in the same context in *1 Henry VI*, IV,i,26. For "contrary to the Kings command" (25), compare "contrary to the king" in *2 Henry VI*, IV,vii,36; "beats his drums to threaten us" (27) might be compared with "the noise of threat'ning drum" in *Richard II*, III,iii,51.

Act III, Scene vi

Contained in this scene are the remaining interpolations from *Cupid's Revenge*, which will be discussed in Chapter VI; for present purposes, we can easily trace the continuing pattern of Shakespearean elements. The most obvious feature is the line "The incertain Changes of a wavering Skie" (17), which instantly reminds us of "The uncertain glory of an April day" in *Two Gentlemen*, I,iii,85. (We can also note "the sky changes" in *As You Like It*, IV,i,149, among similar Shakespearean usages.)

The Shakespearean linkages in this scene that I find most striking are those having a thematic relationship with the canonical works. The aggressive confrontation between the Britons and Artesia in III,vi has several commonalities with the scenes in *Othello* in which Othello and Desdemona have their confrontations. For "Impudent whore" (27), compare "Impudent strumpet" in *Othello*, IV,ii,81; "false as hell" (81) is found in line 39 of the same scene. For "confound and rot thee" (75), we might cite "let her rot" in *Othello*, IV,i,181 (with five "confound thee" phrasings elsewhere in Shakespeare); for "Wildefire and Brimstone" (108), compare "Fire and brimstone" in line 234 of the same scene in the canonical play.

The British divide into factions for civil strife in this scene—which in turn leads to several connections with Shakespeare's history plays, where the theme of such civil conflict is paramount. Artesia calls out for "Rescue" at line 36, in the way Shakespeare's characters sometimes do; see *2 Henry IV*, II,i,55, or *Richard III*, V,iv,1. "Or, which is worse" (80) resembles "And, which is worse" in *Henry V*, II,i,50; "with advantage" (150) occurs in *John*, III,iii,22; for "scorpions / . . .stung you to the heart" (130-1), compare "A serpent that will sting thee to the heart" in *Richard II*, V,iii,58, among similar Shakespearean usages. "Ile set / In bloody lines upon thy Burgonet" (152-3) compares with "I'll write upon thy burgonet" in *2 Henry VI*, V,i,200—similar metaphors employed in similar threats in similar situations. For "gilded rascal" (122), compare "counterfeit rascal" in *Henry V*, III,vi,61, and "emboss'd rascal" in *1 Henry IV*, III,iii,157. (All three of these "rascal" phrasings use terms from metallurgy or coinage; Rowley's closest parallel, "unprofitable rascal" in *Fair Quarrel*, IV,iv,13, is less close, and may derive from Shakespeare via *Merlin*.)

Beyond these thematic commonalities, the scene shows the usual linkages with Shakespeare's works. Links with the later plays recur: the phrase "contemn'd, and lost" (4) recalls "condemn'd to loss" in *Winter's Tale*, II,iii,192; "no man breathing" (47) can be compared to "any lady breathing" in *Kinsmen*, V,iii,89; "my bloods begetter" (48) resembles "blood of your begetting" in *Cymbeline*, V,v,331; "your sacred person" (78) occurs verbatim only once in Shakespeare, in *Henry VIII*, II,iv,41. For "tempest once o'reblown" (148), compare "storm overblown" in *Tempest*, II,ii,110; "Stand on your guard" (97) compares with "stand upon our guard" in II,i,321 of the same play; for "Preserve the person of the King" (143), the closest canonical parallel is "Preserve the king," again in *Tempest*, II,i,307. (Note the double link to a passage in *Tempest*, II,i that similarly deals with factions forming around a king.) For "rob the Kingdom" (99), compare "robb'd this bewailing land" in *Henry VIII*, III,ii,255.

The phrase "try the utmost" (46) occurs in the past tense in *Julius Caesar*, IV,iii,214, with "try him to the utmost" in *Henry VIII*, V,ii,181; "my sick heart" (93) is found in both *Venus*, 584 and *3 Henry VI*, V,ii,8; "traitors all" (132) appears in *Lear*, V,iii,270. For "my brest shall buckler you" (58), compare "I'll buckler thee" in *Shrew*, III,ii,239. (Shakespeare repeatedly uses "buckler" as a verb—see *2 Henry VI*, III,ii,216 and *3 Henry VI*, I,iv,50 and III,iii,99. Rowley doesn't; contrast his closest usage, "Hold that buckler fast," in *Changeling*, I,ii,66.)

"Beat down their weapons" (59) is found in *Romeo*, III,i,86, in a comparable brawl context; and see also I,i,73 of the same play. (Other "beat down" usages occur in Shakespeare; "beat down Edward's guard" in *3 Henry VI*, IV,ii,23, etc.) For "my sword shall bite thee" (60), compare "My sword should bite it" in *Troilus*, V,ii,171, plus "my good biting falchion" in *Lear*, V,iii,277; for "shut you up within some prison" (79), compare "Shut up in prison" in *Romeo*, I,ii,55. For "I have observ'd your passions" (96), compare "I . . . observ'd your fashion, / . . . noted well your passion" in *Love's Labor's Lost*, IV,iii,137-8; for "the worlds Monarch" (111), compare "monarch of the universal earth" in *Romeo*, III,ii,94; "slanderous tongue" (95) occurs four times in various forms in the canonical works.

As with earlier scenes, there are in III,vi some more prosaic and commonplace features that are still consistent with Shakespeare's usage and atypical of Rowley's. The phrase "be wary" (5) appears six times in the acknowledged works, "I am resolved" (47) ten times; "foul Treason" (101) occurs in *Richard II*, V,ii,72. For "instance" (14) and "example" (18), recall our discussion of such elements in connection with a passage in II,iii. Edoll's and Edwin's uses of "by the Gods" (126, 152) conform to that pattern of Christian characters using pagan oaths in this play, that suggests Shakespeare more than Rowley, as we have noted. The phrases "fiery flames" (9) and "poison'd venome" (124) are redundancies, another kind of feature more typical of Shakespeare than Rowley.

Before leaving III,vi, there is one other Shakespearean connection that merits attention. In her opening speech, Artesia, while flirting with Uter, says, "you do but flatter; / What you term Love is but a Dream of blood" (1-2). When Henry is courting Katherine in the final scene of *Henry V*, he uses a similar conjunction of words and ideas: "my blood begins to flatter me" and "my father . . . was thinking of civil wars when he begot me" in V,ii,222-6. Both passages have "flatter" and "blood," and the idea of dreaming or thinking in an erotic context, in courting/flirting conversations between English princes and foreign princesses. There are many other examples of such verbal/contextual linkages between *Merlin* and Shakespeare's acknowledged works; we will survey more of them in the following chapter.

Act IV, Scene i

The Clown, Joan, and Merlin return in this scene; as in the earlier comedy scenes, the Clown's speeches seem to be mainly the work of Rowley with a minor contribution from Shakespeare, while Shakespeare's hand is more substantially present in the speeches of the other characters. Please remember that it is not my contention that any portion of this or any other scene in the play represents Shakespeare's unadulterated work; the signs of close collaboration between Shakespeare and Rowley are, in my judgment, clear and persuasive. While Rowley's hand is most strongly evident in the Clown's part, features suggestive of his presence occur in the speeches of other characters as well.

In lines 54-68 of this scene, Merlin has a speech that describes the large number of magicians flocking to Vortiger's court in Wales; he mentions (60-3):

The Bards, the Druids, Wizards, Conjurers,

Not an Auraspex with his whisling spells,
No Capnomanster with his musty fumes,
No Witch or Juggler, but is thither sent . . .

Compare *Shoemaker*, II,iii,152-4:

I could by Metroposcopie read thy fate
Here in thy fore-head: by Chyromancie find it
In thy Palme . . .

Rowley likes to spice his texts with sesquipedalian words;
"Auraspex," "Capnomanster," "Metroposcopie," and "Chyromancie" are all in keeping with this habit. Another Rowleyism
can be found in the Clown's penchant for referring to people
as birds, usually in sexual contexts—"a Goshawk was his father" (134), etc. The Shoemaker has a similar cluster of these in
Shoemaker, IV,i,194-200. We can also cite the name "Chough"
in *Fair Quarrel*, and "red-shanks" in II,ii,120 of the same
play.[15] Then there is Bellides calling Ismenia a "Pea-Hen" in
Maid in the Mill, V,i, among other examples in various Rowleian works.

Turning from Rowley to Shakespeare, we find that IV,i is
rich in Shakespearean elements. In this scene, Vortiger's courtiers are searching Wales for a "fiend begotten childe" foretold
by Proximus. When found, he will be sacrificed to preserve
Vortiger's castle from destruction—for only "Mortar temper'd
with the fatal blood / Of such a childe" (80-1) will secure the
foundation. Compare "temper clay with blood of Englishmen" in *2 Henry VI*, III,i,311, and "Who gave his blood to lime
the stones together" in *3 Henry VI*, V,i,84. This striking image,
of human blood being mixed with clay or mortar, is hardly a
commonplace of Jacobean dramatic verse. Consider lines 218-21:

Hast thou such leisure to enquire my Fate,
And let thine own hang careless over thee?
Knowst thou what pendelous mischief roofs thy head,
How fatal, and how sudden?

For the first line of this passage, compare "Had you such leisure in the time of death" in *Richard III*, I,iv,34. For the rest,
compare *Lear*, III,iv,67-8: "Now all the plagues that in the
pendulous air / Hang fated o'er men's faults light on thy
daughters!"—the same idea of evils hanging over men's heads,
in similar language. For Joan's "Thus with the Peacock I beheld my train, / But never saw the blackness of my feet" (195-
6), compare "for all the water in the ocean / Can never turn the
swan's black legs to white" in *Titus*, IV,ii,101-2.

The phrase "better knowledge" (55) occurs in *Measure*,
III,ii,150, "enquire further" (101) in *All's Well*, V,ii,52, "by this
intelligence" (173) in *Richard II*, III,iii,1, "By whose direction"
(213) in *Romeo*, II,ii,79, "Dispatch it quickly" (230) in *Merry
Wives*, V,iii,3, "a minutes time" (also 230) in *Love's Labor's Lost*,
IV,iii,180, "expound the meaning" (261) in *Shrew*, IV,iv,79;
"knit together" (281) is found in *Antony*, II,vi,115, in a similar
politico-military context. The phrase "scornful eye" (193) appears in plural form in *Lear*, II,iv,166; "Deny it not" (18), "I
think no less" (143), "As erst" (169), and "so slightly" (264) all
occur twice in Shakespeare's canonical works, "prevail with
me" (103) three times, "unlook't for" (113) and "Be not amaz'd"
(255) four times each, "most excellent" (266) six times.

"Why, wherein" (8) resembles "Why, and wherein" in *Julius
Caesar*, III,i,222; for "strange and fear'd event" (64), compare
"strange event" in *Timon*, III,iv,17; for "labors of the painful
day" (66), compare "painful labor" in *Shrew*, V,ii,149. The
phrase "Most peaceably" (154) is almost identical to "most
peaceable" in *Much Ado*, III,iii,57; for "write thine Epitaph"
(229), compare "write mine epitaph" in *Merchant*, IV,i,118, and
"make thine epitaph" in *Timon*, IV,iii,379; "'Twixt thee and
thy death" (231) compares with "'Twixt me and death" in *Pericles*, II,i,127. For "thou mayest die laughing" (233), compare "I
should die with laughing" in *Shrew*, III,ii,241; "Seek for yor
safety" (287) compares with "seek sweet safety" in *John*,
V,ii,142.

For "search your pockets" (1-2), compare "search his pockets" in *1 Henry IV*, II,iv,530-1; in both instances, the pockets being searched belong to fat-clown characters. For "certifi'd the King" (78), compare Shakespearean usages like "certified the duke," "certifies your lordship," and "princes shall be certified." For "reasons to the contrary" (89), the closest parallel in either man's works is "persuasions to the contrary" in *Henry VIII*, V,i,147. For "wil't thou have more hair then wit" (116-17), compare the "she hath more hair than wit" passage in *Two Gentlemen*, III,i,353-62. When the "antick spirit" steals the Clown's purse, Merlin orders the spirit to "restore it" (24); we might cite "restore a purse" in *Richard III*, I,iv,140.[16] Many points of vocabulary and word usage in IV,i are typical of Shakespeare; to cite only one obvious example, the word "overslip" (76) occurs twice in Shakespeare, in *Lucrece*, 1576 ("overslipp'd") and in *Two Gentlemen*, II,ii,9 ("o'erslips").

Act IV, Scene ii

The middle of Act IV is occupied by three short action scenes, from sixteen to forty-one lines in length, which depict the combat between the forces of Uter and Vortiger. The way in which the military confrontation is handled in IV,ii has strong similarities with the battle between the Romans and the barbarians in Rowley's *Shoemaker*. When Uter orders a halt and a parley with the enemy, with "hold, drum" (1), Edoll instantly contradicts him—"Beat, slave! why do you pause?" (2), etc. In *Shoemaker*, III,iii, the Romans meet the Goths and Vandals in the field; Roderick, king of the Vandals, says "Drummes beate a parley" (3), though the Roman emperor Diocletian immediately rejects the idea—"Death blurre their parley" (4), etc. Edoll accompanies his views with some striking imagery (8-11):

> Fie on such slow delays! so fearful men,
> That are to pass over a flowing river,

Stand on the bank to parly of the danger,
Till the tide rise, and then be swallowed.

Rowley uses similar imagery in the relevant scene in his play,
in III,iii,23-6:

We are a swelling Sea, and our owne Bankes,
Not large enough to bound us, are broke forth
Like a resistlesse Torrent to o'rewhelme
And drowne in blood all Nations that withstand us.

A similar passage occurs in a later scene in the same play; see
Shoemaker, IV,i,4-6:

.... it seemes a shallow Ford,
When first 'tis tride; but when the depth we sound,
It is a gulfe of raging whirle-pooles found.

Yet we should hesitate before assigning this passage to
Rowley alone; as Caroline Spurgeon has observed, this river-
in-flood imagery is very much typical of Shakespeare.[17] At least
one particular in the quoted lines points to Shakespeare: "slow
delays" (8) is a redundancy that appears verbatim in a canonical work, in *3 Henry VI*, IV,viii,40. Here again, we are confronted with a passage that mixes Rowleian and Shakespearean elements in a way suggestive of close collaboration.

As for other features in IV,ii: "why do you pause?" (2) is
nearly identical to "Why dost thou pause?" in *2 Henry VI*,
V,ii,19, a phrase used in a comparable talk-before-battle context. "What articles or what conditions" (30) compares with "I
embrace these conditions, let us have articles betwixt us" in
Cymbeline, I,iv,156-7. "I do applaud thy counsel" (38) can be
classed with "I do applaud thy spirit" in *Two Gentlemen*,
V,iv,140, and "I do applaud his courage" in *Pericles*, II,v,58;
"We'l hear no parly" (39) resembles "we shall admit no parley"

in *2 Henry IV*, IV,i,157; for "death killing words" (40), compare "dead-killing news" in *Richard III*, IV,i,35. Minor features in IV,ii, like "be calm" (19) and "tenth part" (35) among others, also participate in the Shakespearean pattern.

Act IV, Scene iii

For "most unhappy Tyrant" (12), compare "most unbounded tyrant" in *Kinsmen*, I,ii,63; "do hourly seek" (15) fits with other "do hourly" usages in *Lear*, I,iv,203 and *2 Henry VI*, III,ii,283 (with a "doth hourly" phrasing in *Hamlet*, III,iii,6). For "destroyer of thy Native Countrey" (20), compare "Destroy'd his country" in *Coriolanus*, V,iii,147. The phrase "take mercy" (7) is found in *1 Henry VI*, IV,iii,34; "grown great" (14) occurs in *2 Henry VI*, IV,i,83, with "grown so great" in *Julius Caesar*, I,ii,150, and "grow(s) great" four times elsewhere in Shakespeare; "work enough" (25) appears in *Henry V*, IV,ii,19 (in a combat context) and in *Titus*, V,ii,150 (in a killing context).

Act IV, Scene iv

During the battle between Uter's forces and Vortiger's, Cador asks Uter, "How goes our fortunes" (7). Compare "How goes the day with us" in *John*, V,iii,1, and "How goes the field" in *1 Henry IV*, V,v,16, both in battlefield contexts. For "in a golden Beaver" (2), compare "in a gold beaver" in *Troilus*, I,iii,296 ("beaver" being the face protector on a helmet). For "beat down by Edols sword" (9), we can cite several "beat down" usages in Shakespeare—as noted previously in connection with III,vi,59. The phrase "rightful cause" (5) occurs in *2 Henry VI*, II,i,201 (the same phrase occurs in plural form in *All's Lost*, I,i,154, though the political context shared by *Merlin* and *2 Henry VI* is lacking in Rowley's usage); "lag behinde" (6) is found in *1 Henry VI*, III,iii,34. For "dislodge him thence" (15), we might note that Shakespeare's single canonical use of "dislodg'd" occurs in the same context of evicting a military opponent from a strong point—see *Coriolanus*, V,iv,41.

Also in line 15, Uter says that his forces will burn Vortiger out of his fortress with "wilde fire." Middleton, in his version of the story, also has Aurelius and Uter burn Vortiger's castle with "wild-fire"—see *Hengist*, V,ii,2. Beyond this common detail, though, the passage in *Merlin* has a Shakespearean dimension that *Hengist* lacks: immediately after this reference to wildfire, the next scene opens with the prophetic meteor (IV, v,1ff.). In *Lucrece*, 1523-5, we find the same association:

> Whose words like *wildfire* burnt the shining glory
> Of rich-built Ilion, that the skies were sorry,
> And *little stars shot from their fixed places* . . .

The conjunction of wildfire and meteors is shared by *Lucrece* and *Merlin*, but not by the non-Shakespearean *Hengist*.

Act IV, Scene v

With IV,v the series of short combat scenes is over, and we return to a larger dramatic scale. The Clown's inability or unwillingness to be silent when bidden is similar to Bustopha's in *Maid in the Mill*, V,ii. Both clowns have to be silenced with more than verbal commands (the Clown in *Merlin* is deprived of his power of speech by his nephew's magic, while Bustopha is ejected to the porter's lodge). The Clown's use of the phrase "flesh and blood" in line 48 seems worth a mention; while the phrase is one of the most common of commonplaces, Rowley shows an especially frequent use of it, especially in the mouths of his fat-clown characters. Of the four instances of "flesh and blood" in *All's Lost*, three are spoken by Jaques—see III,ii,77 and III,iii,104-5 and 148; Tim Bloodhound uses it in *Match at Midnight*, II,iii,233, Bustopha has it in his exit line in *Maid in the Mill*, II,ii, and Pompey Doodle uses it in *Wit at Several Weapons*, II,ii. Also note that a reference to Arthur's "thirteen Crowns" (117) is found in *World Tossed at Tennis*, 294, in a portion usually assigned to Rowley.

Scene IV,v is dominated by an episode of prognostication
in which Merlin interprets the significance of an enormous and
elaborate comet that has appeared over the battlefield after
Vortiger's defeat. Shakespeare's plays are rich in similar materials; the image of stars leaving their Ptolemaic spheres is a favorite of his, as Caroline Spurgeon has shown—especially in a
context of political and social upheaval reflected or foretold in
the disorder of the heavens.[18] This is not to imply that other
playwrights do not also refer to the traditional belief that meteors and comets portended earthly events—of course they
do; examples can be found in many of the other dramatists of
the era, including Rowley (see *New Wonder*, I,i,112-14, and *All's
Lost*, III,i,26-9). It is worth noting, though, that Rowley's uses
of such imagery tend to be relatively superficial, and often applied for comic effect.

For an extended use of what we can call the meteor/comet
conceit, used for the elucidation of serious socio-political issues, we need to turn to Shakespeare rather than Rowley. The
most blatant Shakespearean example of such material is in *Julius Caesar*, I,iii-II,i, though other instances can also be cited;
see, for one, *John*, III,iv,153-9 ("No natural exhalation of the
sky . . ."). The opening lines of this scene in *Merlin* give us a
similar picture of a disrupted celestial sphere reflecting and
presaging changes in human affairs (1-11):

Uter: Look, Edol:
Still this fiery exalation shoots
His frightful horrors on th'amazed world;
See, in the beam that's 'bout his flaming ring,
A Dragons head appears, from out whose mouth
Two flaming flakes of fire stretch East and West.
Edol: And see, from forth the body of the Star
Seven smaller blazing streams directly point
On this affrighted kingdom.
Cador: 'Tis a dreadful Meteor.
Edwin: And doth portend strange fears.

The phrasing of this passage has elements that are common to the similar usages in Shakespeare: "a bright exhalation in the evening" in *Henry VIII*, III,ii,226; "portentous things" and "exhalations whizzing in the air" in *Julius Caesar*, I,iii,31 and II,i,44; "an exhal'd meteor" in *1 Henry IV*, V,i,19; "some meteor the sun exhal'd" in *Romeo*, III,v,13; etc. The phrase "th'amazed world" (3) is virtually identical to "the mazed world" in *Dream*, II,i,113, while "this affrighted kingdom" (9) recalls "th'affrighted globe" in *Othello*, V,ii,100. For "flaming *flakes* of fire stretch *East* and West" (6), we might compare "*flaky* darkness breaks within the *east*" in *Richard III*, V,iii,86, in a similar "skyey" observation in a context of battlefield prognostication and occultism.

The scene as a whole reflects the pattern of Shakespearean features that occurs in every preceding scene in the play. Here in IV,v, Merlin most prominently fulfills the role of prophet rather than magician; and it is in the same role that he makes his two intrusions into Shakespeare's acknowledged works— "the dreamer Merlin and his prophecies" in *1 Henry IV*, III,i,148, and "this prophecy Merlin shall make" in *Lear*, III,ii,95. (These rather mocking allusions are typical of the skeptical or negative attitude toward most manifestations of the occult that Shakespeare displays in most of his works. In regard to prophecy, it is the cryptic, misleading, "double-meaning prophesier" who dominates, as with the witches in *MacBeth* or the soothsayer in *Antony*. Yet the late romances show a radically different and more positive attitude toward prophecy and other aspects of occultism; and the handling of these elements in *Merlin* is typical of this more positive disposition.) For "And durst I prophecy of your Prophet" (22), note that Shakespeare, in his wide and varied range of repetitive effects, often uses two different forms of the same word in a single line. In *Lucrece*, we can cite "This forced league doth force a further strife" (689), "Devise extremes beyond extremity" (969), and "Extremity still urgeth such extremes" (1337), among others; in Sonnet 5,4, "And that unfair which fairly doth excel" is a good example—and there are many more scattered throughout his canon. Line 22 in IV,v conforms well to this tendency. (While similar lines are not wholly absent from Rowley's style, I find his use of such tricks of repetition to be far more sparing.)

Common phrasings: "large effects" (17) occurs in *Lear*, I,i,131, "disturb him not" (35) in *2 Henry VI*, III,iii,25, "fatal end" (42) in *MacBeth*, III,v,21, "mournful tears" (52) in *2 Henry VI*, III,ii,340, "fair posterity" (77) in *Winter's Tale*, IV,iv,409, "Again behold" (95) in *Romeo*, III,v,47; "Contrary ways" (94) is used in singular form in *All's Well*, III,v,8; "make division" (134) can be found in *Twelfth Night*, III,iv,346, with a past-tense usage in V,i,222 of the same play.

"The fortunes of this day successful to us" (27) can be compared with "Successful fortune" in *3 Henry VI*, II,ii,41; "He told the bloody Vortiger his fate, / And truely too" (29-30) contains an echo of "and tell me truly too" in *Shrew*, IV,v,28, along with similar phrasings elsewhere in Shakespeare ("I tell thee truly" in *Henry V*, IV,vii,83; "And tell me truly" in *Julius Caesar*, I,ii,214.) For "figur'd yonder in that Star" (39), compare "Figur'd quite o'er with burning meteors" in *John*, V,ii,53; for "how swiftly mischief creeps" (41), we can cite "False creeping craft and perjury" in *Lucrece*, 1517, for a similar image of creeping evils. For "his action shows it" (43), "your outward action shows itself" in *Richard III*, I,iii,66 may be a useful comparison; for "hear the rest with patience" (55), "Hear me with patience" in *Shrew*, I,ii,237 is perhaps the closest of many Shakespearean parallels. For "The milde and gentle, sweet Aurelius" (61), note that another English king is "gentle, mild, and virtuous" in *Richard III*, I,ii,104, while other English magnates are "mild and gentle" in *2 Henry VI*, III,ii,392 and *Richard III*, IV,iv,161.

For "cost thousand lives" (72), compare "cost ten thousand lives" in *3 Henry VI*, II,ii,177; for "after times shall fill their

Chronicles" (109), compare "fill up chronicles in times to come" in *1 Henry IV*, I,iii,171, and note that "after-times" is used in *2 Henry IV*, IV,ii,51. For "Monarch of the West" (114), compare "monarch of the north" in *1 Henry VI*, V,iii,6; for "War and Dissension" (133), compare "quarrels and dissensions" in *Henry V*, IV,viii,65. "Prosperity will keep you company" (152) resembles "Prosperity be thy page" in *Coriolanus*, I,v,23, a similar congratulatory remark to a victorious general.

Connections with the late romances are worth noting: for "to satisfie / Your Highness pleasure" (32-3), the closest canonical parallel is "To satisfy your highness" in *Winter's Tale*, I,ii,232; for "the damn'd witch Artesia" (69), compare "this damn'd witch Sycorax" in *Tempest*, I,ii,263. "That Kingdoms Title" (106) compares with "the titles of two kingdoms" in *Kinsmen*, IV,ii,145; for "Knight-hoods honor" (122), compare "knighthoods and honors" in *Cymbeline*, V,ii,6, while "Expect revenge" (165) is nearly identical to "expect my revenge" in III,iv,25 of the same play. "Thou speakst of wonders" (129) compares with "Thou speakest wonders" in *Henry VIII*, V,iv,55, in the comparable instance of patriotic prophecy in that play.

And, as usual in *Merlin*, this scene shows other features, more commonplace in themselves, that still have some potential as pointers toward Shakespeare rather than Rowley. The phrases "be appeas'd" (16), "East and West" (6, 102), and "adde unto" (155) all occur twice in the collected works, "without book" (84) five times, "lawful King" (159) ten times. (As noted earlier, the last phrase has repeated uses in this play; see II,ii,55 and IV,i,277.)

For "met us in the way" (26), note that "met us on the way" occurs twice in Shakespeare; for "his conquering foot" (112), compare "the proud foot of a conqueror" in *John*, V,vii,113; "warlike sword" (110) and "fertile France" (111) are found in *1 Henry VI*, in IV,vi,8 and III,iii,44 respectively. "Forefend it heaven" (63) has various parallels in Shakespeare; for the

Clown's "Me thinks, I see something like a peel'd Onion; it makes me weep agen" (78-9), we can cite several similar references in Shakespeare—see *All's Well*, V,iii,320, and *Antony*, I,ii,169-70 and IV,ii,35. The scene opens, as we have noted, with "Look, Edol" (1); *Julius Caesar*, V,iii opens with "O, look, Titinius, look," in a similar resolution-of-battle context. Various other usages can also be noted—the word form "styl'd" (158), for instance, appears once in *Cymbeline* and twice in *Kinsmen*.

In line 21 we find the tongue-twisting "the best that ever Brittain bred"; since this is the kind of writing that Shakespeare parodied so famously in *Dream*, V,i ("with blade, with bloody blameful blade, / He bravely broach'd his boiling bloody breast," 146-7), one might suppose that Shakespeare is positively unlikely to have written such a line into *Merlin*. Yet Shakespeare also wrote "being bred in broils" in *Coriolanus*, III,ii,81, and "By thy bright beauty was it newly bred" in *Lucrece*, 490, among similar lines. Preconceived ideas about what Shakespeare would have or could have written are of little use in authorship studies.

Act V, Scene i

The first scene of Act V contains the final and the most important of the play's three contests of magic, in which Merlin prevents his mother's abduction into the underworld at the hands of his devil-father, and confines his father permanently within the earth through the force of his incantation. This scene has an interesting general resemblance to III,ii of *A Fair Quarrel*, a scene in that play usually assigned to Rowley. In both, we have a "tempter" character (the Devil; the Physician) trying first to lure, and then to bully a female character for whom the audience has sympathy (Joan; Jane) into illicit sexual relations. Both women are "fallen" women by the standards of their societies, having recently given birth to illegitimate children; yet both are determined to resist the "tempter." In both scenes, the tempter departs and is replaced with a friend or ally of the woman, who depart together at the scene's end (Merlin; Anne).

More striking than this general similarity with Rowley's work, however, is the pattern of Shakespearean commonalities that distinguishes the scene. Joan, at this point in the play, is repentant over her assignation with the Devil; once Merlin has triumphed over his father, he says, "So! there beget earthquakes or some noison damps, / For never shalt thou touch a woman more" (81-2)—and then he turns to Joan with, "How chear you, mother?" (83). The phrase itself is a commonplace; yet Shakespeare reveals a tendency in his usage of it that is individual enough to be worth noting. In the opening scene of *Midsummer Night's Dream*, Theseus warns Hermia of the fate that awaits her if she disobeys her father, and then addresses Hippolyta with, "What cheer, my love?" (I,i,122). In *Cymbeline*, III,iv, Pisanio gives Imogen Posthumus' letter and observes her reaction with a speech on the pervasiveness of slander—and then addresses her directly with, "What cheer, madam?" (39). Hortensio's "Mistress, what cheer?" in *Shrew*, IV,iii,37, and Oliver's "Be of good cheer," spoken to the fainting Rosalind in *As You Like It*, IV,iii,163, also participate in the same psychological situation: a woman in distress or danger because of an unhappy love affair, and a sympathetic male third party who speaks of "cheer" in a comforting or conciliatory manner. We find the same situation here in V,i of *Merlin*.

Repetitive effects in V,i deserve attention. "From Brittain and from Merlin" (42) conforms to a pattern of "from" repetitions in the canonical works; the best examples combine references to a place and a person, as here—see "from Padua, from Bellario" in *Merchant*, IV,i,119 and V,i,268, and "From hence, from Silvia, and from me" in *Two Gentlemen*, III,i,220. (For other instances of repetitions with "from," see *Measure*, II,ii,161 and III,ii,39, *Hamlet*, III,ii,164 and III,iv,190, *Henry VIII*, III,ii,261, etc. etc.)

In lines 57-60 there is an interesting passage worth quoting in full:

> Obedience is no lesson in your school;
> Nature and kind to her commands my duty;
> The part that you begot was against kinde,
> So all I ow to you is to be unkind.

In discussing the previous scene, we mentioned Shakespeare's habit of constructing this kind of repetition with different forms of a single word; for this passage, compare " 'Twixt his kindness and his unkindness" in *Winter's Tale*, IV,iv,552, "A kind overflow of kindness" in *Much Ado*, I,i,26, and "Th' unkindest beast more kinder than mankind" in *Timon*, IV,i,36. Beyond the mere repetition, note that these lines touch upon a standing preoccupation that Shakespeare has with the idea of "human-kindness" in both senses of the term—of humans as a specific "kind" of creature who should therefore treat each other with "kindness." For Shakespeare, "unnatural and unkind" (*Titus*, V,iii,48) are closely related terms and concepts. I do not find a comparable preoccupation with this complex of ideas in Rowley's plays.

As for other features in V,i: "And gently twine thy body in mine arms" (8) resembles "let me twine / Mine arms about that body" in *Coriolanus*, IV,v,106-7; "Thou didst beget thy scourge" (72) compares with "He'll breed revengement and a scourge" in *1 Henry IV*, III,ii,7. "Ile conduct you to a place retir'd" (92) resembles "I'll conduct you to the sanctuary" in *Richard III*, II,iv,73—in a relevant politico-military context, with a male authority figure guiding a female offstage to safety from the play's conflict. (Other "I will/shall conduct you" phrasings also occur in Shakespeare.) "With grones and passions your companions" (95) might be compared with "The sad companion, dull-ey'd melancholy" in *Pericles*, I,ii,2. "Hence, thou black horror" (1) has some relation to "hence in horror" in *Measure*, V,i,436, which occurs in a similar context of a woman being transported into a hostile underworld ("Her brother's ghost . . . take her hence in horror").

The phrase "kindled agen" (2) appears in the present tense in *Pericles*, III,ii,83; "too too much" (4) is found in *Two Gentlemen*, II,iv,205 (with "too much too" in *Cymbeline*, III,ii,69). "Is past already" (5) is almost identical to "is pass'd already" in *All's Well*, III,vii,36; "What hound so e're I be" (10) can be classed with a range of "what e'er I/he/you be" usages in Shakespeare—compare, for instance, "what goddess e'er she be" in *Troilus*, I,i,27. "Why, whither wouldst?" (15) compares with the "Why, whither" phrasings in *As You Like It*, I,iii,106 and II,iii,29; we find a comparable alliteration in "Wit, whither wilt?" in IV,i,166 of the same play. "Ages to ages" (23) resembles "age to age" in *Richard III*, III,i,73 and 76. "Hence from my sight" (29) is another of those "out of my sight" injunctions that recur in Shakespeare; recall "Hence and avoid my sight" in *Lear*, I,i,124, quoted in connection with III,ii,99. "Sweet death" (also 29) occurs in *Venus*, 997, with a plural usage in Sonnet 54,12 and "So sweet a death" in *Titus*, V,i,146. "Thy cursed person" (33) is synonymous with "thy cursed self" in *Richard III*, I,ii,80, "palled Hecat" (39) with "pale Hecat" in *MacBeth*, II,i,52. For "The jaws of Achoron" (69), compare "The jaws of darkness" in *Dream*, I,i,148, and "the jaws of death" in *Twelfth Night*, III,iv,360; for "is all confirm'd" (73), compare "All is confirm'd" in *MacBeth*, V,iii,31. "Thou first shall taste it" (76) compares with "Taste of it first" in *Richard II*, V,v,99; for "weep away this flesh" (96), note the synonymous "weep what's left away" in *Errors*, II,i,115.

Other features in V,i conform to the Shakespearean pattern on a more modest level. For "loud throated thunder" (2), compare "dread-bolted thunder" and "all-shaking thunder" in *Lear*, IV,vii,32 and III,ii,6 respectively, and "deep-mouth'd thunder" in *John*, V,ii,173. The phrase "all bare" (97) occurs in Sonnet 103,3, while "be absent" (91) is used four times in the acknowledged works. In line 67, Merlin tells the Devil to "Put off the form of thy humanity"; compare "spirits can assume both form and suit" in *Twelfth Night*, V,i,235. The "glory/story" rhyme in lines 24-5 is to be found in Sonnet 84,6-8. "Hark, how the sounds of war now call me hence" (88) compares with the five "hark how . . ." phrasings in the collected works, including one in *Kinsmen*, V,iii,56.

(As Merlin leads his mother away to a life of seclusion and repentance at the close of V,i, he tells her that "when you die, I will erect a Monument / Upon the verdant Plains of Salisbury, / . . . A dark Enigma to the memory" (98-103). The identification of Merlin as the builder of Stonehenge is traditional, and is recorded by Geoffrey of Monmouth, the main source for the plot of this play. Inigo Jones, however, came to believe that Stonehenge was an ancient Roman rather than a British creation, after he had conducted a study commissioned in part by William Herbert, Earl of Pembroke.[19] Herbert, of course, was one of the men to whom the First Folio was dedicated; and he is one of the perennial top contenders for the identity of "Mr. W.H." of Shakespeare's Sonnets. His interest in Stonehenge is easily understood, since Wilton House, the Herbert family seat, stands in the neighborhood. The King's Men were at Wilton House on December 2, 1603, to perform before King James; while Shakespeare apparently had retired from active stage performance by this time, he might well have accompanied them. The idea that Shakespeare might have visited Stonehenge in person is purely speculative—but it is such a pleasing speculation that it would be a shame not to entertain it as the genuine possibility it is.)

Act V, Scene ii

In this final scene the Modestia subplot is wound up quickly and perfunctorily in the first thirty lines; a summary of the political and military developments (the defeat of the Saxons, Ostorius' death, and Artesia's capture) is thrown in for good measure. Once the major characters enter at line 38, the last loose ends are tied up, with Merlin's second episode of prophecy and a final display of ritual pomp following in good order.

There is a second mention of Arthur's thirteen crowns in lines 96-7; recall the previous instance in IV,v,117, plus the parallel cited earlier from *World Tossed*, 294. Shakespeare never mentions Arthur's thirteen crowns, so that it seems reasonable to take this as at least a minor indicator of Rowley's presence. Conversely, Rowley's works never allude to either Merlin or Uter Pendragon; Shakespeare's mentions of Merlin have already been noted in our survey of IV,v, and we can also cite his reference to Uter Pendragon in *1 Henry VI*, III,ii,95. Such allusions, though not of major signficance, have interest and relevance in the context of this study.

The pattern of Shakespearean features in all previous scenes is also here in V,ii. The scene's repetitive effects are worth notice: for "Those lost, I am lost: they are lost, all's lost" (8), we might compare "All lost! To prayers, to prayers! All lost!" and "all, all lost, quite lost" in *Tempest*, I,i,51-2 and IV,i,90, plus other "lost" repetitions in *Hamlet*, I,ii,89-90 and *Richard III*, II,ii,11. For "thirteen several Princes shall present / Their several Crowns unto him" (96-7), note that Shakespeare uses this stylistic trick, of repeating the word "several" in successive verse lines, four times in his acknowledged works: see *Tempest*, III,i,42-3, *Love's Labor's Lost*, V,ii,124-5, *Richard III*, V,iii,193-4, and *Julius Caesar*, I,ii,316-17. (Yet again, we find in lines 96-7 an example of Shakespearean and Rowleian features mingled intimately together, signalling a close collaboration.) The "perswade" repetition in lines 12-13 lacks any direct precedent in the canonical works, though it is the type of feature that is common in Shakespeare, less common in Rowley.

As for other elements: for "'Twill be a good Office in you" (14), we can cite similar "good office" lines in *Merry Wives*, I,i,100 and III,i,49; for "thus neglect" (15), compare "thus neglecting" in *Tempest*, I,ii,89. The word "re-deliver" (26), used in reference to the idea of relinquishing political authority over a city, is employed in the same sense in *Measure*, IV,iv,6. For "triumphantly is marching hither" (29), we may compare "Is marching hitherward in proud array" in *2 Henry VI*, IV,ix,27, with three more "marching hitherward(s)" usages elsewhere. For "firm hope" (39), compare "As firmly as I hope" in *2 Henry VI*, III,i,88; for "Uprising Sun" (43), compare "the sun's uprise" in *Titus*, III,i,159, and "O sun, thy uprise" in *Antony*, IV,xii,18; for "let us salute thy glory" (also 43), compare "the golden sun salutes the morn" in *Titus*, II,i,5; for "diet good enough" (69), compare "very good diet" in *Measure*, II,i,112. "What Heaven decrees, fate hath no power to alter" (84) compares with "alter not the doom / Forethought by heaven" in *John*, III,i,311-12. In line 86 Merlin states that the numbers of the opposing Saxons will "still increase"; compare "still his power increaseth" in *Richard III*, IV,iii,48, in a relevant military context. "Succeeding Princes" (90) resembles "succeeding royalty" in *MacBeth*, IV,iii,155.

Other, less striking usages in V,ii have some value in a discrimination between Shakespeare and Rowley. For "fairly promis'd" (5), compare Shakespearean usages like "fairly answer'd," "fairly offer'd," and "fairly spoke"; for "Times joy" (23), we may cite "time's hate," "time's glory," "time's help," etc., from various Shakespearean works. "To be invested" (30) occurs in *MacBeth*, II,iv,32; for "Fairs and Markets" (56), compare "markets, fairs" in *Love's Labor's Lost*, V,ii,318; for "resolve my fears" (79), compare "Resolve my doubt" in *3 Henry VI*, IV,i,135. The phrase "go no further" (11) occurs seven times in the collected works, with "stand apart" (72) and "do him homage" (100) twice each, plus variants; for "a day perpetual" (44), we might note Shakespeare's three uses of "perpetual night." The phrase "latter days" (91) appears in both singular and plural forms in Shakespeare, along with variants like "latter times" and "latter age"; for "future times" (109), compare "future ages" in *Richard II*, IV,i,138, in a relevant death-of-kings context. For "in the middest of" (102), note that the word form "middest" is found in *2 Henry VI*, IV,viii,61, while "in the midst of" phrasings appear four times in Shakespeare, plus variants. The "story/glory" rhyme from V,i,24-5 recurs in 109-10 of this scene; refer to Sonnet 84,6-8 for a canonical example. And "visible apparitions" (88) is another of the play's many redundancies.

I have no doubt that some of the features I have cited in this chapter will appear trivial to some readers. If, however, those readers are willing to inspect Rowley's works firsthand, they will find that these cited particulars do represent points on which *Merlin* is like Shakespeare's work and unlike Rowley's—and that is a fundamental, an essential fact to be recognized in our attempt to understand this play's authorship. As we have seen, there are various lines, speeches, passages, references, plot elements, and stylistic traits in *Merlin* that are symptomatic of, suggestive of, or consistent with Rowley's dramatic style as evidenced in his known works. Taken together, these Rowleian features form a pattern of internal evidence that confirms the external evidence of Rowley's authorship. By the same standard, there are other features in the play that are positively unlike Rowley's work, and very much like Shakespeare's. If we apply to these Shakespearean features the same reasoning and the same judgment that we apply to the play's Rowleian features, it is hard to see why we should not accept the Shakespearean elements as legitimate evidence of Shakespearean authorship.

In a play that purports to be a Shakespeare-Rowley collaboration, it is only logical to compare that play to Shakespeare's and to Rowley's works—just as it is logical to compare *Kinsmen* to the works of Shakespeare and Fletcher. Yet we do not need to stop at that point; we can extend the comparison to a larger body of English Renaissance literature. Any author for whom a concordance is available can be a resource in a study such as this. For present purposes, I have consulted the concordances for the plays, poems, and translations of Christopher Marlowe,[20] and for the poems of Ben Jonson,[21] Edmund Spenser,[22] and John Donne.[23] Such a comparison is revealing in many ways.

In our discussion of III,vi, we cited canonical Shakespearean parallels ("emboss'd rascal," "counterfeit rascal") for "gilded rascal" (122). A check of the Marlowe, Donne, Spenser, and Jonson concordances shows no similar phrasings. For the idea of mixing human blood into clay or mortar, which is shared by *Merlin*, IV,i,80 and Shakespeare's works, we again find no comparable usages in the four concordances. This sort of contrast can be repeated over and over. Consider the following list (by no means an exhaustive one) of phrases that are common to *Merlin* and the acknowledged Shakespearean works, either verbatim or in close variants, and which do not have equally close parallels in the concordances for the other writers:

abortive birth	age(s) to age(s)
airy word(s)	all submission
beat down their weapons	beauteous sister
be not amaz'd	better knowledge
be wary	borrow'd robes
brave Hector	burning tapers
by the rood	by whose direction
careful father	commanded home
dear dear . . .	death or sickness
desire(s) instruction	dispatch it quickly
duty and observance	earth and dust
even already	expect (my) revenge
expound the meaning	false as hell
fertile France	for wisdom's sake
for aught that I can tell/see	foul treason
full commission	hasty marriage
have a fling at	hellish charms

human shape(s)	infernal deep(s)
inhabit here	inquire further
is past/pass'd already	I think no less
kindle(d) again	large effects
latter days	make division
many a weary step	a minute's time
mirth and triumphs	much rather
my sick heart	Oh fate
Oh the good gods	on afore
on equal terms	prevail with me
quickly wooed	slanderous tongue
so many miseries	stand apart
strange alteration	stuck full of . . .
tenth part	tie you to your word
time and fortune	to be invested
to hasten on	too too much
two-legg'd creature	warlike sword
why, whither	winged with (sweet) desire
a woman's fault	work enough
youthful lord	

Admittedly, list-making is a crude recourse; one can debate, almost endlessly, points of inclusion or exclusion. Note, for instance, that the phrase "in a gold(en) beaver," and the image of "writing" or "setting lines" on an enemy's "burgonet" with strokes of a weapon in battle, are common to *Merlin* and Shakespeare's works, but absent from the four concordances used for comparison. Since much of the body of work used for this comparison does not exploit military subject matter (particularly the poetry of Donne and Jonson), one might object to the inclusion of those phrases, and others like "warlike sword," on that basis. (On the other hand, the fact that *Merlin* employs subject matter typical of Shakespeare is hardly irrelevant to the question of the play's authorship.)

It is not my contention that any of these phrases is unique

to Shakespeare; "abortive birth" can be found in Fulke
Greville's *A Treatie of Human Learning*, stanza 14, and no
doubt instances of other phrases on the list can be located in
the works of other authors of the period. (A few of the listed
phrases *might* be unique to Shakespeare; "duty and observance" is one good candidate, since the word "observance" is
fairly common with Shakespeare but rare elsewhere. Yet this
cannot be determined with any degree of certainty; as Eric
Rasmussen has written, "until concordances are available for
the entire corpus of English Renaissance literature, it will be
impossible to claim with absolute assurance that any phrase is
unique to any particular author."[24]) On a more limited scale
than absolute uniqueness, such a comparison can still be quite
revealing: it shows that if *Merlin* is like Shakespeare's works in
ways and to degrees that set it apart from Rowley's, it is also
like Shakespeare's works in ways and to degrees that set it
apart from Elizabethan/Jacobean literature in general, as represented by the works of four major poets of the age.

Or consider another feature cited in this chapter, one that
might seem especially vulnerable to objection in that it draws
upon proverbial material. In IV,i, I compared lines 195-6 of
that scene, "Thus with the Peacock I beheld my train, / But
never saw the blackness of my feet," with "For all the water in
the ocean / Can never turn the swan's black legs to white" in
Titus, IV,ii,101-2. Both of these images are rooted in the proverb, "The peacock has fair feathers but foul feet," and it can be
asserted that any writer could draw upon that proverb to form
a similar image with the same meaning and significance.
When, however, we consult R.W. Dent's compendium of proverbial allusions in Tudor and Jacobean drama, we find that
the only other passage based on this proverb is from *Sappho
and Phao*, a play by John Lyly dating from 1584: "I will pull
those plumes, and cause you to cast your eyes on your feet, not
your feathers" (V,ii,79).[25] The Lylian usage is the weaker parallel—it does not, for instance, specify the blackness of the

bird's feet or legs—and of course Lyly is a poor prospect as a potential author of *Merlin* both on stylistic and chronological grounds (he died in 1606 after fifteen years of inactivity as a dramatist). The parallel between the passages in *Titus* and *Merlin* is much closer.

This broader comparison can negate one abstract objection to this survey, based on the disparity in size between Shakespeare's canon and Rowley's. It could be argued that any phrase or usage in *Merlin* is more likely to have a parallel in Shakespeare's works than in Rowley's, through mere chance resemblance and regardless of any factor of common authorship, simply because Shakespeare's canon is so much larger than Rowley's. I do not find this a strong argument: specific features present in Shakespeare's works are not due to some random distribution, but because Shakespeare consciously put them there. The essential difference between Shakespeare's and Rowley's canons is not that Shakespeare wrote more plays, but rather that he wrote in a very different style to very different effects and ends, generating a very different aesthetic achievement. I do concede, though, that disparity in canon size could be a problem for readers with other viewpoints. The extension of the range of comparison, from Rowley's works alone to a much larger sample of English Renaissance literature, should vitiate this objection.

Another point worth considering: if the possession of a concordance for a given author's work is a tremendous advantage in the study of that writer (as I believe is indisputably true), the lack of a concordance can be a real limitation and hindrance. Throughout this survey, Shakespeare's hand has appeared to be far more noticeable, more distinguishable, than Rowley's. In part this is because Shakespeare's style is simply more distinctive than Rowley's in a great many details, and in part it is a distortion caused by the existence of a concordance for one writer but not for the other. The employment of concordances for other contemporary writers allows us to be more

certain that the apparent "Shakespeareanness" of *Merlin* is
real, and not an illusion projected by an imbalanced and preju-
diced method.

(I have noted a number of lines in *Merlin* that appear to
indicate a very close and intimate collaboration between the
two authors; in my judgment, these lines are typical of the
style of the play, and tell us something fundamental about the
genesis of *Merlin*. A Rowley concordance would allow us to
refine our perception of his hand in the play—though the lack
of such a resource is not a crucial inhibition to our comprehension of the play. In one key respect, I believe that this survey of
the stylistic elements in *Merlin* is true to the nature of the poets
involved: it gives an accurate picture of the repetitiveness of
Shakespeare's usage of many words and phrases. Many readers
might expect Shakespeare to be the more "original" of the two
collaborators, and Rowley to "repeat himself" more frequently. Yet Shakespeare's greater commitment to regularity in his
verse leads him to re-use elements that fit well into the iambic
pentameter framework; Rowley, in contrast, is willing to write
very irregular verse, and so does not have the same motivation
to repeat words and phrases that fill out a line. The majority of
features that *Merlin* repeats from the Shakespearean canon partake of this tendency to verse regularity.)

Stylistic parallels and common phrasings are a basic aspect
of any writer's distinctive style; yet there are other aspects of
style that are similarly useful in discerning Shakespeare's hand
in *Merlin*, as we shall see in the following chapters.

CHAPTER V

Further Stylistic Considerations

GIVEN OUR desire to pursue this authorship inquiry further, there are several paths open to us. Various scholars have devised methods for addressing authorship questions, and several of these approaches yield interesting results when applied to *Merlin*. MacDonald Jackson, for one, has concentrated attention on what he has called "function words," the most common words in English and in any writer's vocabulary: "the," "a," "and," "but," "by," "for," etc.[1] When two writers can be shown to use function words in differing frequencies, that difference can be used to distinguish between them. (As with the more common forms of textual evidence, this use of function words is strictly relative; a pattern of usage that allows distinctions to be drawn between Authors A and B might be useless for distinguishing between Authors A and C or B and D, etc.)

It is our good luck that a clear distinction exists between Shakespeare and Rowley in their relative frequencies of use of the words "a" and "and." Shakespeare uses "and" significantly more often than "a." The Harvard Concordance shows that "and" is the second most common word in the acknowledged Shakespearean works, while "a" is only the sixth most com-

mon. For Rowley, the reverse is true: "a" appears to be consistently more common in his work than "and."[2] When we
look at the totals of these words in *Merlin*, we find that there
are 508 uses of "and" in the play, but only 315 of "a," a proportion that clearly indicates Shakespeare, not Rowley.[3]

If we narrow our focus, we find that the differing patterns of
the two authors hold true: in the speeches of the Clown, the
most strongly Rowleian aspect of the play, there are only 61
instances of "and" against 114 of "a." If we turn to II,ii, which
seems to me perhaps the most strongly Shakespearean single
scene in the play, we find thirty-two uses of "and" but only
eight of "a." Obviously, we need to be cautious about our employment of such evidence, and to recognize that such patterns
are most meaningful when they occur on a large scale, less so
when the samples are smaller. In the scope of the entire play,
however, this test of function words does appear to tell us
something useful about the play's authorship.

Shakespeare's relatively frequent use of "and" can sensibly
be related, I think, to his passion for word pairs, noted by various commentators.[4] The very frequent word pairings in
Merlin—"this *and* that," rather than "this" alone—are quite
typical of Shakespeare's habits. Lines like "My will *and* rule
shall stand *and* fall together" and "So high *and* noble to my
fame *and* Country" (I,ii,136 and 147) provide good examples,
though there are many others (see II,ii,104-5, III,iii,1-5, etc.
etc.) Passages quoted in Chapter IV to illustrate other Shakespearean aspects of the play (like II,ii,82-6) also illustrate this
taste for multiple terms. This is not to imply, of course, that
every word pair in *Merlin* is the work of Shakespeare or that
Rowley never uses similar features; yet the overall picture is a
sound one. The "and/a" proportion in *Merlin* is quite unprec-
edented for Rowley, but quite in keeping with the hypothesis
of a Shakespearean contribution.

It can be objected that this function-word test is not, if we
can use such a phrase, "Shakespeare-specific"—other play-

wrights of his era (Heywood, for one) also show a more frequent usage of "and" than "a." Let's turn, then, from the most
common words to the least common. It is known with certainty that Shakespeare had an unusually large vocabulary, the
largest of any of the English Renaissance dramatists; and several scholars have used this fact in tests of authorship. Alfred
Hart demonstrated that Shakespeare used a significantly larger
and richer vocabulary than his contemporaries;[5] he then
showed that the portions of *The Two Noble Kinsmen* most often assigned to Shakespeare display this characteristic Shakespearean vocabulary in a way that the other sections of the
play, usually assigned to Fletcher, do not.[6] Yet the differences
between *Kinsmen* and *Merlin* complicate the application of
Hart's test to *Merlin*. While the traditional delineation of the
authorship shares in *Kinsmen* is by no means unanimous or
certain (see Appendix I), that play can still be divided with reasonable plausibility into predominantly Shakespearean and
predominantly Fletcherian portions; I do not see the same opportunity in *Merlin*, where the shares appear to be much more
closely intertwined, often, in my judgment, in inextricable
ways. In a more limited sense, the vocabulary test can still have
some relevance: Shakespeare's vocabulary is so large that each
of his major works, his plays and narrative poems, shows an
ample supply of "nonce words"—words that do not occur
elsewhere in the Shakespearean canon. The plays in the recognized canon tend to possess one hundred or more such words
(depending on the degree of rigor with which one discrimi-
nates between word forms). Any work that is Shakespearean
in authorship should, insofar as it is Shakespearean, show a
similar pattern of nonce words. This test has been applied to
the non-canonical Shakespearean plays *Edward III* (by Hart
and others) and *Edmund Ironside* (by Eric Sams)[7] with what I
and others consider persuasive results.

Here again, though, *Merlin* presents difficulties. The pattern
of Shakespeare's distinctive vocabulary will inevitably be dilut-

ed in a close collaboration with another author. Also, vocabulary tests, like any other means of distinguishing between two
collaborators, have a relative worth dependent on the differences between the artists involved. Rowley, as many commentators have noted, reveals a penchant for using large and
unusual words, so that the difference between his manner and
Shakespeare's, as far as vocabulary is concerned, is not as great
as the differences between Shakespeare and other writers of
the era. These factors need to be kept in mind as we consider
the nonce words in *Merlin*, the words that are found in this
play but not in Shakespeare's acknowledged works. A list of
such words would include:

abearing	ague-days	artichoke
atheism	Auraspex	authentical
begetter	bi-form'd	bloodshot
blue-fac'd	Capnomanster	coadjutors
contributory	covey	dampish
dead-killing	decretals	deliverer
Druids	earth-bred	examining
explanation	extirpation	eyesight-killing
fiend-begotten	flame-feather'd	flame-hair'd
forestside	goshawk	health-lov'd
heaven-blessing	heaven-knit	heptarchy
hieroglyphic	hindrance	hoarseness
idolaters	igniferent	judgement-seat
loadstone	loud-throated	low-bred
martyrdom	miscarriage	murd'ress
night-hag	nonplus	obtaining
o'er-awes	overgrow	palpably
pentagoron	restorer	Sabalists
sea-crab	secluded	sparrowhawk
speckled	splendent	squint-ey'd
strongholds	Stygian	tiding
torture-monger	unastonish'd	unbottom'd

| valid | verdant | wish'd-for |
| werewolf | woman-fury[8] | |

We need to stress that some of these words are "nonce" words only in regard to Shakespeare; while they do not occur in his cannon, they can be found in Rowley's—"martyrdom" and "verdant" fall into this category. Others, like the previously cited "Capnomanster" and "Auraspex" in IV,i,61-2, or the mysterious and definition-defeating "Sabalists" in V,i,23, have something of the "feeling" of Rowley's manner more than Shakespeare's. Still others, however, both from their forms and the contexts in which they are used, seem to point more in Shakespeare's direction. Terms like "unastonish'd" and "unbottom'd" are unsurprising in a putatively Shakespearean work, since Shakespeare has a habit of making such "un-" prefix coinages. Some of the hyphenated compounds have close parallels in his acknowledged works: for the *Merlin* terms "dead-killing," "bi-form'd," "earth-bred," "woman-fury," "flame-hair'd," and "flame-feather'd," we can cull "death-killing," "bi-fold," "earth-bound," "woman-queller," and "flame-color'd" from Shakespeare. (Interestingly enough, "flame colours" is used in one of *Merlin*'s stage directions; see II,iii,90 s.d.) Still, caution is wise; Rowley also uses many original compound coinages, and some of his (like "bi-neck'd" in *Shoemaker*, I,i,26) can stand comparison with words used in *Merlin*. Overall, though, the nonce words in the play are compatible with the hypothesis of Shakespeare's presence.

We can also take the opposite approach, turning away from the words in *Merlin* that Shakespeare does not employ in his known works to study those that he does. A range of unusual words or word forms in *Merlin* can be found in Shakespeare's canon but not in Rowley's:

| a-breeding | aerial | after-times |
| all-admiring | assisting | augery |

cardecues	circumscribe	constellation
credulity	dislodge	ebon
exorcisms	footstool	inequality
local	manlike	marted
monastery	monopoly	mussel
overslip	parling	pendulous
ragamuffin	recant	redeliver
repugnant	sepulchre	streaming
tenement	two-legg'd	uprising
vaulted	zodiac	

All of these words occur in *Merlin* and one to three times in Shakespeare's works. By extending the list to a higher limit, we could add still other terms. I hope, however, that even a limited list can help show that *Merlin* is written in a vocabulary symptomatic of Shakespeare.

List-making is a technique that can exaggerate the significance of some features while under-representing the distinctiveness of others. In *Merlin*, elements like the use of "emblem" as a verb (IV,v,102), and the phrase "some hell- or earth-bred monster" (V,i,27), have an imaginative resourcefulness that no list can capture. We can refine our list somewhat, and accentuate its usefulness, if we apply to it the same comparison applied to Shakespearean phrasings at the end of the last chapter. The following terms, common to *Merlin* and to Shakespeare's works, are absent not only from Rowley's but from the concordances for Marlowe, Spenser, Jonson, and Donne as well:

a-breeding	aerial	all-admiring
cardecues	exorcisms	inequality
local	manlike	marted
monopoly	mussel	parling
pendulous	overslip	ragamuffin
repugnant	two-legg'd	

At the risk of stating the obvious, let me observe that uniqueness is a criterion even less applicable to vocabulary than to phraseology. Certainly, some of Shakespeare's more radical and original compound coinages are unique to him—though these are precisely the words least likely to be repeated. ("Castalion-king-urinal" in *Merry Wives*, II,iii,33 provides an excellent example.)

The compound word "all-admiring" occurs in *Henry V*, I,i,39 and in *Merlin*, III,iii,27. It is an interesting commonality; most writers would have used "all-admir'd" in the relevant line in *Merlin*. Note too the similar contexts of the two uses: both refer to the high mental and intellectual abilities of men coming into sudden prominence—the "Knowledge, Arts, / Learning, Wisdom" of the newborn Merlin and the "reason ... debate ... discourse ... policy" of the newly crowned Henry.

Such shared contextuality is by no means rare in *Merlin*; it is easy to show that the play not only uses a Shakespearean vocabulary, but uses it in Shakespearean ways. Some examples of this were given in Chapter IV ("imperfect" and "inequality" in I,i,123 and 125; "pendulous," IV,i,220; "dislodge," IV,iv,15; "redeliver," V,ii,26); more can be added from the word list given above. Both uses of "two-legg'd creature" occur in fat-clown contexts, as do both uses of "ragamuffin" (see *Merlin*, II,i,231 and III,iv,94-5, and *1 Henry IV*, II,iv,188 and V,iii,36); both uses of "footstool" occur in high-authority contexts, either that of God or king (*Merlin*, I,ii,252; *3 Henry VI*, V,vii,14); both uses of "after-times" occur in political-prediction and English-royalty contexts (*Merlin*, IV,v,109; *2 Henry IV*, IV,ii,51); all three uses of "ebon" occur in personifications of malevolent forces, of Mischief, Revenge, and Death (*Merlin*, III,iii,38; *2 Henry IV*, V,v,37; *Venus*, 948).

The roster of examples could be extended much farther; this contextual consistency is valid not only for the rare words cited above, but for more common words too, as we observed in some cases in the previous chapter ("employ'd" in I,i,33, etc.

etc.). To add more examples here would only belabor what I believe is a by-now obvious point: the vocabulary of *Merlin* clearly confirms rather than contradicts the hypothesis of Shakespeare's presence.

Another productive avenue of approach is the study of Shakespeare's imagery, especially in those groupings of associations that have come to be called image clusters. Beginning with Walter Whiter in 1794,[9] and continuing through the works of twentieth-century scholars like Caroline Spurgeon and Wolfgang Clemen, among many others, much attention has been paid to the ways in which Shakespeare tends to link certain ideas and images. This tendency toward image clustering, though not unique to Shakespeare, is strong in his work, and is expressed in specific clusters that seem quite peculiar and individual. Various commentators have applied image-cluster tests for Shakespearean authorship, with, in my judgment, generally sound results. Edward Armstrong, in his excellent book *Shakespeare's Imagination*, studied Shakespeare's clusters in *Kinsmen*;[10] others have taken the same approach to *Edward III*[11] and to *Edmund Ironside*.[12] (Some critics have attempted to develop fairly rigid and schematic approaches to image clusters; others have stressed the flexible and evolutionary nature of the clusters themselves as an argument against such rigidity.)

As with any other technique of authorship study, there are cautions to be observed. In his discussion of the possible uses of image clusters as evidence of authorship, Edward Armstrong notes two complicating factors: there is the possibility that another playwright might have picked up some of Shakespeare's image-clustering habits, motivated by anything from overt plagiarism to unconscious influence; and there is the chance that both Shakespeare and another dramatist might derive similar clusters from a common source.[13] Some critics have doubted the uniqueness of specific Shakespearean clusters—though such questioning can be, and has been, carried to comically unrealistic extremes. (Schoenbaum, in *Internal Evidence*, notes that MacDonald Jackson has found one of Shakespeare's clusters "in a poem by Shelley. 'The possibility that Shakespeare wrote *The Boat on the Serchio*,' Jackson drily concludes, 'can presumably be discounted,'"[14] as can the possibility that Shelley wrote any Jacobean plays. When scholars are reduced to inane quibbles in their attempts to refute conclusions they don't favor, it is often a sign that the unwanted conclusions are correct.[15]) Certainly, image clusters do not constitute any sort of skeleton key to unlock the secrets of English Renaissance authorship; no such key has yet been found, in textual evidence or in any other technique, and it is doubtful such a thing could exist. The fact remains that image clusters have been used in authorship studies in insightful and revealing ways; they are productive tools with a valid role in authorship inquiries.

As noted above, Edward Armstrong surveyed *Kinsmen* for signs of Shakespearean image clustering; he came to the conclusion that Shakespeare's hand is indeed present in the portions of that play generally assigned to him. Yet Armstrong also quotes C.F. Tucker Brooke's opinion that "when we consider individually the parts of *The Two Noble Kinsmen* which have been ascribed to Shakespeare, we find invariably that each act, scene, or verse falls just short of what it should be. Always there is the strong Shakespearean reminiscence, but nowhere quite the full and perfect reality that we could swear to."[16] Armstrong blames this deficiency on a diminution of power and vigor on the poet's part, which he finds typical of the late plays as a group, and which reaches its extreme in *Kinsmen*. In that play, "peculiarities in style and imagery indicate that here we are dealing with the poet's work when his creative imagination was past its prime. Thus may be explained the deterioration in dramatic power and characterization in the later plays, noted by many critics, and peculiarities in the imagery such as the loosening of linkages and dispersal of the clusters. . . . The spontaneous fluidity of association seems to be impeded."[17]

In *Kinsmen*, Armstrong finds that Shakespeare's "dependence on his later and more recently written plays . . . is particularly apparent," and that "some of these borrowings . . . lack the richly associative character of his best earlier imagery"; "there is intermittency in his inspiration, occasional lack of care or, on the other hand, evidence of straining after the right expression, as if the conscious mind had to take over what the subconscious could previously have been trusted to do."[18] If, as I believe, *Merlin* is roughly contemporaneous with and perhaps even later than *Kinsmen* in its date of authorship, all these considerations would have relevance to *Merlin* as well. Indeed, Armstrong's descriptions of the deficiencies in *Kinsmen* seem to apply even more fully to *Merlin*, accentuating the impression that the latter is a very late Shakespearean work.

In reference to this perceived weakening in inspiration in Shakespeare's late collaborations, it is also important not to neglect the fact that the plays are collaborations and not solo works. Commentators tend to treat the sections of *Kinsmen* assigned to Shakespeare as though they must be either purely Shakespearean or non-Shakespearean; yet there are at least a few hints that Fletcher's hand is not wholly absent from them (see Appendix I). If, in the relevant portions of *Kinsmen*, we are looking at "predominantly Shakespearean" rather than "purely Shakespearean" work, some of the difficulties noted by Armstrong and other readers may be accounted for. This factor of collaboration has even greater relevance to *Merlin*, in my view, since I find that the authorship shares in this play to be inextricably intertwined, with an inevitable dilution of the Shakespearean impression the play makes on the reader.

Concrete examples are easy to find: *Merlin* does show a pattern of Shakespearean image clustering—though in some cases the clusters appear even more diffuse than they do in *Kinsmen*, let alone in Shakespeare's solo plays. Consider the version of Shakespeare's "blot" cluster that occurs in II,iii: in Uter's encounter with Artesia as his brother's bride, we find "blotted" (202), along with several of the associations suggestive of Shakespeare—"heaven" (202), night ("Wedding-night," 176), and "eye" (160), in a context of sovereignty and constancy. One can complain that this is a weak example of the "blot" cluster compared to the strongest canonical examples (as in *Love's Labor's Lost*, IV,iii,212ff.). Simultaneously, one can observe that some of Shakespeare's other instances of the cluster are also comparatively weak—Muir notes that there are only "traces" of the cluster in eleven Shakespearean works.[19] It is also worth remembering Armstrong's caution that Shakespeare's clusters are dynamic rather than static, and that attempts to define them must always be partial and limited. Among the list of elements in the "blot" cluster cited by Muir, the idea of ebbing and flowing tides is not mentioned; yet we find "To lowest ebbes men justly hope a flood" in *Merlin*, II,iii,204, and "The sea will ebb and flow" in the relevant portion of *Love's Labor's Lost*, IV,iii,212.

A more substantive objection might be raised by turning to the use of "blot" in Rowley's *All's Lost*, III,iii,226, which also occurs with "night" (206) and "heaven" (228) in a constancy context. Clearly, some chance groupings of some of the more common elements in a Shakespearean cluster can mimic weak versions of that cluster, yet not be indicators of Shakespearean authorship. I would assert that the cluster in *Merlin* is closer to Shakespeare's canonical uses of his "blot" cluster than the grouping in *All's Lost*; I concede, though, that skeptical readers might not find this very meaningful or persuasive evidence.

At first sight, the version of Shakespeare's "hum" cluster in IV,v is more striking, though it is also vulnerable to qualification. Kenneth Muir has pursued the development of a cluster of images around the word "hum" in Shakespeare's plays.[20] By noting variants of the root word, we can add other instances to the dozen cited by Muir, so that more than twenty installments of this cluster can be identified in the collected works. For example:

In *Henry V*, I,ii,202 we find "hum," plus the ideas of food ("honey," 199), music or song ("singing," 198), sleep ("yawning," 204), wealth ("gold," 198), and death ("executors," 203).

In *Hamlet*, II,ii,588 we find "hum," plus food ("fatted," 579), hearing ("ears," 566), sleep ("John-a-dreams," 568), adultery ("bawdy" and "lecherous," 580-1), and plot (the plot to "catch the conscience of the King," 605).

In *Hamlet*, V,i,103, we have another "hum," along with death ("skull," 99, and "grave," 118), plot ("tricks," 100), and wealth ("fines . . . vouchers . . . recoveries," 105-6, etc.).

Similar versions of the cluster, stronger or weaker, adding various other elements, are to be found with uses of "hum" in *1 Henry IV*, III,i,156, *Merry Wives*, III,v,139, *Henry V*, IV,Pr.,5, *Othello*, V,ii,36, *Lear*, I,ii,55 and III,iv,47, *MacBeth*, III,ii,42, III,vi,42, and IV,iii,203, *Coriolanus*, V,i,49 and V,iv,21, *Pericles*, III,i,63 and V,i,83, *Cymbeline*, III,v,103, *Winter's Tale*, II,i,71-4, *Tempest*, II,i,317 and III,ii,138, and *Kinsmen*, I,iii,75. Muir sums up his consideration of the "hum" cluster by writing that "any use of the word after 1610 would be likely to evoke some of the following associations: death, plot, food, sleep, music, song, flowers, wealth or value, ears, spirit, adultery or bastardy."[21]

And this is precisely what we find in *Merlin*. In IV,v Merlin prophesies on the comet. To stop his uncle's constant interruptions, Merlin deprives the Clown of his voice by magic, so that all his uncle can say is "Hum, hum, hum"—and say it he does, repeatedly through the rest of the scene (IV,v,88, 107, 118, 127, 141). With these multiple uses of "hum" appear virtually all of the associations Muir predicts for a post-1610 Shakespearean play.

Merlin describes the comet as "that Star, that *sings* / The change of Brittians State and death of Kings" (39-40). He reads in it the death of Aurelius (59-61), at the hands of "that *devil* Ostorius / And the damn'd witch Artesia" (68-9). Merlin continues to prophesy about the coming of Arthur, his triumphs and conquests, including the allegiance of "contributory Kings" (115); he mentions the "feast" at "his Royal Table" (124), and also "Prosperity" (152), "Sweet rest," "soul," and "spirit" (164). There are repeated references to hearing: "hear a happy story" (76), "silent" (80), "words authentical" (137), etc. Merlin himself is both a spirit and a bastard, the product of an adulterous union (cf. "adulterate," V,i,3).

In IV,v, then, we find not some but nearly all of the associations Muir predicts—the only missing ingredient being the relatively rare and unimportant association with flowers. I cannot help but find this a very telling point: here we have a prediction of what a post-1610 Shakespearean work should possess in terms of a given stylistic feature—a prediction made with no reference to *Merlin*; and when we examine *Merlin* we find that it fulfills the prediction almost perfectly.

Here again, though, some qualification is necessary. Rowley uses this trick of multiple "hums" in *All's Lost*, III,iii (see lines 39 and 53, plus 24), and interspersed with these "hums" we find a few of the more common Shakespearean associations. (Note the similarity of circumstance: both in *Merlin*, IV,v and in *All's Lost*, III,iii, fat-clown characters use their triple "hums" to attract attention in order to speak. If *All's Lost* is chronologically the later play, as I and many others believe, then Rowley's usage of this material in his solo play might derive from the prior collaboration with Shakespeare.) Because of this partial parallel in Rowley's play, the instance of the "hum" cluster in *Merlin*, like the instance of the "blot" cluster, is more provocative than demonstrative. Yet there are other features in the play that are not compromised in the same way.

(Before continuing, we should pause to note once more the couplet about "that Star, that sings / The change of Brittians State and death of Kings" in IV,v,39-40. Both Shakespeare and Rowley use the "sing/king" rhyme in singular form in their works; see *Winter's Tale*, IV,iii,6-8, *Richard II*, II,i,262-3 and III,iii,182-3, *2 Henry IV*, V,v,107-8, and *Shoemaker*, III,v,50-1. But it is Rowley who has the closest single parallel, in his lines about the raven "whose dismall beake now sings / The sudden ruine of two barbarous Kings," in *Shoemaker*, III,iii,19-20. Note, however, that in *Merlin* the singing comes not from a bird or any other usual source of song, but from a star. The usage, though curious, is not wholly inexplicable: both men have "music of the spheres" references in their plays, along with related allusions and images. It is Shakespeare, though, who gives us similarly intimate anthropomorphic references to stars: "a star danc'd," *Much Ado*, II,i,335; "charitable star," *All's Well*, I,i,191; "comfortable star," *Lucrece*, 164. Given its place in the "hum" cluster in IV,v, I suspect that this singing star is more likely the work of Shakespeare than Rowley. Here again as elsewhere in this play, we might have a sign of intimate collaboration between the two men. If the "sings / . . . death of Kings" is Rowley's, the star that does the singing may well be Shakespeare's, so that the couplet as a whole is the product of both men working closely together.)

At the start of III,vi there is a remarkably revealing passage that deserves quotation in full; consider lines 1-23:

> *Artesia:* Come, come, you do but flatter;
> What you term Love is but a *Dream* of *blood*,
> Wakes with enjoying, and with *open eyes*
> Forgot, contemn'd, and lost.
> *Uter:* I must be wary, her words are dangerous.—
> True, we'l speak of Love no more, then.
> *Artesia:* Nay, if you will, you may;
> 'Tis but in jest, and yet so *children* play
> With *fiery flames*, and covet what is bright,
> But, *feeling his effects, abhor the light*.
> Pleasure is like a *Building*, the more high,
> The narrower still it grows; *Cedars do dye*
> *Soonest at top*.
> *Uter:* How does your instance suit?
> *Artesia:* From Art and Nature to make sure the *root*,

And lay a fast *foundation*, e're I try
The *incertain Changes of a wavering Skie*.
Make your example thus.—You have a kiss,—
Was it not pleasing?
   Uter: Above all name to express it.
   Artesia: Yet now the pleasure's gone,
And you have lost your joys possession.
   Uter: Yet when you please, this *flood* may *ebb* again.
   Artesia: But where it never *ebbs*, there runs the *main*.

Several of the elements in these speeches were discussed in Chapter IV; now I wish to focus on the imagery in this passage, since the emphasized terms comprise a pattern of Shakespearean associations. Compare this passage from *King John*, IV,ii,103ff.:

They *burn* in indignation. I repent.
There is no sure *foundation* set on *blood*;
No certain life achiev'd by others' death.
A *fearful eye* thou hast. Where is that *blood*
That I have seen *inhabit* in those cheeks?
So foul a sky clears not without a storm . . .
O, where hath our intelligence been drunk?
Where hath it *slept*?

Some of the commonalities are obvious—but some are more subtle. This speech of King John's occurs in a scene dominated by a rumor of Prince Arthur's death; in the preceding scene in *John*, IV,i, occurs that memorable encounter in which Arthur pleads with Hubert not to burn out his eyes. In the quoted passage from III,vi of *Merlin* we have "children," "eyes," "flames," and the idea of children being burned and thereafter fearing the effects of fire, along with a range of connections with John's speeches quoted above.

Armstrong, in his discussion of *Kinsmen* mentioned earlier, points to the "Green Neptune" passage in that play as being derivative of two passages in *The Tempest* compounded together;[22] I would suggest that something very similar has happened here in *Merlin*. Perhaps it was the common name "Arthur" that acted as a subconscious trigger; though King Arthur is not present as a character in *Merlin*, he is a strong subliminal influence (IV,v, V,ii). The opening of III,vi combines elements from IV,i and IV,ii of *John*: we have children, eyes, fire, burning, fear, plus foundation, blood, sleep, the building metaphor ("inhabit"), and a concise one-line weather report as well. To apply Armstrong's verdict on the passage in *Kinsmen* to these speeches in *Merlin*: "It is certain that Shakespeare wrote the passage . . . because no other writer would, or could copy images to such an extent wittingly or unwittingly."

Yet there is more. The building metaphor—for the human body inhabited by a soul, or for some element of the individual personality, among other meanings—is a commonplace, used repeatedly by Shakespeare, by Rowley, and by most other writers of the age. In some of Shakespeare's uses, though, and especially when the word "foundation" appears, we find a portrayal of a whole landscape of imagery, with trees and plants and structures, even sea and sky and weather, along with associations with blood, sleeping and dreaming, and fire and flames.

The quoted passages from IV,ii of *John* give one installment of this bundle of imagery; another occurs in *MacBeth*, IV,i,48-67—it begins with "secret, black, and midnight," the world of sleep, and then proceeds into the landscape:

> . . . untie the *winds*, and let them fight
> Against the *churches*; though the yesty *waves*
> *Confound and swallow navigation up*;
> Though bladed *corn* be lodg'd, and *trees* blown down,
> Though *castles* topple on their warders' heads,
> Though *palaces* and *pyramids* do slope
> Their heads to their *foundations*;

Soon after follow "blood" and "flame."

In *Winter's Tale* there are two selections of this imagery: in I,ii,417ff. we find "blood," "sea," "heaven," "foundation," "grow" and "grown" (trees, plants), and "ships." In II,i,100ff. we get "foundation," "burns," "tears drown," along with Hermione's lines:

> There's some ill planet reigns;
> I must be patient, till the heavens look
> With an aspect more favorable . . .

The unfavorable heavens are reminiscent of the "foul sky" and "wavering sky" of *John* and *Merlin*.

In *Cymbeline*, IV,ii,342-66, the word "foundation" is absent, though the conjunction of "ruin" and "building" suggests the same picture:

> . . . what *trunk* is here?
> Without its *top*? The *ruin* speaks that sometime
> It was a worthy *building*.

As in the passage in *Merlin*, we have here an association of a dead or dying tree with the foundation imagery. With these lines is an appropriate grouping: "wind," "sunbeams," "dream," "sleeping," and "bed," "bloody pillow," "sad wreck." "From the spongy south to this part of the west" suggests the sweep of landscape that Shakespeare's "foundation" cluster tends to encompass. Again, such a listing of elements tends to neglect other associations that sometimes crop up in the relevant passages—but the general pattern is, I think, clear.

The passage that begins III,vi in *Merlin* is certainly not great dramatic verse; it can be taken as an illustration of the tendencies that Armstrong sees in late Shakespearean works—a kind of careless or unfocused quality, a lack of concentration and power, and a dependence on recently written works. Yet its various Shakespearean connections point squarely to Shakespeare as partial author.

The specification of "churches" and "pyramids" in the quoted lines from *MacBeth*, IV,i is interesting, since these are precisely the types of buildings that grow narrower with height, as mentioned in the *Merlin* excerpt. This, in turn, can lead us to another relevant consideration: Shakespeare has a standing preoccupation with the image of tall things brought low. Sometimes the tall structures are man-made, buildings, wall, towers, that "topple" or "crash," as do the "castles" in the *MacBeth* passage; other times they are trees, cedars or pines that "bend" or "stoop" with the wind.

Rowley does not show the same preoccupation; if we look at his similar images (the cedar imagery in *All's Lost*, I,iii,11, for instance), the idea of tall structures brought low does not appear. This idea is implicit (not explicit) in the opening of *Merlin*, III,vi, with its building that needs a "sure foundation" and a tapering shape to stand against the weather, and the cedars that die soonest at top. It receives a more blatant expression earlier in *Merlin*, in II,i,69-73, where these lines occur:

> How like a voice that Eccho spake, but oh,
> My thoughts are lost for ever in amazement.
> Could I but meet a man to tell her beauties,
> These trees would bend their tops to kiss the air
> That from my lips should give her praises up.

The mention of "echo" in a love-and-forest context recurs in Shakespeare (*Venus*, 695, 834, 840; *Dream*, IV,i,111; *Titus*, II,iii,17, etc.); I do not find similar allusions in Rowley. More pertinently, the image of trees bending their tops has various precedents in the acknowledged works: see *2 Henry VI*, II,iii,45, *Cymbeline*, IV,ii,175, *Richard II*, III,iv,30-2, etc.

Indeed, the quoted lines from II,i of *Merlin* contain a striking combination of two characteristically Shakespearean images, the bending trees and the amorous air. In Shakespeare, air and wind have basic sexual associations: the wind is strumpet, inconstant, merry, light, easy, and wandering; the wind bestows kisses in *Othello*, IV,ii,78 and in *Venus*, 1082. To be sure, this imagery is not unique to Shakespeare; examples can be found in the works of other dramatists, including Rowley ("this halcion gale / Playes the lewd wanton with our dancing sayles, / And makes'm big," *New Wonder*, I,i,3-5). Yet the Shakespearean parallels are striking nonetheless; if the trees kiss the air in *Merlin*, it is the wind that kisses the trees in *Merchant*, V,i,2-4:

> ... the sweet wind did gently kiss the trees,
> And they did make no noise, in such a night
> Troilus methinks mounted the Troyan walls ...

which leads in turn to *Troilus*, IV,v,219-21:

> For yonder walls that pertly front your town,
> Yon towers, whose wanton tops do buss the clouds,
> Must kiss their own feet.

These lines from *Troilus* yield precisely the same combination, of the amorous air and the tall structure brought low, that we find in II,i,72-3 of *Merlin*. Given the proximity of other Shakespearean features in the same scene, I have to find this a telling detail.

These connections between *Merlin* and Shakespeare's acknowledged works tend to be the kind of subtle links that would be natural in the mind of a single author, but difficult for any other writer to replicate. Consider another example: in the same speech in which she uses peacock imagery in IV,i,186-204, Joan Go-too't also has the line, "My glass the Altar was, my face the Idol" (190). In one of Shakespeare's earliest plays, another Joan is the focus of related material: in *1 Henry VI*, III,iii,6ff., Joan of Arc applies a peacock metaphor to Talbot, though in the context of her character it reflects back on her, and brings sacrilegious associations similar to those in *Merlin*. Alencon says to Joan, "We'll set thy statue in some holy place, / And have thee reverenc'd like a blessed saint" (14-15)—sheer idolatry, given the portrayal of Joan's character throughout the play, and comparable to the later Joan's references to "Altar" and "Idol." Here again, as earlier with "Arthur," the common name "Joan" may have served as a trigger for the same subconscious associations. *1 Henry VI* was a very old and uncurrent play at the time of *Merlin*'s (likely) authorship, though it was not yet in print (see Chapter VI for the play's date); it seems highly improbable that anyone other than Shakespeare could have possessed the close familiarity with *1 Henry VI* needed to forge such a commonality.

At one point in his *Shakespeare's Imagination*, Armstrong discusses the associations with the folklore figure Tom Thumb.[23] There is a mention of Tom Thumb in *Merlin*, III,iv,65, in a context of sexuality and folklore occultism that is appropriate for such a Shakespearean reference. I do not find any mention of Tom Thumb in Rowley's works. Armstrong points to the witches' speeches at the beginning of IV,i of *MacBeth* (which immediately precede MacBeth's "foundation" speech already quoted) as an example of various Tom Thumb associations; and it is revealing to compare the witches' speeches with the materials surrounding the Tom Thumb reference in *Merlin*. Both feature "baboon," "tongue," "tooth" or "teeth," "hog" or "hedgehog"; the witches' "birth-strangled babe / Ditch-deliver'd by a drab" is suggestive of Merlin's "abortive birth" and "birth prodigious"—it is stressed that Merlin, though fully grown, is yet a "baby," and therefore a "monster"; the Clown repeatedly calls him a "witch." If as "witch" Merlin has connections with the witches in *MacBeth*, his identity as "monster" links him to that other late-Shakespearean monster, Caliban, another half-human, half-devil prodigy. In *Merlin*, III,iv, we find "moncky," "baboon," "urchin," "hogs"; compare Caliban's speech in *The Tempest*, II,ii,1-

14, which offers us "apes," "urchin-shows," and "hedgehogs." (There are some intriguing common elements among these three plays, *Merlin*, *MacBeth*, and *The Tempest*; all three deal with usurpation of royal authority in a heavily occult setting; all three use borrowed-clothing imagery.)[24]

Significant connections can be traced beyond the realm of imagery per se; there are points where similar concepts and ideas find expression in similar sequences of terms. The first scene of *Merlin* contains discussions of what we today would call sexual politics: Cador leads off with "You teach me language," and follows with "The Debt of Love I owe unto her Vertues"; references to "oaths" and "time" ensue. In *Cymbeline*, III,iii,66ff., in a scene with various links to *Merlin*, we find "oaths," "pious debts to heaven," "time," and "language." In *The Tempest*, I,ii,352ff., we have "You taught me language" and "learning me your language," "print of goodness," "curse," and "hour."

It is evident, I think, that this study of images and conceptual associations would, if pursued diligently enough, intersect with a study of the Shakespearean word contexts noted earlier. Both approaches have potential for refining our definition of Shakespeare's contribution to the play; this chapter only begins to tap that potential. Yet enough has been shown of the Shakespearean nature of the play in these respects to warrant a judgment: it would have been extremely difficult for any other writer to create this complex web of Shakespearean elements.

This last point can be illustrated very tellingly by posing the reader a direct question: In what context does Shakespeare use scorpion imagery? I wager that virtually none of the readers of this paragraph will be able to answer this question without consulting concordance and text—and there is no good reason you should be able to do so, reader, for this is a very minor point in Shakespeare's general style. Yet the authors of *Merlin* knew the answer, because a scorpion metaphor appears in III,vi,130 in its proper Shakespearean context.

There are only three instances in which forms of the word "scorpion" are used in Shakespeare's acknowledged works: *2 Henry VI*, III,ii,86, *MacBeth*, III,ii,36, and *Cymbeline*, V,v,45. The context is the same in each: royalty and usurpation and the sex-power relationship between a uxorious king and the strong, willful queen who manipulates him. Scorpion imagery occurs in conversations between Henry and Margaret and between MacBeth and Lady MacBeth; Cornelius uses it while speaking to Cymbeline about his queen—and Edoll uses it while speaking to Aurelius about Artesia. (Contrast Rowley's use of scorpion imagery in *Shoemaker*, II,iii,173, which does not share this common context.) The person who was responsible for inserting this bit of imagery in *Merlin* has a closer and more particular familiarity with Shakespeare's style than most of us today have, despite the fact that we benefit from more than three centuries worth of study and scholarship. There is only one plausible identity for that person, and that is Shakespeare himself.

CHAPTER VI

Themes and Content

BEFORE WE bring this survey to a close, there are several other matters that demand attention. The previous three chapters have concentrated on specific and sometimes minute details of the play—but the larger aspects of the play have import for this argument too. If *The Birth of Merlin* is the work of Shakespeare to any significant degree, it should, insofar as it is Shakespearean, express Shakespeare's values and outlook—it should be Shakespearean in matter as well as in manner. Some material along these lines has already been presented; we have noted some of the broad connections between *Merlin* and the canonical plays, especially the late romances. This present chapter will explore further the content of the play for signs of Shakespeare's hand. (One important caveat: Shakespeare was not a philospher, not, primarily, an original social or political thinker. In general terms, he occupied a place securely within the established intellectual world view of his historical era. Still, Shakespeare's place within that system is identifiable, vis-à-vis his contemporaries. *Merlin* reveals a significant consistency with the thought-world of Shakespeare's plays.)

We can start with the politics of the play. Some of the phrases noted in Chapter IV, like the repeated uses of "lawful king(s)" (II,ii,55; IV,i,277; IV,v,159), are traces and tokens of Shakespeare's characteristic political outlook, amply expressed in this play. Another occurs in IV,iv,4-5, where Edwin says to Cador: "Justice is with her, / Who ever takes the true and rightful cause." This type of "Just cause" or "Rightful cause" reference recurs in Shakespeare's works. The most famous instance is found in *2 Henry VI*, III,ii,232-5 (the well-known "What stronger breastplate than a heart untainted!" speech), though other examples appear in II,i,200-1 of the same play, plus *1 Henry IV*, V,i,120 and V,ii,87-8 and *Henry V*, IV,i,127-8. And this is more than just a felicitous phrase; while Shakespeare is not oblivious to the conditions of real politics, there remains for him a level on which Right makes Might, where God rewards the virtuous and punishes the guilty—politics as Morality Play. This tendency is strongest in the English history plays, where the kings who are both strong and good (Henry V, Henry VII) triumph, while those who are weak (Henry VI) or evil (Richard III) fall. This motif can also be found in various forms and permutations throughout his works. For a Shakespearean ruler, it is critically important to possess a balance and a harmony between the personal and the public realms. When the personal usurps the public (as happens, in varying ways, to a number of Shakespeare's rulers, including Lear and Prospero), the results are unfortunate in the extreme.

King Aurelius in *Merlin* fits this pattern perfectly. He is almost the ideal ruler of a Shakespearean divine-right monarchy: "loud fame" testifies to his "humanity" and "mild and vertuous life" (I,ii,119-20); he is "gentle" and "sweet," "the glory of our Land" (IV,v,60-1). His single failure lies in allowing his judgment and his noble qualities to be overwhelmed by his blind love for Artesia; in consequence, he loses his kingdom and his life. Hamlet's "stamp of one defect" could hardly apply more fittingly. Aurelius is a recapitulation of Marc Antony, suffering the same flaw to a similarly fatal end.

One might complain that this is all too general to be useful as evidence of authorship; yet once again, a contrast with Rowley's plays is instructive. In the opening scene in *Shoemaker* the English king Allured dies of wounds received in battle against the Romans; he dies not because he has failed to fulfill the highest demands of his office, as is true of Shakespearean figures and of Aurelius, but simply because kings sometimes fall in battle. Later in the same play, the Romans conveniently and wordlessly forget about their virulent persecution of Britain's Christians when the play's happy ending requires them to. In *All's Lost*, IV,i, Julianus' soldiers join his rebellion against their king with an almost comical readiness, with hardly a moment's hesitation. (Compare the more Shakespearean sentiments about loyalty expressed in *Merlin*, II,ii,117-18.) Rowley manifests no real interest in political matters; he indulges in caricatures of political affairs without any sign of self-consciousness or self-awareness. *Merlin* may not be a strongly or overtly political play in the class of *Julius Caesar* or *Coriolanus*, but it does take its politics seriously, which points away from Rowley and toward Shakespeare.

The contrast can also be drawn with other writers of the era; Middleton, since he has been suggested as a possible author of *Merlin*, is a good candidate. Apart from his early and atypical play *The Phoenix*, Middleton's dramas are not dominated by virtuous rulers; quite the contrary, it is the usurper and the despot—the Tyrant in *The Second Maiden's Tragedy*, the Duke in *The Revenger's Tragedy*—who stand out most prominently. And just so, in *Hengist, King of Kent*, Middleton's version of the Aurelius/Uter story, it is the Machiavellian "Realpoliticians" Vortiger and Horsus who dominate; the virtuous king Constantius is little more than a figure of fun. The contrast between Middleton's political world and Shakespeare's is easy to draw—and *Merlin* falls squarely on Shakespeare's side.

If *Merlin* is not primarily a political play, one might ask what it is actually about. Theme-hunting is not always a productive approach to English Renaissance dramas; if one were to insist on finding a theme to *Merlin*, one might say that its controlling idea is the superiority of a commitment to spiritual chastity over sensual indulgence—whether that indulgence is nakedly sexual and egocentric (Joan and the devil) or dressed up in romantic idealization (Aurelius's passion for Artesia). The first- and third-level plots of the play illustrate the effects of failures of chastity, while the second-level plot shows chastity's triumph. Having said this, one should go on to note that the play achieves limited success in its advocacy of this idea, especially to a modern sensibility. The effect of the play is more to demonstrate the insufferable dullness of chastity when compared with the comedy and adventure that ensue from sensuality. This is partially an anachronistic view—though not wholly; there are confusions in the play that inflict serious wounds upon its efficacy as a plea for chastity. The most serious of these is that the most egregious moral lapse in the play, Joan's sexual liaison with the devil, produces the play's central event, the birth of Merlin the Magician.

We can clear up at least some of this confusion by taking note of two couplets in the play that might otherwise pass unobserved and unremarked upon. These two couplets, in II,iii,173-4 and 260-1, tell us something important about the value system operating below the surface of *Merlin*. First, it must be understood that Shakespeare was fascinated by ideas of opposites attracting and interacting, of opposites being inextricably linked with and generating each other. In part, this preoccupation, this mindset, is a reflection of some of the more esoteric currents in the thought-world of the poet's era, as expressed in the views of men like Montaigne and Bruno;[1] but more directly and more fundamentally it reflects the natural bent of the poet's mind.[2] There are many displays of this tendency in the acknowledged works; perhaps the most blatant of them is Friar Lawrence's thirty-line speech, "The grey-

ey'd morn smiles on the frowning night," at the beginning of
Romeo and Juliet, II,iii. To quote the two lines (21-2) that best
sum up the whole:

> Virtue itself turns vice, being misapplied,
> And vice sometime by action dignified.

(Which is certainly one of the strangest statements ever put
into the mouth of a Catholic clergyman in all of literature, and
which indicates the peculiarity of the poet's moral vision quite
clearly when compared to what a real friar might have to say in
response.) Shakespeare's thought is sometimes so strongly influenced by such duality concepts that he applies them to subjects for which he ordinarily has the most positive feelings, like
music—see *Measure*, IV,i,14-15:

> 'Tis good; though music oft hath such a charm
> To make bad good, and good provoke to harm.[3]

It is in light of this dualistic attitude that we should read the
two couplets from II,iii of *Merlin*—in lines 173-4:

> The Day's most prais'd when 'tis ecclipst by Night,
> Great Good must have as great Ill opposite

—and in lines 260-1:

> Vices are Vertues, if so thought and seen,
> And Trees with foulest roots branch soonest green.

We can see applications of this dualistic thinking beyond
these two couplets; the Shakespearean preoccupation with tall
things brought low, discussed in the previous chapter, conforms to this tendency. More significantly, the larger plot of
Merlin shows the same influence: the idea of Joan's sexual in-
tercourse with the devil leading to the birth of Merlin makes

sense in a dualistic context—it is an instance of great ill having as great good opposite, to paraphrase the play. The contrast between Shakespeare's more sophisticated mindset, with its pronounced capacity for savoring multiplicity and duality, and Rowley's conventional and simplistic and pietistic morality, is clear. *Merlin* constitutes a hybridization of the two men's moral stances.

The links between Rowley's Winifred in *Shoemaker* and Modestia in *Merlin* assure us that Rowley had a major share in her creation; Shakespeare consistently shows a negative attitude toward what we might call the nun's option—see *Dream*, I,i,65-78, or compare Isabella in *Measure*, Modestia's closest counterpart in the collected works, who nonetheless begins in a nunnery and ends as a bride-to-be, the reverse of Modestia's progress. In Shakespeare's final plays, however, there is a strong emphasis on chastity that makes the contrast between Modestia and most of Shakespeare's heroines less jarring. Prospero's warnings against premarital sex (IV,i,14-23 and 51-4) are vehement enough to have caused comment among generations of critics; and in *Kinsmen*, V,i,137-68, Emilia expresses a reluctance to marry ("I am bride-habited, / But maidenhearted," 150-1) that resembles Modestia's.

The linkage between *Merlin* and Shakespeare's late romances is more complex and intimate than we have yet seen; to understand how and why this is true, we can turn to the works of Frances A. Yates. In her *Majesty and Magic in Shakespeare's Last Plays*, Yates studies the late plays as expressions of a specific cultural, political, and religious milieu, which she calls the Elizabethan Revival.[4] To sum up the argument very briefly: it is generally recognized that the social, political, cultural climate of Shakespeare's England shifted markedly during the poet's lifetime; the post-Armada optimism and expansionism of the 1590s was followed, in the closing years of Elizabeth's reign and the opening of James', by a more negative, more pessimistic period. Our stereotypical notions of the

Elizabethan versus the Jacobean eras, while oversimplified, are grounded in historical reality.

Around the beginning of the second decade of the seventeenth century, however, an alternative cultural climate was manifested in a nostalgia for the glorious days of the previous reign that coalesced about the appealing figures of Prince Henry and Princess Elizabeth, James' elder children. This Elizabethan Revival can be characterized as strongly nationalistic and expansionist, anti-Spanish and anti-Catholic, and opposed to James' policies of Spanish appeasement; militantly Protestant, but with a significant irenist element, tending toward broad nonsectarianism rather than narrow dogmatism, and with a chivalric and idealistic orientation like that represented by the late Sir Philip Sidney; and possessing at least a tolerance for the Neoplatonist, Hermetist, and Cabalist strains in Renaissance thought. (This mixture of magic with political expansionism and militant Protestantism is a strange one to us; yet, as Yates has shown in several of her works, figures like John Dee could and did assimilate these different elements into a single coherent outlook.[5])

Politically and religiously, the Elizabethan Revival was intimately involved with the idea of Imperial Reform, the concept of a just ruler having the right and duty to institute wide-ranging reforms of national institutions, including religious institutions, without control or interference from any extra-national authority (such as the Church of Rome). This concept, as Yates has shown,[6] was essential to the moral position of the Tudor dynasty, since it justified Henry VIII's break with Rome and establishment of Anglicanism, as well as legitimizing his multiple marriages and the heirs produced by Jane Seymour and Anne Boleyn. The Elizabethan Revival encompassed not only Tudor political theory, but Tudor political symbolism and mythology as well: the Tudor dynasty had attempted to bolster its weak genealogical claim to the English throne by maintaining that the ascent of the Welsh Tudors constituted the return of the original ancient line of British kings, which had been displaced by the Anglo-Saxon invasions in the early Christian era. (And the Stuarts, who based their claim to the English throne on their descent from the first Tudor monarch, Henry VII, in their turn embraced the same mythology once they came to power in England.)

All these elements of the Elizabethan Revival found expression in a cluster of literary works produced around the years 1610-14, especially in works dedicated to Prince Henry and Princess Elizabeth, by authors like Michael Drayton and John Selden, Francis Beaumont and John Fletcher, and, as Yates has shown, by Shakespeare too. Yates offers a convincing analysis of Jonson's *The Alchemist* and Shakespeare's *The Tempest* as embodying contrasting negative and positive views of Elizabethan-Revivalist values;[7] Jonson's Spanish sympathy, his treatment of magic as fraud, and his dressing up of a whore in the Faerie-Queen guise of the late queen's mythological identity all place him in clear opposition to the entire atmosphere and spirit of the Revival. It would undoubtedly be a mistake to conceive of the Revival as anything approaching a "movement"; I would suggest words like "atmosphere" and "spirit" are most appropriate to what was more a climate of thought and feeling than anything formal or organized.

Yet this Revival spirit is distinctive enough to be recognizable, both by its presence and its absence, in the literary works of the period. One good example of its absence is George Chapman's *Masque of the Inner Temple and Lincoln's Inn*; although written for the 1613 wedding of Princess Elizabeth and the Elector Palatine of the Rhine (the central event of the Revival era), Chapman's masque is devoid of elements that would suggest sympathy with the Revival viewpoint. (Chapman's other works, like Jonson's, yield other indications of a pro-Catholic disposition that would naturally be antipathetic to the Revival.) Conversely, Beaumont and Fletcher's *Philaster* of ca. 1610, with its opposition to a Spanish match and its Sidneian Arcadian chivalry, is much in sympathy with Revivalist sentiments.[8]

The Birth of Merlin shares many of the Elizabethan-Revival values that Yates finds in Shakespeare's romances; it partakes, with *Cymbeline*, of the Tudor/Stuart ancient-British political mythology, and it shares with *The Tempest* a positive disposition toward magic and an interest in the magus as social and political reformer. Also, *Merlin* contains an expression of the ideas of Imperial Reform and British expansionism. In the play's climactic scene, IV,v, Merlin's prophecies on the coming of Arthur offer a picture of Arthur as the ultimate British religious-political imperator, conquering pagans over an area of western Europe as large as Charlemagne's empire, spreading justice and order and plenty (IV,v,108-26). The tale is fantastic, but has to be given serious consideration for its political implications, since such material held legitimate meaning for people of the era: in his heyday in the 1570s, John Dee used the mythical North Atlantic possessions of Arthur (the Orkneys, Shetlands, and Faeroes, Iceland, and Greenland) as precedents for a more vigorously expansive English naval and colonial policy.

These elements in *Merlin* are important not only for our ability to place the play with the historical and cultural context of Shakespeare's late works, but also for their implications for the play's date of authorship. My dating of *Merlin* to ca. 1613-15 is dependent upon its commonalities with the late romances, *Pericles* through *Kinsmen*; from the way the play utilizes and develops themes and materials from the late plays as a group (and especially from *Cymbeline*, *The Tempest*, and *Henry VIII*), *Merlin* appears to be a successor and debtor to all of these works, which implies a date of authorship between 1613 and Shakespeare's death in 1616.

The values of the Elizabethan Revival allow us to approach the question of date from another perspective. I know of no commentator on the play who disagrees with C.F. Tucker Brooke's judgment that *Merlin* is a Jacobean play rather than an Elizabethan or Caroline one: "From the language and grammar ... it is clear that *The Birth of Merlin* was not composed later than the reign of James I; nor is it at all likely that it antedates James's succession."[9] Various individual scholars have dated the play anywhere from 1608 to 1622. Yet the most credible interval for the authorship of *Merlin* is that period in the first half of the second decade of the seventeenth century when the Elizabethan Revival was at its zenith, coinciding with the brief public career of Prince Henry and the marriage of Princess Elizabeth, the years that saw the appearance of Beaumont and Fletcher's *Philaster* (ca. 1610), Drayton's *Poly-Olbion* (1612), and Shakespeare's late plays.

The duration of the Revival was quite short in historical terms: by the early 1620s the mood had dissipated with Elizabeth and Frederick's disastrous Bohemian adventure and the start of the Thirty Years' War.[10] The significance of this shift in mood can be seen by comparing the pristinely naive and positive treatment of British-Imperialist elements in *Merlin* with the bitingly satiric and blackly comic handling of similar national political themes in Middleton's *A Game at Chess* in 1624. The height of the Elizabethan Revival is the most likely time for *Merlin* to have been written; each year removed from that brief period involves a diminution of that likelihood.

(And of course, the date of the play is crucial for any hypothesis of imitation rather than Shakespearean authorship. Given the numerous, varied, subtle, and specific Shakespearean stylistic features found in *Merlin*, it is very hard to imagine any hypothetical imitator achieving such a result without intimate knowledge of, and constant access to, the texts of Shakespeare's plays; and half of those plays, including many of those with the closest links to *Merlin*—like *MacBeth* and *Cymbeline*, *The Tempest* and *Henry VIII*—were not in print until the appearance of the First Folio in 1623. It is unlikely on artistic, cultural, and political grounds that *Merlin* would have been written as late as the early 1620s; if *Merlin* is a work of Shakespearean imitation, it could hardly have been written before 1623. The one sensible solution to this riddle is to accept *Merlin* as being what it gives every sign of being, a work of partial Shakespearean authorship.)

This dating of *Merlin* to the time of Shakespeare's collaborations with Fletcher is supported, I believe, by the implications of the relationship between *Merlin* and Beaumont and Fletcher's *Cupid's Revenge*. Since the materials common to these two plays have been cited by earlier commentators as evidence of common authorship, it may be wise to pause and consider what such shared materials may or may not mean in the plays of the period. One example of such shared materials occurs in the plays *Love's Pilgrimage* and *The New Inn*. *Love's Pilgrimage* is one of the Beaumont-Fletcher works that was first printed in the 1647 folio of their works; it is thought to have been written ca. 1615, with a possible revision for a new production in 1635. That possible revision provides one explanation for the fact that *Love's Pilgrimage* contains lines and passages that are also found in Ben Jonson's *The New Inn* of ca. 1629. The passages in question are, *Love's Pilgrimage*, I,i,25-63 and 330-411, and *The New Inn*, II,v,48-73 and III,i,57-93 and 130-68. Two alternatives present themselves: either an anonymous reviser interpolated some of Jonson's work into the Beaumont-Fletcher play around 1635, or Jonson adapted material that was original with Beaumont and Fletcher for his own use. One can assign different degrees of plausibility or probability to these alternatives (the first seems far more likely than the second), but either is possible. The common materials have no bearing on the authorship of either play: *Love's Pilgrimage* is as certainly and unequivocally Beaumont and Fletcher's work as *The New Inn* is Jonson's.[11]

While the facts in regard to *Merlin* and *Cupid's Revenge* are slightly different, the implications of their shared materials are not far removed from what we conclude of the plays discussed above. The crucial passages in *Cupid's Revenge* are I,v,5-11,

IV,i,2-7 and 37-9, and V,ii,44-9,[12] which are paralleled in *Merlin*, II,ii,35-9 and 72-81, and III,vi,83-4 and 108. (Larger-scale plot elements shared by the two plays—the missing prince, the ruler and his heir falling in love with the same woman—might be attributed to the fact that both works draw inspiration and source material from Sidney's *Arcadia*; but the common passages assure us that these two plays have a specific relationship with each other apart from any common source.) Unlike the common material in the Beaumont-Fletcher and Jonson plays, which consists of long comedy passages only tangentially connected with the plays' plots, the shared material in *Merlin* and *Cupid's Revenge* comprises short speeches and lines that are more difficult to abstract from their settings within the plays. *Cupid's Revenge* was in performance in 1611-12, and was probably written a year or so earlier (though this is not certain); it was first printed in 1615. If one accepts (even if only provisionally) my dating of *Merlin* to 1613-15, then *Cupid's Revenge* would predate that play by a few years.

William Wells was the first person to draw attention to these common features in *Cupid's Revenge* and *Merlin*; both he and E.H.C. Oliphant accepted these elements as evidence that Beaumont and Fletcher were part-authors of *Merlin*.[13] Yet apart from the common materials, *Merlin* shows little sign of those writers' presences—in clear contrast to *Cupid's Revenge*, which reveals itself to be a fairly standard Beaumont-Fletcher collaboration.[14] *Merlin* is as much like Shakespeare's and Rowley's work as *Cupid's Revenge* is like Fletcher's and Beaumont's; the common materials seem no more indicative of common authorship in this case than in the similar case of *The New Inn* and *Love's Pilgrimage*.

When the various possible explanations for the shared elements in *Merlin* and *Cupid's Revenge* are considered, I find it most plausible to view the Beaumont-Fletcher play as the "model" for *Merlin*. There is a direct precedent for this kind of connection between a late-Shakespearean collaboration and another artist's work, in the pairing of *Henry VIII* and Samuel Rowley's 1604 play *When You See Me You Know Me*. (Samuel is the "other" Rowley of English Renaissance drama; *When You See Me* is his only extant solo work. Nineteenth-century speculation sometimes linked Samuel and William as father and son, though there is no evidence either for or against any kind of a connection between them.)

Samuel Rowley's play about Henry VIII was first printed in 1605; a second quarto, reprinted from the first, was issued in 1613, the year in which *Henry VIII* was being performed and described as "new." A tandem reading of the two plays reveals their close relationship in terms of subject matter and structure: both deal with Wolsey's power and ambition, with the English lords' resentment of him, and with Wolsey's eventual rejection by the king; both feature King Henry venturing out in disguise with his courtiers, as well as the birth of an heir (Edward; Elizabeth); both show an innocent English queen persecuted by a pair of clergymen, and a loyal Protestant supporter being subjected to undeserved opposition. The verbal parallels are not as striking as those that unite *Merlin* with *Cupid's Revenge*, though there are some noteworthy points of contact. The two Henries' shared habit of using the interjection "Ha!" when angry is noted by Herschel Baker in the Riverside edition; in the portion of *When You See Me* that concerns Jane Seymour's lying-in with the soon-to-be-born Edward VI (B1v), the King and his jester Will Summers have these lines:

> *King:* Ladies attend her, Countesse of Salisburie, sister Mary,
> Who first brings word that Harrie hath a Sonne
> Shall be rewarded well:
> *Will:* I, ile be his suretie: but doe you heare wenches, shee that brings the first tydings howsoever it fall out, let her be sure to say the Childs like the father, or else she shall have nothing.

Compare the lines of the Old Lady in *Henry VIII*, V,i,157-76.[15]

Given the fact that the Shakespeare-Fletcher *Henry VIII* appeared in the same year as Q2 of Samuel Rowley's play, it is hard not to see meaningful connections between the two; *When You See Me* may well have prompted or inspired the other work. And Q1 of *Cupid's Revenge* might in turn relate to *Merlin* in the same way that Q2 of *When You See Me* relates to *Henry VIII*. The plot similarities between the first two are not dissimilar to those that unite the last two; and the close verbal parallels from *Cupid's Revenge* found in *Merlin* are like those that Shakespeare's plays sometimes show with their source materials. The versified borrowings from North's translation of Plutarch in *Antony and Cleopatra* are perhaps the best known of many possible examples of this tendency in the acknowledged works. (Interestingly, the critical and biographical literature tends to treat these borrowings from sources as though they must have been intentional—but they could have been, to a large extent, inadvertent. Shakespeare might have had one of those rare minds gifted with intense and facile recall of works read, as Coleridge had; and he may have recapitulated other men's words in his works in an almost-unconscious or half-conscious way. Scholars tend to assume, unthinkingly, that Shakespeare worked rather like a scholar, with his sources open before him; but Shakespeare was a poet, not a scholar, and may have worked often from memory—a real, if unverifiable, possibility.)

The common passages are worth quoting verbatim in their *Cupid's Revenge* versions. First, I,v,3-11:

> *Timantus:* If I had a companie my Lord—
> *Ismenus:* Of Fidlers: Thou a Companie?
> No, no, keepe thy companie at home, and cause cuckolds:
> The warres will hurt thy face, theres no semsters, Shoe-
> makers, nor Taylors, not almon milk ith morning, nor
> poacht egges to keepe your worship soluble, no man to
> warme your shyrt, and blow your roses: nor none to rever-

ence your round lace breeches: If thou wilt needes goe, and
goe thus, get a case for thy Captainship, a shower will spoil
thee else. Thus much for thee.

Second, IV,i,1-7:

Leucippus: And thus she has usd me, ist not a good mother?
Ismenus: Why killed you her not?
Leucippus: The Gods forbid it.
Ismenus: S'light, if all the women ithe world were barren,
shee had dyde.
Leucippus: But tis not reason directs thee thus.
Ismenus: Then I have none at all, for all I have in mee directs
me . . .

Third, IV,i,37-9:

The usage I have had, I know would make
Wisedome her selfe run frantick through the streetes,
And Patience quarrell with her shaddow.

Fourth, V,ii,44-9:

Bacha: Doe you not know me Lords?
Nisus: Yes deadly sin we know ye, would we did not.
Ismenus: Doe you heare Whore, a plague a God upon thee,
the Duke is dead.
Bacha: Dead!
Ismenus: I, wild-fire and brimstone take thee . . .

These four selections from *Cupid's Revenge* contain the key
lines reproduced in *Merlin* —though there are a few other minor links too (compare, for example, "Tis a truth / That takes
my sleepe away" in *Cupid's Revenge*, III,ii,93-4 with "It is a
thought that takes away my sleep" in *Merlin*, II,ii,32). The relevant passages occur both in Fletcher's and in Beaumont's
shares of *Cupid's Revenge*; they are mainly in prose, whereas
they are re-cast into verse in *Merlin*—and such rewriting of

prose material into verse is typical of Shakespeare. The relevant sections of *Cupid's Revenge* are written in Beaumont's and Fletcher's usual styles; Consider the long speech from which the third excerpt given above derives (IV,i,25-39):

> *Leucippus:* O strange carriages!
> Sir, As I have hope that there is any thing
> To reward doing well, my usages
> Which have beene (but tis no matter what)
> Have put me so farre from the thought of Greatnes,
> That I should welcome it like a disease
> That grew upon me, and I could not cure.
> They are my enemies that gave you this,
> And yet they call me friend, and are themselves
> I feare abus'd. I am weary of my life,
> For Gods sake take it from me: it creates
> More mischiefe in the State then it is worth.
> The usage I have had, I know would make
> Wisedome her selfe run frantick through the streetes,
> And Patience quarell with her shaddow.

The style is wholly typical of Beaumont, easily distinguishable from that of Shakespeare, and indicative of the overall stylistic contrast between *Merlin* and *Cupid's Revenge*. Indeed, we can point out this contrast by noting that the common material from the Beaumont-Fletcher play is rephrased in *Merlin* in ways suggestive of Shakespeare. This is most obvious in II,ii of *Merlin*, where the more substantive of the borrowings occur. "Smooth up your brows" (38) compares with "smoothed brows" in *1 Henry VI*, III,i,124, among many similar Shakespearean usages; for "spoil'd your faces" (also 38), compare "spoil upon my face" in *Henry V*, V,ii,231. For "few will now regard you" (39), we might cite "unregarded" in *As You Like It*, II,iii,42, and "Neither regarding" in *Two Gentlemen*, III,i,70. For Edoll's "your gross *mistake* would make / Wisdom her self run *madding* through the streets" (72-3), compare "mad mistaking" in *Shrew*, IV,v,49, and note that "madding" and "madded" are word forms that recur in Shakespeare. For "The great devil take me" (76), compare "A burning devil take them" and "the devil take thee" in *Troilus*, V,ii,196 and V,vii,23, and "The devil take Henry of Lancaster and thee" in *Richard II*, V,v,102, among similar canonical phrasings. For "had I been by" (also 76), compare "Would I had been by" in *Winter's Tale*, III,iii,107, and "hadst thou not been by" in *John*, IV,ii,220; for "married her / On these conditions" (78-9), note a use of "these conditions" in a courting context in *Kinsmen*, III,vi,264. In *Coriolanus*, IV,v,172ff., there is a conversation that touches upon some of the same points about idle soldiers; just as the soldiers in *Merlin* are told to stay home and "increase Cuckolds" (II,ii,36), the servants in *Coriolanus* claim that peacetime only serves to "increase tailors" (IV,v,219-20).

The relevant materials in III,vi of *Merlin* are only one or two lines long; yet even there we catch a hint of the same Shakespearean transformation. Fletcher's "Yes deadly sin we know ye, would we did not" becomes "Yes, Deadly Sin, we know you, / And shall discover all your villany" (III,vi,83-4). For "discover all your villany," note that Shakespeare has similar-sounding canonical phrasings: "discover such integrity" in *Two Gentlemen*, III,ii,76, and "discover thine infirmity" in *1 Henry VI*, V,iv,60. Consistently, the borrowings from *Cupid's Revenge* sound more like Shakespeare's work in their *Merlin* versions than they do in the Beaumont-Fletcher versions—which certainly seems to suggest a Shakespearean rewriting of lines and passages original in the other play.

As we have already noted, *Cupid's Revenge* was likely written not long before 1611, and was first printed in 1615. Shakespeare was collaborating with Fletcher, one of the authors, in 1613, and might well have seen the play in manuscript; it is not necessary for us to suppose that he must have had access to a printed text. Yet his apparent use of *When You See Me* for *Henry VIII* certainly does coincide with that play's reappearance in print. As we have seen, *Merlin* gives various indications of being a very late Shakespearean work, written around the time of the collaborations with Fletcher, and perhaps even later; the connections with *Cupid's Revenge*, if they are linked to that play's published text, point toward the same conclusion. I suggest the period 1613-15 as the most likely chronological interval for Shakespeare's and Rowley's authorship of *The Birth of Merlin*, with special emphasis on 1615 as the most probable single year.

This dating conflicts with the traditional idea of Shakespeare's retirement from playwriting late in his career, and has been criticized on that basis; I confess that I cannot find this a substantive argument. The idea of Shakespeare's retirement was first recorded by Nicholas Rowe in the account of Shakespeare's life prefixed to his 1709 edition of the Works. It is apparently rooted in tradition and is not necessarily more reliable than the deer-poaching story and other elements of specious biography recorded by Rowe and other early commentators.[16] The tradition is thin in supporting detail: "Of Shakespeare during his years of retirement, tradition says nothing ..."[17] The gap has been filled largely by imagination. In previous generations, the idea of *The Tempest* as Shakespeare's "farewell to the stage" was popular; the fact of the late collaborations with Fletcher complicated this romantic notion, but only slightly—one commentator imagined Shakespeare emerging from retirement to speak the Prologue to *Henry VIII* in the theatre.[18]

The facts that we do possess, however, yield a more vigorous picture of Shakespeare's last years. We know that he was in London in the spring of 1612 to testify in the Belott-Mountjoy suit; in the following year he was paid, along with his old colleague Richard Burbage, for working up an *impresa* (heraldic design and inscription) for the Earl of Rutland.[19] Around this time he was working with Fletcher on *Henry VIII* and *Kinsmen*, plays that first appeared on the stage in 1613 and were almost certainly written not long before. And in a telling fact, we can note that in March of 1613 Shakespeare purchased a house in London, the so-called Blackfriars Gatehouse, apparently as a real-estate investment.[20] Thus there is more evidence for an active Shakespeare than a retired Shakespeare in his final years. The best argument for Shakespeare's abandonment of active playwriting after 1613 has been the lack of any works from those years; but *Merlin* helps to fill that gap. If we credit, at least as possibilities, the reports of a lost Shakespeare-Fletcher collaboration in *Cardenio*,[21] and even the lost plays *Henry I* and *Henry II* that Shakespeare may have written with Robert Davenport, another younger contemporary,[22] we get a picture of quite regular collaborative dramatic composition in the last years.

The 1615 dating is also interesting from the obvious alternative viewpoint—that of William Rowley. If *Merlin* dates from 1615, then the play that Rowley worked on next was likely *A Fair Quarrel*, one of his collaborations with Middleton; and the Rowleian sections of *Fair Quarrel* do show a number of interesting links with *Merlin*, as noted in Chapter IV—links that could be considered compatible with a close chronological connection between the two plays. I do not place too much stress on such links, because their interpretation is highly problematical; yet in a general way, the sequence of *Merlin* and *Fair Quarrel* does have some plausibility.

Collateral to the subject of the play's date of authorship is the matter of its date of publication. Some people might find the date 1662 suspiciously late for a Shakespearean work; yet it is not far out of the ordinary for plays in the seventeenth century. Note that *Kinsmen* was first printed in 1634, twenty-one years after it was written. Note that several of Shakespeare's earliest plays—*1 Henry VI*, *The Comedy of Errors*, *The Two Gentlemen of Verona*—first appeared in print in the First Folio in 1623, some three decades after they were composed; and in an extreme case, note that the partially Shakespearean *Sir Thomas More* was only published in 1844, some two and a half centuries after its likely date of authorship. Long delays between authorship and publication do not necessarily cast doubt on authenticity. Note too that only a few of Rowley's works were printed before his death in 1626; some were published comparatively late like *Merlin*—*The Witch of Edmonton* (1658), *The Spanish Gypsy* (1653), *The Old Law* (1656), *The Changeling* (1653), *A Cure for a Cuckold* (1661), *Fortune by Land and Sea* (1655), *Wit at Several Weapons* (1647).

If we turn to other writers, we can observe that Marlowe's *The Jew of Malta* appeared in print in 1633, four decades after its author's death, and that many of the plays of Fletcher and his collaborators were first published in the folio of 1647, twenty to forty years after their authorship. Further examples could be added, but the point would be the same; the late publication of *Merlin* was not unusual for the era in question, and need not be a factor in affirming Shakespeare's connection with the play.

CHAPTER VII

Conclusion

THIS STUDY IS meant to be introductory in nature and not definitive; it is designed not as the final word on the authorship of *The Birth of Merlin*, but as the first in what I hope will be a fruitful reconsideration of the play. The reader who has been annoyed by the prevalence in these chapters of phrases like "seems to be" and "appears to be" should understand that their use is quite deliberate; I have consciously attempted to avoid the "vocabulary of confidence" criticized by Schoenbaum[1]—and to remain cognizant of the genuine difficulties and limitations inherent in this type of work. Nevertheless, "there must be conclusions," as Corporal Nym says. Let's consider what a reasonable, prudent, objective, fair-minded reader might justifiably conclude about the authorship of *The Birth of Merlin*—for if the consideration of the play's evidence of authorship has hardly been exhausted by this survey, its coverage of the more fundamental aspects of the question should allow at least a tentative verdict.

I believe it is fair to say that attribution questions in English Renaissance dramas (like attribution studies in other fields—musicology, art history, etc.) vary greatly in difficulty; if some are complex and challenging, others are relatively easy to resolve. If, for instance, we ask, "Who wrote *The Two Noble Kinsmen*?" we are faced with a relatively easy question. The 1634 quarto of *Kinsmen* contains a title-page attribution to Shakespeare and Fletcher; Shakespeare and Fletcher wrote in recognizably different styles, with many distinguishing traits between them; both men's distinctive styles are present in the play's text. The internal evidence confirms the external evidence: *Kinsmen* was written by Shakespeare and Fletcher. Can we regard this as proven absolutely? Perhaps not. In the abstract, almost anything is possible, and almost anything can be disputed. It is not difficult to assert that a proposition is unproven, or even unprovable; one merely needs to demand ever-higher standards of proof. (I tend to see much Shakespearean commentary as falling into this trap: much higher standards of proof of authorship are demanded for Shakespeare than for his contemporaries.) In the real world of the sensible and the probable, however, we can observe that the evidence for Shakespeare's and Fletcher's authorship of *Kinsmen* is abundant, and that countervailing evidence is nil. We can determine that Shakespeare and Fletcher wrote *Kinsmen* and rely on that conclusion as certain beyond reasonable doubt.

I would assert that the authorship of *The Birth of Merlin* is, by the same standard, another relatively easy attribution question. The external evidence from seventeenth-century sources unanimously assigns the play to Shakespeare and Rowley; Shakespeare and Rowley wrote in recognizably different styles, with many distinguishing traits; both men's distinctive styles are present in the play's text. The internal evidence confirms the external evidence; *Merlin* was written by Shakespeare and Rowley. We can be as certain of this as we are that Shakespeare and Fletcher wrote *Kinsmen*.

This comparison that I draw between *Kinsmen* and *Merlin* does have one problem: allowing for dissenters and doubters, the Shakespearean contribution to *Kinsmen* has been recognized for a long time, while Shakespeare's share in *Merlin* has been generally denied for equally as long. As I have indicated repeatedly in this study, I believe that this is largely because *Merlin* is a close and intimate collaboration between the two poets, which in effect dilutes the Shakespearean impression of the work as a whole. The numerous specific indications of close collaboration in the text confirm the blending of Shakespearean and Rowleian elements that the work displays on larger and more general levels.

There are essentially two reasons given for the dismissal of the idea that Shakespeare had a hand in *Merlin*; one, that the play simply is not good enough to be his work; and two, that it lacks Shakespeare's stylistic traits. The second point is patently and demonstrably false; as this study has shown, there is abundant evidence of Shakespeare's style in *Merlin*. The first point is also unsound; it violates Schoenbaum's seventh rule for authorship studies, quoted in Chapter I, which states that subjective judgments have no value in determining the authorship of disputed works.

I confess that my estimation of the literary worth of *Merlin* is higher than anyone else's that I know of. Having spent, perhaps, as much time studying the play as anyone has ever spent on *Merlin*, I still find it a rewarding and satisfying play; at a degree of familiarity at which Rowley's solo works can only leave me numb, *Merlin* still pleases. I consider it a better play than *Kinsmen*; I find that it provides some of the same aesthetic satisfactions that Shakespeare's romances provide. And yet, I have to recognize that my positive valuation of the play is as irrelevant to the authorship question as are other people's negative valuations. The question of the play's authorship can be resolved only on the evidence. As we noted earlier in this book, Shakespeare's title to some of his lesser works has frequently been disputed by individuals who judged those works to be "not good enough" for Shakespeare. But disliking *Titus Andronicus*, say, or finding *A Lover's Complaint* a weak poem, is not justification for supposing that Shakespeare couldn't have, wouldn't have written the offending work.

I believe it is simply accurate to say that Shakespeare has been elevated to a totemic, talismanic role in our literary culture, a prominence that interferes with our ability to make rational judgments about his works. While this is less severe now than it was in previous generations, it still remains a significant obstacle. Even scholars who readily apply coolly rational and objective standards of judgment to the other English Renaissance dramatists and poets can sometimes lapse into subjectivity and emotionalism concerning Shakespeare—which is understandable as far as aesthetic experience is concerned, but risky when it involves the historical record. The reception of *Kinsmen* betrays this tendency clearly, I think: despite the abundant evidence of Shakespeare's hand in the play, its full acceptance into the canon has been very slow (it has only rarely been included in editions of the "complete" works) and even painful, as though scholars were embarrassed by an act of literary miscegenation on Shakespeare's part. To me, the recognition that Shakespeare collaborated on plays like *Kinsmen* and *Merlin* is an enrichment of his canon, not an adulteration of it; more Shakespeare, even minor Shakespeare, is good to have.

Readers who remain skeptical about the hypothesis of partial Shakespearean authorship of *Merlin* will surely raise the alternative explanation of imitation of Shakespeare—but the hypothesis of imitation is wholly inadequate to deal with the totality of the evidence. Examples of Shakespeare's influence on his contemporaries and immediate successors, and instances in which other writers have imitated him, are readily available; Rowley's works contain some noteworthy imitations. As noted in Chapter II, the spectral procession in *All's Lost*, V,ii seems clearly derivative of *MacBeth*, IV,i. Or consider the final scene of *The Maid in the Mill* (in Rowley's portion of that play), where Gillian reveals that Florimell, her supposed daughter, is actually the child of a nobleman—Gillian having rescued the girl as an infant when her nurse was "seiz'd on by a fierce and hungry Bear." This, of course, is a borrowing from *The Winter's Tale*.

Can we distinguish between such borrowing and common authorship? Easily: the relationship between *Winter's Tale* and *Maid in the Mill* is limited and relatively superficial, the kind of relationship that normally indicates a non-authorial connection.[2] In contrast, the external evidence assigning *Maid in the Mill* to Fletcher and Rowley is confirmed by abundant internal evidence: the two men's characteristic styles, readily distinguishable, permeate the text, so that scholars are unanimous in acceptance of the external attribution as valid. (Again, the standard of evidence that tells us that *Maid in the Mill* is the work of Fletcher and Rowley is the same standard that tells us that *Kinsmen* is the work of Fletcher and Shakespeare—and the same standard that tells us that *Merlin* is the work of Shakespeare and Rowley.)

The distinction between authorial and non-authorial commonalities is no more insuperable in the case of *Merlin* than it is in the case of *Maid in the Mill*. Instances of Shakespearean influence or imitation are normally few and far between in any given work. The elements from Shakespeare's works that are imitated, or that influence other writers, tend to be the most memorable and striking effects—the ghostly procession in *MacBeth* and the bear in *Winter's Tale* being precisely this type of feature. Authorial connections, on the other hand, tend to be abundant, varied, subtle, and specific. We have seen something of the pattern of Rowleian elements in *Merlin*, a pattern that stands as sound evidence of his authorship. The fact that the play shows a similar pattern of Shakespearean elements (the same kind of pattern that *Kinsmen* reveals) points to a similar conclusion in favor of Shakespearean authorship.

The idea of imitation of Shakespeare, especially in the context of the late works, can be pursued one step farther with productive results—because imitation was once proposed, most prominently in recent years by Una Ellis-Fermor, as an explanation for the Shakespearean aspects of *Kinsmen*.[3] Kenneth Muir considers this hypothesis of imitation at length in his study of *Kinsmen*, even postulating an identity for the supposed imitator ("Henry Tomkins") to test the theory; yet the verdict Muir reaches on this anonymous imitator is negative.[4]

First of all, there are the strictly practical considerations: *Kinsmen* is universally dated to 1613, and was in performance by 1619,[5] while Shakespeare's late plays (excluding *Pericles*) were not in print until 1623, so that "Henry Tomkins" had to acquire an extensive and intimate familiarity with Shakespeare's later works in some circuitous, circumstantial way ("he bribed the prompter to lend him copies of *The Tempest* and *The Winter's Tale*," in Muir's scenario). (Since *Kinsmen* was not printed until 1634, a resourceful obscurantist could argue that "Henry Tomkins" could have performed an extensive revision of the play between 1623 and 1634. The total lack of evidence in favor of such a revision, though, should stand as a barrier to that theory.)

Beyond the practical considerations, there are larger concerns of motivation and method, questions as to why and how "Henry Tomkins" made his imitation of Shakespeare. Once Shakespeare was perceived as a unique, towering figure in English literature, the spectre of forgery and falsification became a real factor: in the climate of Bardolatry that prevailed in the late eighteenth century, an escapade like William Henry Ireland's *Vortigern and Rowena* is comprehensible.[6] "Henry Tomkins," however, did not live in such a climate of opinion; Shakespeare's contemporaries and immediate successors, even those who had an appreciation of his work, did not feel any temptation to canonize or deify him. (Jonson might have been a better candidate for such imitation; there were self-proclaimed Sons of Ben, but not, as far as we know, any Sons of Will.) It would have been as difficult for "Henry Tomkins" to have anticipated the world of William Henry Ireland as it is for those of us in the late twentieth century to foresee the cultural atmosphere that will prevail in the early twenty-second.

Yet, for the sake of the argument, let us grant this unlikelihood—that "Henry Tomkins" anticipated his culture by generations in his grasp of Shakespeare's achievement and his perception of Shakespeare's art, *and* that he felt a desire to write the way Shakespeare did. If we grant the "why," we are still faced with the "how" of the imitator's accomplishment— for, unlike the lamentable effort of Ireland, "Henry Tomkins" created in *Kinsmen* an imitation of such high quality that it passed the tests of Shakespearean authorship that scholars would devise over the ensuing three centuries, tests of style, textual features, imagery, prosody. The imitator was able to master all the features of Shakespeare's style, from the largest to the most minute, anticipating three hundred years' worth of intensive intellectual and critical activity—*and* was able to replicate all of these Shakespearean elements in original yet convincing ways. And, on top of this mountainous improbability, this imitator—despite his possession of such a remarkable range of cognitive and artistic abilities, despite being one of the most striking minds of his age—remained completely anonymous, and left no trace of his existence other than his contribution to *Kinsmen*. It is hardly surprising that Muir finds the hypothesis of "Henry Tomkins" untenable, or that he quotes Marco Mincoff's opinion that the idea is "too fanciful for refutation."

I have to point out that most of these factors apply to *Merlin* as well as to *Kinsmen*; the hypothesis of imitation of Shakespeare rather than Shakespearean authorship is no more sound in the former instance than in the latter. Even if one were to take the willfully obstinate position and maintain that *Kinsmen* and *Merlin* might *both* be the work of "Henry Tomkins," one would still be confronted with the same problems of the imitator's motives and methods. It is worthwhile to be mindful of Gerald Eades Bentley's assertion that a "power of almost irresistible anachronism" taints our views of Shakespeare and his age. To us, Shakespeare is, in Alfred Harbage's phrase, "the poet of our idolatry," and the idea of a contemporary imitator may attain an illusory plausibility as a result. Yet to the people of his own era, Shakespeare, though often admired, was much less than he is to us. "Henry Tomkins" is clearly an anachronism, a figment of modern imagination. Where we find strong evidence of Shakespeare's style, we find strong evidence of Shakespeare's authorship.

The past several years have been unusually productive in Shakespearean authorship studies; a list with no pretensions to completeness could include Eric Sams' book on *Edmund Ironside*, Gary Taylor on the poem "Shall I Die?,"[7] Eric Rasmussen on the additions to *The Second Maiden's Tragedy*,[8] Eliot Slater on *Edward III*,[9] and Donald Foster on the "Funerall Elegie" for William Peter.[10] The sheer plenitude of this activity might appear suspicious to a remote observer; in my judgment, it merely shows that while the core of Shakespeare's canon is certain and solidly established, the periphery is still being defined.

Professor Foster's book contains a passing comment on *Edward III* that is worth quoting here. In surveying problematical alleged Shakespearean works, Prof. Foster observes that "There is a general consensus also that Shakespeare had a hand in *Edward III*...."[11] Stop and think what this means. The Shakespearean nature of *Edward III* was first pointed out by Edward Capell in 1760; over the ensuing two centuries various individuals advocated the Shakespearean hypothesis, though consensus opinion remained resistant and skeptical. If that consensus is shifting, or has shifted, now, it would constitute one demonstration of the fact that individual dissenters are sometimes right when the received opinion, the established view, is wrong (a phenomenon not unknown in other fields of inquiry as well).

I ask the reader to keep this in mind when considering the authorship of *Merlin*. Those who are willing and able to set aside *ad hominem* and *ad auctoritatem* considerations to take a fresh and objective look at the play and its evidence of authorship will find ample support for the hypothesis of this study. If this occurs, I believe that a gradual shift in the consensus on *Merlin* will come about, comparable to the one that *Edward III* now enjoys. (Perhaps, in the case of *Merlin*, only one century will be needed instead of two—but this may be wild optimism on my part. . . .)

There are many avenues for further investigation of this play open to us; one that seems particularly profitable to me involves potential for a greater refinement of both the texts of *Merlin* and the plays of the acknowledged canon. Consider the song at the start of *Kinsmen*; in line 16, the original quarto reading of "angle" is often jettisoned from modern editions (like the Riverside) in favor of the reading "angel" from the second Beaumont and Fletcher folio of 1679:

> Not an angle of the air,
> Bird melodious, or bird faire,
> Is absent hence.

The word "angle" sounds strange when applied to "air"; yet the lines could be read as meaning that fair and melodious birds are not absent from any part ("angle") of the sky. In this connection, recall the line "any angle underneath the Moon" in *Merlin*, II,iii,74, which, with its application of "angle" in a "skyey" context, might be taken as offering support for the original quarto reading of "angle" over the folio's "angel." In the opposite direction, editors like Delius and Tucker Brooke have emended the original "stallion" in II,i,140 of *Merlin* to the more commonplace "scullion"; yet Shakespeare's use of "stallion" in the same context in *Hamlet*, II,ii,587, might be interpreted as confirming the quarto reading. This type of textual adjustment would be possible once *Merlin* is accepted into the Shakespeare canon.

APPENDIX I

The Shakespeare-Fletcher Collaborations

OUR EVALUATION of *The Birth of Merlin* as a partially Shakespearean work will be colored by our preconceptions concerning collaboration in general and Shakespearean collaboration in particular. Consensus opinion allows that Shakespeare collaborated only in a few instances toward the close of his career, with John Fletcher, in efforts that produced *Henry VIII* and *The Two Noble Kinsmen* (and maybe, just possibly, the lost play *Cardenio*). Critics and scholars over succeeding generations have expended great effort to define and differentiate the respective shares of each man in these plays—though often in an overly schematic and mechanical way. The assumption has often been that the plays can be broken down into individual units (usually single scenes) that are either Shakespearean or Fletcherian in authorship. I believe it can be shown that both *Henry VIII* and *Kinsmen* are more complex products of collaboration than such schema indicate, and that both plays reveal a more subtle and intricate interaction between the two authors—a kind of dramatic composition relevant to what we find in *Merlin*.

A few modern commentators have denied Fletcher a hand in *Henry VIII*, and have argued that the play is wholly the work of Shakespeare. Their position, however, is not strong, in my opinion, and fails to convince. Some portions of *Henry VIII* show such clear Fletcherian characteristics that it seems mere recalcitrance to insist upon Fletcher's absence from the play's authorship (Buckingham's two long speeches in II,i,55-78 and 100-36 are perhaps the best and the best-known examples of the play's Fletcherian materials). Conversely, however, the advocates of Fletcher's presence in *Henry VIII* have over-estimated his share, and have underestimated Shakespeare's—as I think is revealed by a close look at the play's text.

The strongest arguments that have been made in favor of Fletcher's contribution to *Henry VIII* depend upon the play's textual evidence, and upon the wide disparity between the known habits of the two dramatists involved—Fletcher's frequent uses of "ye" and "'em" in preference to "you" and "them," Shakespeare's penchant for "the peripharstic auxiliary verb 'do,' used as a mere expletive, in affirmative statements,"[1] and other similar peculiarities. The main problem with this approach is that it yields a schematic breakdown of the two authors' shares that is slanted too heavily on the side of Fletcher, assigning him more than half the play. (In attempting to summarize a large and varied body of scholarship and commentary, there is always risk of oversimplification and distortion. Many individual students of *Henry VIII* have recognized the possibility of cross-writing, of "intrusive elements" in the portions given to each man, of close and intimate collaboration between them. But the general tendency has been to adhere to a division of the play along the lines of the scheme reproduced here.)

A number of people have found the idea of Fletcher's having the majority share in *Henry VIII* unpersuasive; after all, Shakespeare and Fletcher are very different writers in many respects,[2] and the play generally resembles Shakespeare's work much more than Fletcher's. The truth, as is often the case, lies between the two extremes: Fletcher does have a share in the play, but a smaller one than the maximum estimate given by a schematic breakdown of the two men's portions.

Cyrus Hoy, in his study of textual evidence in the canon of Fletcher and his collaborators, recognized this to be true: he argued that the scenes designated with asterisks in the accompanying table—II,i and ii, the second half of III,ii, and IV,i and ii—are actually the work of Shakespeare and Fletcher together rather than Fletcher alone.[3] I argue that the remaining scenes assigned wholly to Fletcher—I,iii and iv, III,i, and V,ii through iv—can also be shown to possess Shakespearean contributions, so that there is not a single scene in the play from which Shakespeare is entirely absent. (*Henry VIII* provides a good illustration of Schoenbaum's point that textual analysis has limited applicability to intimate collaborations. We can see that textual studies have exaggerated Fletcher's share, once we realize that the play is an instance of close collaboration.)

We can begin sensibly at I,iii, the earliest scene in the play that is assigned to Fletcher alone. The claim for Fletcher rests on the textual evidence: there are seven examples of the contraction "'em" in the scene, but none of "them," and one use of

The respective shares of Shakespeare and Fletcher
in Henry VIII, *as traditionally assigned:*

SHAKESPEARE	FLETCHER
I,i-ii	I,iii-iv
II,iii-iv	*II,i-ii
III,iia	III,i
(to exit of King)	*III,iib
V,i	(after exit of King)
	*IV,i-ii
	V,ii-iv

*Cyrus Hoy assigns the indicated scenes to Shakespeare and Fletcher, rather than to Fletcher alone.

"has" against none of "hath"—proportions that do point to Fletcher rather than Shakespeare. Yet there is an important caveat to be made: the scene is colloquial in tone, and six of the seven instances of "'em" occur in the speeches of Lord Sands, who describes himself as "An honest country lord" (44) and who is clearly meant to reflect that status in his manner of speaking. This sort of linguistic realism is hardly unusual for Shakespeare; consider Stephano's "Flout 'em and scout 'em, / And scout 'em and flout 'em" in *Tempest*, III,ii,121-2, a plethora of "'em" uses that if found in *Henry VIII* would most likely be taken as more evidence of Fletcher's hand.

A purely quantitative approach to textual features may not always lead to the soundest conclusions; authors may vary their normal patterns of usage for specific reasons. After looking at the stylistic evidence in I,iii, I think we should be extremely cautious about assuming Shakespeare's absence and assigning the whole of the scene to Fletcher; while I do not dispute Fletcher's substantial presence, I also see valid indications of a Shakespearean contribution.

The Lord Chamberlain opens I,iii with, "Is't possible the spells of France should juggle / Men into such strange mysteries?" (1-2); Lord Sands replies with a remark about the "unmanly" nature of the French customs that some English courtiers have recently acquired (2-4). In *MacBeth*, V,viii,18-19, the same ideas are connected: when he hears of MacDuff's Caesarian birth, MacBeth says that the news "hath cow'd my better part of man," and he curses the "juggling fiends" who inspired his murderous ambitions. Both passages link the ideas of "juggling" and unmanliness. We can note too that Shakespeare uses forms of the word "juggle" in occult contexts: "juggling witchcraft" in *John*, III,i,169, "jugglers ... sorcerers ... witches" in *Errors*, I,ii,98-100, etc. Lord Sands' first speech, "New customs, / Though they be never so ridiculous ..." (2-4), uses a "never so" construction that recurs in Shakespeare—see *Dream*, III,i,136 and III,ii,334 and 442 for three of the score of instances in the collected works: "Who would give a bird the lie, though he cry 'cuckoo' never so," "Never so little show of love," and "Never so weary, never so in woe."

For "you would swear directly" (8), we can note that Shakespeare has a habit of using the word "directly" in reference to speech acts: compare "directly tell," "answer me directly," "answer'd directly," "give me directly to understand," etc., from the acknowledged works. For "The lag end of their lewdness" (35), compare a similar alliterative effect in "the lag end of my life" in *1 Henry IV*, V,i,24. Lord Sands' "Held current music too" (45-7) might be compared to Hotspur's "pass them current too" usage in *1 Henry IV*, II,iii,94; both passages occur in contexts with overtones of flirtation. The medical metaphor in lines 36-7 is rather more suggestive of Shakespeare's manner than Fletcher's. There are other, more minor features in I,iii that also suggest Shakespeare more than Fletcher—for "black mouth" (58), for instance, we might compare "thy mouth or black or white" in *Lear*, III,vi,66. Much in the scene, therefore, seems continuous with the preceding two undoubtedly Shakespearean scenes, I,i-ii. It seems precipitous to rule out Shakespeare's participation in I,iii merely because of a quantitative interpretation of the textual evidence.

This does not mean that I,iii is wholly Shakespearean; quite the contrary, I believe that clear indices of Fletcher's hand are very much in evidence. The style of bawdry in this scene is generally more typical of Fletcher than Shakespeare; see *The Chances*, III,iii,6ff. ("mad colts," 26) for one example, though of course there are many others in his plays. Specifically, for the Lord Chamberlain's words to Lord Sands, "Your colt's tooth is not cast yet" (48)—referring to the mark on the incisor teeth of a horse that indicates its age—note that Fletcher uses similar references in *Monsieur Thomas*, II,iii,132 and *Wit Without Money*, IV,v,72-3, while the same phrase, "colt's tooth," occurs in *The Elder Brother*, II,iii,60, in a section of that play ascribed to Fletcher rather than Massinger.

Both Shakespeare and Fletcher habitually indulge in the use of word pairs; Fletcher, however, frequently makes alliterative pairings, something that Shakespeare normally avoids. The paired terms "fool and feather" (25), "fights and fireworks" (27), and "tennis and tall stockings" (30) conform to this Fletcherian tendency; we can compare "Fooling and fiddling," "cavaliers and captains," and "'larums and loud howlings" in *The Mad Lover*, II,ii,23, 55, and 61, among a vast supply of similar phrasings throughout Fletcher's oeuvre. Other usages in I,iii, like "Death" as an oath (13), also point to Fletcher rather than to Shakespeare; and for similar ridicule of travelled Englishmen's Frenchified manners, see Fletcher's portion of *A Very Woman*, III,i. In this scene, then, I argue that we have a mixture of Shakespearean and Fletcherian elements, revealing that the scene was composed in an intimate collaboration between the two dramatists, and not by Fletcher alone.

In I,iv, the next scene in *Henry VIII* often assigned to Fletcher, we find a somewhat different profile. Here, signs of Shakespeare's hand are much more rare, while the presence of clear Fletcherian characteristics assures us that the latter playwright is dominant. Nevertheless, there are a few points in I,iv where Shakespeare's hand may be indicated. In the scene's opening speech, Sir Henry Guilford welcomes guests to Wolsey's banquet, claiming that the Cardinal "would have all as merry / As, first, good company, good wine, good welcome, / Can make good people" (5-7). Twice in his acknowledged solo works, Shakespeare forms similar "good" repetitions with "good wine": in *As You Like It*, Ep.,3-9 occurs "good wine . . . good bushes . . . good play(s) . . . good epilogue(s)"; in *Othello*, II,iii,309-11 we find "good wine . . . good familiar creature . . . good lieutenant."

Further along in I,iv, Anne Bullen asks Lord Sands if his father was mad, to which he replies, "O, very mad, exceeding mad, in love too; / But he would bite none" (28-9). Compare "Though I am mad, I will not bite him" in *Antony*, II,v,80, and for "very mad, exceeding mad," compare "very good, exceeding good" in *2 Henry IV*, III,ii,274. There are a few other possible indices of a Shakespearean contribution: for "confirm my welcome" (37), compare "Confirm his welcome" in *Two Gentlemen*, II,iv,101; for the use of "cold weather" in an amorous context (22), compare *Venus*, 402 and *Love's Labor's Lost*, I,ii,144; for "fair assembly" (67, 87), see the uses of the same phrase in pre-nuptial contexts in *Romeo*, I,ii,71 and *Much Ado*, V,iv,34.

In my view, though, line 28 is the most interesting single feature in I,iv. Fletcher has a habit of writing verse lines with an extra stress—he composes a fairly standard pentameter verse line and then adds a sixth accented monosyllable, most often "sir," but also "too" or "next" or "still" among other possibilities. Shakespeare simply does not use this same trick of versification, so that this trait is a very useful discriminator between the two poets. Here in I,iv we find some of these six-stress lines; consider lines 27-8:

> *Sands*: If I chance to talk a little wild, forgive me;
> I had it from my father.
> *Anne*:　　　　　　　　Was he mad, *sir*?
> *Sands*: O, very mad, exceeding mad, in love *too*;
> But he would bite none . . .

I have already cited line 28 as evidence of Shakespeare's presence in this scene; and I am sure that some readers will protest that the same line cannot be both Shakespearean and Fletcherian simultaneously. Yet my point is precisely this, that the same line can indeed be the work of both men; in itself it stands as one piece of evidence of intimate collaboration. There were no preordained rules that Shakespeare and Fletcher had to follow as they composed this play; they could have worked in any way, and with any degree of intimacy, that suited them. It would be foolish of us to insist upon a rigid dichotomy between their contributions if the play itself does not suggest it. The essential task is to approach the play with as few preconceptions as possible, so that we can see what the play reveals about its authorship.

When we turn to III,i, the third of the scenes in *Henry VIII* attributed to Fletcher alone in Hoy's authorship breakdown, we once again find, as in I,iii, strong evidence of Shakespeare's presence—indeed, the signs of his contribution are quite substantial here. This scene bears striking similarities to III,ii of *The Winter's Tale*; in both we have an innocent and persecuted queen being subjected to, and reacting against, a quasi-legal but blatantly biased proceeding, in which her main attacker dissimulates his opposition under a show of higher ideals. There are interesting verbal parallels as well: both Wolsey and Hermione make parenthetically qualified remarks about their integrity (*Henry VIII*, III,i,51-3; *Winter's Tale*, III,ii,26-8); for Katherine's "weigh out my afflictions" (88), compare Hermione's "As I weigh grief" (43); for Wolsey's "this is a mere distraction" (112), compare Leontes' "this is mere falsehood" (141).

If Katherine in II,i resembles Hermione, she also talks like some other Shakespearean heroines who share similar predicaments. For Katherine's statement that she is a "wretched lady" (146) and "the most unhappy woman living" (147), who continues to pray for her abandoning husband (180), compare Octavia's picture of herself in *Antony*, III,iv,12-14, "A more unhappy lady, / If this division chance, ne'er stood between, / Praying for both parts." We might also compare Ophelia's "I, of ladies most deject and wretched" in *Hamlet*, III,i,155, among similar usages elsewhere.

If Katherine resembles Hermione, Octavia and other Shakespearean women, then Wolsey here in III,i follows the examples of other Shakespearean manipulating villains, especially Edmund in I,ii of *Lear*. Both Wolsey and Edmund, in their respective scenes, busy themselves claiming affection between people they are actually working to separate (Henry and Katherine, Gloucester and Edgar). For Wolsey's "The hearts of princes kiss obedience" (162), compare Edmund's "the heart of his obedience" (85); for Wolsey's "if you please / To trust us in this business" (172-3), compare Edmund's "I do serve you in this business" (178).

These consistencies of characterization, theme, and verbal expression are supported by a range of other Shakespearean features in III,i. Consider, for example, Katherine's speech in lines 102-11:

> The more shame for ye! Holy men I thought ye,
> Upon my soul, two reverend cardinal virtues;
> But cardinal sins and hollow hearts I fear ye.
> Mend 'em for shame, my lords! Is this your comfort?
> The cordial that ye bring a wretched lady,
> A woman lost among ye, laugh'd at, scorn'd?
> I will not wish ye half my miseries,
> I have more charity. But say I warn'd ye;
> Take heed, for heaven's sake take heed, lest at once
> The burthen of my sorrows fall upon ye.

Partisans of Fletcher will immediately recognize his characteristic verse rhythm, and his typical use of "ye" and "'em"; but let us also consider some of the stylistic elements in this speech. For Katherine's use of "hollow hearts" (104) in reference to Wolsey and Campeius, compare the use of "hollow heart" in *1 Henry VI*, III,i,136, which refers to the Cardinal of Winchester, a character with broad resemblances to Wolsey. We find usages like "hollow bosoms" and "hollow-hearted friends" elsewhere in Shakespeare—but note especially, in comparison with Katherine's conjunction of "hollow hearts" and "comfort" (104-5), King Henry's "crying comfort from a hollow breast" in *2 Henry VI*, III,ii,43. The situations involved are very similar: royal victims rebuking the hypocritical words of false counselors. Katherine urges the churchmen to "Mend" their hearts (105); Shakespeare repeatedly uses similar phrasings in his works: "mend my soul," "mended faiths," "Our worser thoughts heaven mend," "the thought of hearts can mend," etc. For Katherine's linking of "comfort" and "cordial" (105-6), compare "cordial comfort" in *Winter's Tale*, V,iii,77.

Other features in this speech, perhaps more general, nonetheless have parallels and precedents in Shakespeare's solo work. The triplet "lost among ye, laugh'd at, scorn'd" (107) is typical of Shakespeare's habits: compare "baited, scorn'd, and storm'd at," "slander'd, scorn'd, dishonor'd," and "scoffs and scorns and contumelious taunts" among similar canonical usages; note too that "laugh'd to scorn" usages appear in *Mac-Beth*, IV,i,79, V,v,3, and V,vii,12, in *As You Like It*, IV,ii,18, and in *Venus*, 4. For the "I will not wish" in line 108, we can cite the similar "I may/will not wish" phrasings in *John*, III,i,333-4; "I rather wish you foes than hollow friends," in *3 Henry VI*, IV,i,139, may also be worth noting. For "say I warn'd ye" (109), compare "say you are well warn'd" in *1 Henry VI*, II,iv,103; for "burthen of my sorrows" (111), compare "burthening grief" in the same play, *1 Henry VI*, II,v,10. These recurring links with the *Henry VI* plays make good sense thematically—providing we accept the idea of an authorial contribution from Shakespeare; if we insist on Fletcher's sole authorship of the scene, they become surprising and problematical. Here in this speech, we have more evidence of intimate collaboration between the two poets.

Other speeches in III,i show similar evidence. We find a noteworthy concentration of Shakespearean features in lines 149-53, where Katherine pictures herself as:

> Shipwrack'd upon a kingdom, where no pity,
> No friends, no hope, no kindred weep for me,
> Almost no grave allowed me. Like the lily,
> That once was mistress of the field, and flourish'd,
> I'll hang my head and perish.

For the image of hanging one's head and dying like a lily, compare "I hang the head / As flowers with frost" in *Titus*,
IV,iv,70-1; for the sequence "grave ... lily ... flourish'd"
(151-2), we might compare "pale and angry rose ... grave ...
flourish" in *1 Henry VI*, II,iv,107-11 (the trilogy once again).
For Katheine's list of woes, "no pity, / No friends, no hope, no
kindred" (149-50), we can cite a wide range of similar usages,
Queen Elizabeth's "cozen'd / Of comfort, kingdom, kindred,
freedom, life" in *Richard III*, IV,iv,223-4 being one good example among many.

At line 164, Wolsey says that the "hearts of princes," in response to opposition, "swell and grow, as terrible as storms."
Shakespeare frequently uses verse images of "swelling" tides
and stormy seas: "The water swell before a boist'rous storm"
in *Richard III*, II,iii,44, "Th'ambitious ocean swell" and "swell
billow" in *Julius Caesar*, I,iii,7 and V,i,67, "tide swell'd up" in
2 Henry IV, II,iii,63, etc. Sometimes, as here, the imagery is
used as a metaphor for rising anger: see *Richard II*, III,ii,109,
Titus, IV,ii,139, and *Lucrece*, 646 for apposite instances. We
might also note the "terrible seas" in *Cymbeline*, III,i,27, and,
for "swell and grow," the similar-sounding "flowing and swelling" in *Troilus*, IV,iv,78. I do not assert that Fletcher never uses
similar imagery—but I do think it's fair to say that this imagery is more typical of Shakespeare than Fletcher.

Throughout the scene, we find phrasings that show consistency with Shakespeare's style as displayed in his unquestioned
solo works. These features vary widely in significance, yet they
can all be cited as elements in the general Shakespearean style
of III,i. "Out with it boldly" (39) occurs in *Richard II*, II,i,233;
"deep suspicion" (53) appears in *Richard III*, III,v,8. The
phrases "full cause" (29), "main cause" (93), and "sick cause"
(118) conform to a pattern of Shakespearean usage—"full
cause" occurs in *Lear*, II,iv,284, while uses like "great cause,"
"weighty cause," and "distemper'd cause," among others, are
found elsewhere in Shakespeare. For "a point of weight" (71),

compare Shakespearean usages like "any matter of weight," "some things of weight," "a matter of more weight," and "a plea of no less weight." If Shakespearean characters speak "directly," as noted in connection with I,iii,8, they also tend to speak "rightly"; for "He tells you rightly" (97), compare Shakespearean phrases like "rightly say," "rightly said," "rightly sounded," "English'd rightly," and "inform you rightly." For "such men or such business" (76), we can cite many "such" repetitions in Shakespeare—*As You Like It*, II,vii,78 and IV,iii,85, *Twelfth Night*, I,v,265, *1 Henry IV*, III,ii,13-14, *Troilus*, II,iii,71-2, etc.; for "If you have any justice, any pity, / If ye be any thing but churchmen's habits" (116-17), we can note other triple uses of "any" in *Much Ado*, II,ii,4 and *Winter's Tale*, IV,iv,318-19.

We have already compared "this is a mere distraction" (112) with "this is mere falsehood" in *Winter's Tale*, III,ii,141; we can also cite "'twas but distraction" in *Twelfth Night*, V,i,68, "this is mere digression" in *2 Henry IV*, IV,i,138, and "this is mere madness" in *Hamlet*, V,i,284. For "h'as banish'd me his bed" (119), compare "A banish'd woman from my Harry's bed" in *1 Henry IV*, II,iii,39, and "I banish her my bed" in *2 Henry VI*, II,i,193. For Katherine's statement that she "lov'd him next heav'n" (130), referring of course to Henry, compare Helena's "next unto high heaven / I love your son" in *All's Well*, I,iii,193-4, and see *Winter's Tale*, I,ii,176 and *The Tempest*, I,ii,68-9 for comparable usages.

For "gentle, noble temper" (165), it is interesting to note that both canonical uses of "noble temper" are spoken by insincere characters for manipulative effect, as here—see *John*, V,ii,40 and *Cymbeline*, II,iii,4-5; we might also cite "ungently temper'd" in *Troilus*, V,iii,1. For "set footing here" (183), we find similar "set footing" phrasings in *1 Henry VI*, III,iii,64, *Richard II*, II,ii,48, and *Troilus*, II,ii,155, with "set no footing" in *2 Henry VI*, III,ii,87. "She should have bought her dignities so dear" (184) resembles "A borrowed title hast thou bought too dear" in *1 Henry IV*, V,iii,23.

"Your rage mistakes us" (101) might be compared to "'tis your passion / That thus mistakes" in *Kinsmen*, III,i,48-9—a strongly Shakespearean scene. For Katherine's statement that Wolsey and Campeius have "angels' faces" (145), we can note a comparable use of "angel's face" in a betrayal context in *Pericles*, IV,iii,47. "Most honor'd madam" (61) has its closest Shakespearean parallels in later works: "Mine honor'd lady" in *Cymbeline*, V,v,232, "most honor'd lord" in *Timon*, IV,iii,518, and "Most honor'd Cleon" in *Pericles*, III,iii,1. Similarly, "Almost forgot" (132) appears four times elsewhere in Shakespeare, always in later works—*MacBeth*, *Antony*, *Cymbeline*, and *Winter's Tale*.

Scene III,i is rich in the word pairs and triplets that are so common in Shakespeare's style, and many specific phrases have strong parallels in Shakespeare's works. Thus, for "peacemakers, friends, and servants" (167), compare "brothers, friends, and countrymen," "fellows, soldiers, friends," "tenants, friends, and neighboring gentlemen," "Wife, children, servants," and "servants, daughters, wives," among many other Shakespearean usages. For "Zeal and obedience" (63), compare "zeal and charity" in *John*, II,i,565; for "gravity and learning" (73), compare "gravity and patience" in *Merry Wives*, III,i,54, and "gravity and stillness" in *Othello*, II,iii,191; for "time and counsel" (79), compare "use and counsel" in *1 Henry IV*, I,iii,21.

Many other features in III,i can be cited as consistent with the idea of a Shakespearean contribution: "grown so desperate" (86), "loving and most gracious" (94), "All your studies" (123), "Never yet" (128), "add an honor" (137), "the good we aim at" (138), "consider what you do" (159), etc. Overall, the stylistic presence of Shakespeare is so clear in III,i that it seems merely willful to insist upon his absence.

I do not dispute the point that Fletcher has a hand in III,i; among other signs of his presence, we find a sixth-stress line with "sir" at line 92. The assignment of the scene to Fletcher alone relies on a quantitative approach to the textual evidence, which at first does indeed seem to favor Fletcher strongly: there are five instances of "'em" in the scene but none of "them"; instances of "ye" almost equal those of "you" (twenty to twenty-three); there are three instances of "has" but none of "hath." Yet here again, as in I,iii, we find that the linguistic alternatives are distributed in a naturalistic speech pattern. Katherine, in this scene, is intensely emotional, while the Cardinals are more calm and rational; Katherine speaks all three instances of "has," along with four uses of "'em" and nineteen instances of "ye" against only seven of "you." The Cardinals, in contrast, have only one "'em" between them, and only one instance of "ye" against sixteen of "you". Fletcher generally deploys his uses of "ye" and "you" in a random way; while there are occasional points in his works where the distribution can be interpreted as reflecting the emotional states or social positions of his characters, the clear dichotomy found in III,i is very much uncharacteristic for him.

For Fletcher's normal habit in this respect, we might cite the generally indiscriminate uses of "ye" and "you" in the emotionally charged dialogue between Celia and Antigonus in *The Humorous Lieutenant*, IV,v,40-93; many other examples are possible. Consistently, the Cardinals in III,i speak in the more formal, traditional language idiom of Shakespeare's serious protagonists, while Katherine, under the stress of intense emotion, employs a less formal, more colloquial range of usage. The textual profile of III,i appears to combine Fletcher's normal preferences with the kind of linguistic naturalism often found in Shakespeare's works. In conjunction with the abundant stylistic evidence of Shakespeare's hand in the scene, I would say that the sum total of the evidence indicates once again a closely collaborative authorship.

The remaining scenes assigned to Fletcher alone in Cyrus Hoy's modification of the standard authorship scheme are the final three scenes in the play, V,ii, iii, and iv. If we take a purely quantitative approach to the textual evidence, it is easy to see why this is so: Fletcher's preferences rather than Shakespeare's predominate. Taken together, these three scenes show four uses of "has" but none of "hath," and two of "does" but none of "doth"; "'em" is used exclusive of "them," with no less than twenty instances in the three scenes; "ye" is common, with twenty-five instances (against forty of "you"). Yet here again, the distribution of the features is worth noting. "You" is standard when social equals are speaking to each other (the Councillors in V,ii,36-115, the Porter and his man in V,iii), when an inferior is speaking to a superior (the Keeper in V,ii,4-5), or when a superior wishes to treat an inferior with respect (thus the King addresses Cranmer in V,ii exclusively with "you"). Conversely, "ye" appears when the characters show emotional stress (as in the heated Council exchanges in V,ii,116-48), or when a social superior is reproving inferiors (King to Council in V,ii,149ff., Lord Chamberlain to Porter in V,iii,67ff.). (In V,iv, "ye" seems to be used primarily to add to the Biblical sound of the verse and the providential atmosphere of the final scene.) Here again we find Fletcher's general preferences applied with the linguistic realism of Shakespeare. When we look at the style of the last three scenes, we find that telltale Shakespearean features abound.

In V,ii, perhaps the most striking Shakespearean aspect is this scene's close relationship with III,i of *2 Henry VI*. In both scenes we find a loyal servant of the king—Humphrey, Duke of Gloucester in one, Archbishop Cranmer in the other—persecuted and threatened with arrest by a group of hostile and powerful men, led in each play, interestingly enough, by a Bishop of Winchester. The situational and verbal parallels between the two scenes are extensive. In each, the sympathetic victim enters to confront his accusers, and makes an eloquent

and effective response to the accusations laid against him
(*2 Henry VI*, III,i,93-132; *Henry VIII*, V,ii,43-85). But his self-
defense is cut short by one of his persecutors, who tells him
that once in custody he will face more accusations that will not
be so easy to rebut. Compare *2 Henry VI*, III,i,133-8:

> My lord, these faults are easy, quickly answer'd;
> But mightier crimes are laid unto your charge,
> Whereof you cannot easily purge yourself.
> I do arrest you in his Highness' name,
> And here commit you to my Lord Cardinal
> To keep, until your further time of trial

with *Henry VIII*, V,ii,86-92:

> My lord, because we have business of more moment,
> We will be short with you. 'Tis his Highness' pleasure
> And our consent, for better trial of you,
> From hence you be committed to the Tower,
> Where being but a private man again,
> You shall know many dare accuse you boldly,
> More than (I fear) you are provided for.

The accused persists in his defense, and the following
speeches in both scenes are couched in similar terms: compare
Henry VI's "That you will clear yourself" (140) with Cranmer's "That I shall clear myself" (100). The discussion in each
scene becomes so heated that one party intercedes—compare
Winchester's "his railing is intolerable" (172) with the Lord
Chamberlain's "This is too much. / Forbear for shame" (120-1).
Winchester calls Humphrey "the offender" (176), while the
other Winchester terms Cranmer "this great offender" (156). It
is worth noting, too, that these commonalities are not fully
represented in the text of *2 Henry VI* that was in print when
Henry VIII was written;[4] they are, however, reflected fully in
the First Folio text of that play. Whoever wrote these Shakespearean features into V,ii of *Henry VIII* had intimate knowl-

edge of a thematically related play that was two decades old in 1613, the relevant text of which would not see print for another ten years. Obviously, this points to Shakespeare rather than Fletcher.

Indeed, the relationship between this scene in *Henry VIII* and the *Henry VI* trilogy goes far beyond these parallels with Duke Humphrey's arrest scene; there are other elements in V,ii that have significant verbal and situational commonalities with Shakespeare's earliest canonical histories. When Winchester tells Cranmer, "Your painted gloss discovers, / To men that understand you, words and weakness" (106-7), he echoes the earlier Winchester in *2 Henry VI*, I,i,163-4, "for all this flattering gloss, / He will be found a dangerous Protector," lines spoken in reference to Duke Humphrey. For Cranmer's "of purpose ... To quench mine honor" (14-16), compare "Of purpose to obscure my noble birth" in *1 Henry VI*, V,iv,22; "and draw the curtain close" (34) occurs in *2 Henry VI*, III,iii,32 (at the end of a verse line, as here, and also in connection with Winchester).

For "forthwith / You be convey'd to th' Tower a prisoner" (123-4), the closest parallels in the collected works are "he be convey'd unto the Tower" and "See that forthwith Duke Edward be convey'd" in *3 Henry VI*, III,ii,120 and IV,iii,52. "Then thus for you, my lord, it stands agreed" (122) has its closest Shakespearean parallel in "it is thus agreed" in *1 Henry VI*, V,iv,116 (another prisoner-and-accusers scene); "the proudest / He" (165-6) occurs in *3 Henry VI*, I,i,46 (and in *Shrew*, III,ii,234); for "the King / Shall understand" (9-10), compare "your grace shall understand" in *2 Henry VI*, II,i,173 (and in *Merchant*, IV,i,150, all three usages in contexts of malicious accusation). The phrase "dance attendance" (31) appears in past or present tense in *2 Henry VI*, I,iii,171 and in *Richard III*, III,vii,56; for "misdemean'd yourself" (49), the closest canonical parallel is "ill demean'd himself" in *2 Henry VI*, I,iii,103, in a similar official-misconduct context; for "Defacers of a public peace" (76), note that cities and towns are "defac'd" by war in *1 Henry VI*, III,iii,45. For the Lord Chamberlain's "In our own natures frail" (46), we can note that the closest Shakespearean parallel is again in a context of official misconduct: "corrupt frail nature with some bribe" in *3 Henry VI*, III,ii,155.

And again, it should be stressed that these features in V,ii of *Henry VIII* reflect authorial knowledge of the *Henry VI* trilogy, and not merely a familiarity with the texts available in 1613: *1 Henry VI*, of course, was not printed until 1623, while commonalities with the other two parts depend, in some cases, on elements (like "proudest he" and "convey'd unto the Tower") that are not found in the early quarto versions, but only in the First Folio.

Shakespearean features in V,ii are not confined to parallels with the *Henry VI* plays. There are some interesting links with *Henry V*. Cranmer's "My good lords . . . I have labor'd" speech (67-83) resembles Burgundy's "Great Kings of France and England: I have labor'd" speech in *Henry V*, V,ii,24-67; both men speak about their desire to promote the public peace and welfare, in similar terms—"my office / my life and office," 29 and 68; "face to face," 30 and 82. (Yet again, note that this speech of Burgundy's is not contained in either the 1600 or 1602 quarto of *Henry V*, and would only appear in print in 1623.) For "contagious sickness" (61) as a metaphor for political disruption, see *Henry V*, III,iii,31-2 and IV,viii,21 ("contagious treason"). And for Winchester's flattering description of Henry VIII as a prince who, "in all obedience, makes the Church / The chief aim of his honor" (152-3), compare Canterbury's mention of "obedience" as "an aim" in *Henry V*, I,ii,186-7, in a very similar context: a political churchman makes a flattering speech to his king, with manipulative intent.

As for other features in V,ii: for "wagging of your tongue" (162), compare "wagging of your beards" in *Coriolanus*, II,i,87, "wag thy tongue" in *Hamlet*, III,iv,39—and "wag his tongue" in an earlier and certainly Shakespearean scene in *Henry VIII*, I,i,33. Other elements in this scene partake of this same pattern of links with both the larger Shakespearean canon and the unquestionably Shakespearean scenes of this specific play, showing a clear continuity of Shakespeare's style. (Shakespeare frequently re-uses lines and phrases in a given play.[5]) For "I came this way so happily" (9), compare "I am happily come hither" in V,i,85 of *Henry VIII* (a Shakespearean scene), plus usages like "happily arriv'd" and "happily I have arrived" elsewhere in Shakespeare; for "their pleasures / Must be fulfill'd" (18-19), compare "Your pleasure be fulfill'd" in II,iv,57 of *Henry VIII* (another Shakespearean scene), plus "fulfill your pleasure" in *Julius Caesar*, III,i,159.

"More out of malice than integrity" (180) resembles both "more in policy than in malice" in *Othello*, II,iii,274 and "more made of malice than of duty" in *Cymbeline*, III,v,33. Line 66 reads, "Yet freshly pitied in our memories"; pentameter verse lines beginning with "Yet" and ending with "memory" occur in *Coriolanus*, V,vi,153 and in *Errors*, V,i,315. The latter instance is interesting in that it occurs in conjunction with "witnesses" (318); we have "witness" in the preceding line in V,ii of *Henry VIII*, in a comparable context, both Cranmer and Egeon defending themselves in unfair legal proceedings. The equine metaphor in lines 56-9 ("obey the manage") resembles the similar metaphor in *As You Like It*, I,i,11-16 ("taught their manage"). The "Become a churchman better than . . ." phrasing in line 98 compares with the "become me better than . . ." usage in *Julius Caesar*, III,i,202, and the "becomes him better than . . ." usage in *Troilus*, I,ii,122. For Norfolk's lines about King Henry not allowing "but the little finger / Of this man to be vex'd" (140-2), we can note that Shakespeare repeatedly employs similar figures of speech; see *Henry V*, II,ii,102 and *Coriolanus*, V,iv,4-5 for two good examples.

"Make me no more ado" (193) occurs in *Titus*, IV,iii,102, with an almost-identical "makes me no more ado" in *Two*

Gentlemen, IV,iv,28, plus "made me no more ado" in *1 Henry IV*, II,iv,201. The word pair "love and service" (192) appears in both *Merchant*, IV,i,414 and *Othello*, III,iii,18. Many other phrases in this scene occur in the Shakespeare canon either verbatim or in close variants: "high promotion" (23), "can dearly witness" (65), "Speak to the business" (36), "strong course" (70), "single heart" (73), "straying souls" (99), "fairly out on't" (144), "in all obedience" (152), "At chamber-door" (175), "forget yourselves" (177), "noble partners" (202), "we trifle time" (212), etc. For "half so honest" (117), we can cite sixteen comparable "half so ..." phrasings elsewhere in Shakespeare: "half so good," "half so old," "half so great," etc. Line 122 begins with "Then thus," as do five verse lines in other Shakesperean plays; line 201 begins with "Come, come," as do thirty-three other Shakespearean verse lines; line 204 begins with "Once more," as do nineteen other Shakespearean verse lines. Overall, the scene seems rich with signs of Shakespeare's contribution; denying him any hand in V,ii is a highly questionable proposition.

In V,ii as in the other scenes we've looked at, Fletcherian traits are mixed with Shakespearean features, sometimes in very close connections. The word pair "words and weakness" (107) is typical of Fletcher's alliterative word pairing—and in fact appears verbatim in *Valentinian*, III,iii,127. For "men of some understanding" (170), the closest parallel in either man's work is "men of understanding" in *The Island Princess*, II,v,7; the lines that follow, with the repetitive "this man ... This good man ... This honest man" (172-4), are also suggestive of Fletcher. Once again, close collaboration is indicated.

The next scene, V,iii, conforms to the same pattern. This scene possesses a significant parallel with the opening of Fletcher's *The Humorous Lieutenant*; in both, we have minor court functionaries (porters, ushers) warding off commoner gatecrashers at a royal ceremony (christening, audience for ambassadors). In Fletcher's play, one of the ushers ridicules the appearance of one of the commoners ("fish-face," I,i,29), who attempts to claim a personal connection to ease his way in (33-4); here in V,iii of *Henry VIII* we find the same kind of ridicule of a gatecrasher's appearance (39-46), and a similar claim of right of entry (4-5). And see also *A Wife for a Month*, II,iv, where the Citizens and their wives are trying to get in to see Valerio's and Evanthe's wedding; "We will get in, we'l venture broken pates else" (36). In V,iii, the Porter and his man beat back the encroaching crowds (7-9, 43ff.). Note too that the phrase "running banquet" (65) occurs in *The Loyal Subject*, V,iv,14, in a similarly sarcastic context.

But if the scene is Fletcherian in these respects, it also contains evidence of Shakespeare's presence. At lines 22-3, the Porter's Man says, "I am not Sampson, not Sir Guy, nor Colbrand, / To mow 'em down before me"; we find a strikingly similar passage in *Coriolanus*, IV,v,200-2:

> He'll go, he says, and sowl the *porter* of Rome gates by th'ears. He will *mow all down before him* ...

Traces of the large-scale relationship between *Henry VIII* and the *Henry VI* trilogy surface in V,iii: for the boys who deliver "such a show'r of pibbles" (56-7), we can compare the street-fighters and their "pebble stones" in *1 Henry VI*, III,i,78-83; and for the Lord Chamberlain's threat to "Clap round fines" on the Porter and his man (80), the closest canonical parallel is "O'ercharging your free purses with large fines" in *1 Henry VI*, I,iii,64.

In his opening speech, the Porter wonders if the crowds pressing in to see the christening of the future Queen Elizabeth mistake the place for "Parish Garden" (2)—Paris Garden being the bull- and bear-baiting ring on the south bank of the Thames. Later in the scene, his man uses the phrase "cuckold or cuckold-maker" (25), which is nearly identical to "the cuckold and the cuckold-maker" in *Troilus*, V,vii,9, a usage that also occurs in a bull-baiting connection. The red-faced man described in lines 39-46 ("twenty of the dog-days now reign in's nose," 41-2), resembles Falstaff's compatriot Bardolph, who is consistently described in similar terms ("Bardolph, whose zeal burns in his nose," *2 Henry IV*, II,iv,329-34; see also II,i,39-40 in the same play, plus *Henry V*, II,i,83-4 and II,iii,40-2).

The phrase "ale and cakes" (10) immediately reminds us of the famous "cakes and ale" in *Twelfth Night*, II,iii,116; for "leave your gaping" (3), compare "leave gaping" in *Pericles*, II,i,33; "the poor remainder" (20) occurs in *Titus*, V,iii,131. The phrase "able to endure" (63) is found in both *2 Henry VI*, IV,ii,56 and *Richard II*, III,ii,52; for "Great store of room" (73), we can note a similar "great store of . . ." phrasing in *Shrew*, III,ii,186, with other "store of . . ." usages elsewhere in the acknowledged works. "An army cannot rule 'em" (77) compares with "the dev'l cannot rule them" in the Shakespearean riot scene in *Sir Thomas More*, II,C,54, both lines applying to disorderly crowds.

V,iv, the play's final scene, continues in the same vein. Early in the scene, we find these lines (6-8):

> All comfort, *joy*, in this most gracious lady
> Heaven ever laid up to make parents happy
> May *hourly fall upon ye*!

In *The Tempest*, IV,i,106-8 appears a very similar passage, in a similar ritual-ceremonial context:

> Honor, riches, marriage-blessing,
> Long continuance, and increasing,
> *Hourly joys be still upon you!*

Interestingly, both scenes follow those parallel passages with an abundance of agricultural imagery. In *The Tempest* comes Cere's speech in the wedding masque, "Earth's increase, foison plenty" (110-17) and the dance of the reapers. In *Henry*

VIII, Cranmer's prophecy in lines 14-55 contains repeated agricultural images. Let's consider one of these images, "Her foes shake like a field of beaten corn, / And hang their heads with sorrow" (31-2). Shakespeare employs comparable imagery recurringly in his solo works; compare, for instance, "Why droops my lord, like over-ripen'd corn, / Hanging the head at Ceres' plenteous load" in *2 Henry VI*, I,ii,1-2, and "what valiant foemen, like to autumn corn, / Have we mow'd down in tops of all their pride" in *3 Henry VI*, V,vii,3-4. "Like to a harvest-man that's task'd to mow" in *Coriolanus*, I,iii,36 gives the same metaphor of foes being like corn; and recall the images of plants hanging their heads in *Henry VIII*, III,i,153 and *Titus*, IV,iv,70-1, cited earlier. (Fletcher's closest usages are less strikingly similar; cf. *Valentinian*, IV,iv,149-50.)

For "all the virtues that attend the good, / Shall still be doubled on her" (27-8), note that Shakespeare has a habit of making abstract qualities "attend" on his characters like human servants (as we saw in connection with *Merlin*, II,iii,127): "Grace and good disposition attend your lordship" in *Twelfth Night*, III,i,135, "Fair thoughts and happy hours attend on you" in *Merchant*, III,iv,41, "Success and conquest to attend on us" in *Henry V*, II,ii,24, "honorable peace attend thy throne" in *2 Henry VI*, II,iii,38, etc.

In the preceding line (26), the newborn Elizabeth is referred to as a "mighty piece"—a usage that rings strangely to a modern ear, but one that is typical of Shakespeare: Hermione is described as a "peerless piece" and a "royal piece" in *Winter's Tale*, V,i,94 and V,iii,38; Imogen is called, metaphorically, "a piece of tender air" in *Cymbeline*, V,iv,140 and V,v,437; and other women have the phrase "piece of virtue" applied to them in *Antony*, III,ii,28, *Pericles*, IV,vi,111, and *Tempest*, I,ii,56. For "Our children's children" (54), note that "Your children's children" occurs in *Richard III*, V,iii,262, in a similar patriotic-oratorical context.

For the list of Elizabeth's future "servants," "Peace, plenty, love, truth, terror" (47), compare Duke Vincentio's "Lent him our terror, dress'd him with our love" in *Measure*, I,i,19, in the same political-authority-figure context. (Also, note that "peace" and "plenty" occur in conjunction four times in Shakespeare, all four instances to be found in *Cymbeline*.) The phrase "too prodigal" (12) appears in *Merchant*, I,i,129, at the end of a verse line, as here; "truly known" (36) appears three times in various forms in the solo works (recall our discussion of *Merlin*, I,i,130); and for "new create" (41), we can compare "create me new" in *Errors*, III,ii,39. Many other usages in V,iv are at least consistent with Shakespeare's stylistic habits as reflected in his acknowledged works; he is no more absent from this last scene than from any of the previous ones.

Once we see that it is unsound to draw any supposed scene-by-scene breakdown between the Shakespearean and Fletcherian portions of *Henry VIII*, we find that a major obstacle to our fuller comprehension of the play has been removed. We can see, for example, why Heminges and Condell included *Henry VIII* in the First Folio while excluding *The Two Noble Kinsmen*: the former is predominantly Shakespearean with only a minor contribution from Fletcher, while the latter, upon examination, shows itself to be much more of an equal collaboration. The scenes in *Henry VIII* traditionally assigned to Shakespeare seem to be his alone (I find no evidence of Fletcher's hand in them; I don't know of anyone who has), but the scenes often assigned to Fletcher are actually the work of both men, writing in close collaboration. Cyrus Hoy recognized this in part when he re-attributed half of the allegedly Fletcherian scenes to the two dramatists together. I believe that the evidence cited above justifies the same re-attribution for the remainder.

Turning to *The Two Noble Kinsmen*, we find a play that is similar in kind, though different in degree: another joint work between Shakespeare and Fletcher, though one in which Fletcher's share is much more substantial. One good indication of this, I think, lies in the number of Fletcherian sixth-stress verse lines in the two plays. If we consider the two words that Fletcher most commonly adds to his pentameter verse lines to gain this extra accented syllable, "sir" and "too," we find that there are only nine six-stress lines ending in either "sir" or "too" in *Henry VIII*,[6] while there are fully twenty-seven in *Kinsmen*.[7] After studying the two plays in detail, I strongly suspect that these numbers give us more insight into the different proportions of Fletcher's input than do some other textual indicators that have been more widely cited.

Scholars have generally applied the same approach to *Kinsmen* as to *Henry VIII*, in that they have attempted to divide the play between the two men by relying on quantitative evaluations of the textual and prosodic evidence. In *Kinsmen*, however, the task of defining such a schematic breakdown of the authors' shares has proved to be difficult and ambiguous. While the accompanying table gives an often-cited division of authorship, other commentators have quarreled with the assignments of I,iv-v, III,ii, IV,ii, and the first thirty-odd lines of V,i as recorded in this scheme. And here again, it is important to avoid generalizing too broadly: individual scholars have not been uniformly indifferent to the possibility that the shares blend together at points in the play.[8]

I certainly concede that the traditional breakdown yields a

The respective shares of Shakespeare and Fletcher
in The Two Noble Kinsmen, *as traditionally assigned:*

SHAKESPEARE	FLETCHER
I,i-v	II,ii-vi
II,i	III,iii-IV,ii
III,i-ii	V,ii
IV,iii	
V,i and iii-iv	

fair outline of the sections in the play where the relative contributions of Shakespeare and Fletcher are dominant. Yet, in
Kinsmen as in *Henry VIII*, I think it can be demonstrated that
there is a more intimate collaboration than has been recognized, and that any attempt to divide the play into purely
Shakespearean and Fletcherian portions is doomed to failure.
For considerations of space, I will not discuss all of the scenes
in *Kinsmen*; I believe that a sampling of the play's materials
can be adequate to make the basic point.

Scene II,v, for instance, is one scene in *Kinsmen* usually
ascribed to Fletcher alone. When we examine it closely,
though, we find intriguing echoes of Shakespeare's style
blended with obvious Fletcherian traits. Let's begin with the
strong situational parallel with the second scene in *As You Like
It*. In the respective scenes, both Orlando and Arcite are
shown after winning victory in wrestling matches witnessed
by the local rulers; the winners are congratulated by the rulers,
and admired by their future brides, Rosalind and Emilia; they
are asked about their parentage, and reveal that they are the
younger sons of gentlemen, though far inferior in rank to the
women they eventually marry. (Arcite, let us qualify, is a relative of the king of Thebes—but he conceals this fact in the
scene in question.) We can note other connections: Arcite is
"most unworthy" of Emilia (40), as is Orlando "most unworthy" of Rosalind in *As You Like It*, IV,i,193 (and Leontes is
"most unworthy" in *Winter's Tale*, II,iii,113); for Emilia's "If
you deserve well" (42), spoken to Arcite, compare Rosalind's
"Doth he not deserve well," spoken of Orlando, in *As You Like
It*, I,iii,36-7 (with three other "deserve well" usages in other
Shakespearean plays).

The discussion of Arcite's worthiness in II,v has significant
parallels with the similar discussion of Coriolanus in II,ii of his
play. Here in II,v we find "well-found" and "worth" in the
same line (27), plus "noble service" (34); compare, in the scene
from *Coriolanus*, "well-found" and "worthy" within a line of

each other (44-5), plus "noble service" (40), all embedded in a comparable passage extolling the hero's virtues and honor. A pair of linkages to *A Midsummer Night's Dream* are also worth noting: for Arcite's statement that he has "hollow'd / To a deep cry of dogs" (11-12), compare the hunting-dog reference in *Dream*, IV,i,124-5, "A cry more tuneable / Was never hollow'd to"; for Theseus' intent that the assembled company will go out at dawn the next morning "to do observance / To flow'ry May" (50-1), compare "To do observance to a morn of May" in *Dream*, I,i,167. (Another "do observance to ..." phrasing can be found in *2 Henry IV*, IV,iii,15.)

As for other features in II,v: when asked why he has come to the Athenian court, Arcite says he wants "To purchase name" (26); compare "say I sent thee forth to purchase honor" in *Richard II*, I,iii,282. When Arcite kisses Emilia's hand, he says, "Thus let me seal my vow'd faith" (39); Oxford makes a nearly identical statement, "thus I seal my truth," when he kisses the king's hand in *3 Henry VI*, IV,viii,29, and there are comparable usages elsewhere in Shakespeare's plays. (Fletcher's closest phrasings are less close; see *The Chances*, III,i,133, or *Philaster*, V,iii,193.)

The phrase "a proper man" (16) occurs ten times in Shakespeare, not counting variants; "fiery mind" (22) is found in *Hamlet*, II,i,33; "too cruel" (41) appears four times in other Shakespearean works; "beshrew my heart" (62) occurs in *Dream*, V,i,290,with variants elsewhere; for "you shall receive all dues / Fit for the honor you have won" (60-1), compare "All dues be rend'red to their owners" in *Troilus*, II,ii,174. (And for Theseus' words to Emilia, "you have a servant / That if I were a woman, would be master," 62-3, we have the same thought in "had I been a woman, these kind words would have won me" in *Merlin*, II,i,114-15.)

Other elements in II,v could also be mentioned—the comparison of Arcite to "a hidden sun" (23) recalls *1 Henry IV*, I,ii,197ff., among other Shakespearean usages—but the general nature of the scene is clear. In a play that is certainly Shakespearean to a significant degree, it would be rash to insist on Shakespeare's absence from II,v.

The fifth scene in the second act of *Kinsmen* is flanked by two short scenes, both consisting of soliloquies by the Jailer's Daughter; both scenes are written in Fletcher's typical style—though both also reveal traces of contributions from Shakespeare. The first of these soliloquies, in II,iv, serves to communicate the Daughter's infatuation with Palamon, which she expresses as a series of developments: "First, I saw him . . ." (7), "Next, I pitied him . . ." (11), "Then, I lov'd him . . ." (14). A similar progression occurs in *As You Like It*, V,ii,32-7: "no sooner met but look'd; no sooner look'd but they lov'd; no sooner lov'd but they sigh'd," etc. We can also note that such "First . . . Next . . ." constructions are common with Shakespeare: see *Pericles*, IV,vi,49-54, *Merchant*, II,ix,10-16, *Julius Caesar*, III,i,185-9, and *Hamlet*, IV,v,79-94 for a few examples. (This usage in *Kinsmen* is more in Shakespeare's manner than Fletcher's; cf. *Women Pleased*, III,ii,38-9, *The Loyal Subject*, IV,v,44, and *Monsieur Thomas*, II,iii,5-7 and III,i,274-86.)

For "He will never affect me. I am base" (2), we might compare the passage in *Love's Labor's Lost*, I,ii,167ff. ("I do affect," "base," etc.), with an infatuation involving a commoner female and a socially superior male. "Out upon't" (5) occurs only once in Shakespeare's solo works, in *Merry Wives*, I,iv,165—though it occurs there in the context of a young woman's secret marriage plans, as here in *Kinsmen*. "'Tis odds" (1) appears in *Coriolanus*, III,i,244, with variants elsewhere; for "what a coil he keeps" (18), we can cite Shakespearean usages like "kept a coil," "what a coil's here," "what a coil is there," etc. (Comparable uses in Fletcher are very rare; cf. *Humorous Lieutenant*, V,iv,20.) For the Daughter's protest that she will free Palamon from prison without concerning herself for "law or kindred" (32), we can cite the lines around "law, kindred" in *A Lover's Complaint*, 270, a similar point in a similar context.

The second soliloquy, in II,vi, in which Jailer's Daughter reveals that she had freed Palamon and expounds her love for him, follows the example of II,iv: generally Fletcherian in style, but with persistent hints of a minor contribution from Shakespeare. For the use of the word "whoobub" in line 35, note that Shakespeare's sole use of the word in his other works occurs in *Winter's Tale*, IV,iv,616, in essentially the same context: a prince or nobleman makes an escape connected with the affection of a young woman commoner, causing a "whoobub." Fletcher's uses of the same word do not occur in comparably close contexts; see *Monsieur Thomas*, IV,ii,19, and *Women Pleased*, IV,i,89.

"I love him beyond love and beyond reason" (11) echoes Imogen's statement in *Cymbeline*, III,ii,56 that her love for Posthumus is "beyond beyond"—both women are innocently eager to be reunited with the men they love, and both have some unpleasant surprises in store for them. For "Dying almost a martyr" (17), compare "martyrs, slain in Cupid's wars" in *Pericles*, I,i,38, and "martyrs in love" in *2 Henry IV*, IV,i,191; in "such prisoners and such daughters" (38), we have another of those "such" repetitions to be found in Shakespeare, as we mentioned in connection with *Henry VIII*, III,i,76. "Or wit, or safety" (12) might be compared to "wit and safety" in *Twelfth Night*, V,i,211; and we can note in passing that the Jailer's Daughter and Viola tend to talk about their similar predicaments in similar terms. The daughter describes herself as "desperate" (13) as does Viola in II,ii,37 of her play; when the Daughter goes on to express her forebodings about rejection and death (15-17), we can observe that Viola thinks similar thoughts in II,iv,107ff.

In concentrating on some of the scenes in *Kinsmen* normally assigned to Fletcher, I do not wish wholly to neglect the scenes usually given to Shakespeare; there too, I would argue, we can find some signs of mixed authorship. Indeed, a large part of the reason these scenes have caused so much uneasiness among critics and readers may be that they are not "pure Shakespeare." The scenes in question are strongly Shakespearean to be sure, but they also offer us hints of subsidiary contributions from Fletcher. Consider, for example, the word "flurted," meaning "scorned" or "cast off," which occurs in I,ii,18, in a scene usually ascribed to Shakespeare alone. Nowhere else in Shakespearean works does any form of this word appear; but it is found repeatedly in Fletcher's plays, as in *The Chances*, III,i,34, *Rule a Wife and Have a Wife*, III,v,55, *The Spanish Curate*, V,ii,9, *The Pilgrim*, I,i,25 and III,iii,90, and *The Wild Goose Chase*, II,iii,109. This is not to say, of course, that Shakespeare could not have used the word one time in *Kinsmen*; yet in a play that indisputably has a major Fletcherian element, it seems merely sensible to read the word as Fletcher's. Features that could be traces of Fletcher's hand occur elsewhere in the scene as well; see I,ii,107ff.

If space permitted, I believe that this survey could be extended over the whole of the play, to show that intimate collaboration is common throughout. There are portions of the play where Shakespearean and Fletcherian elements are relatively stronger or weaker, where one man or the other is the dominant voice; but any insistence on a clear-cut division between their respective shares is clearly wrongheaded.

This partial survey of some scenes in the two Shakespeare-Fletcher plays clearly does not take the place of a complete overview; I hope, however, that it is adequate to make the essential point, which is that the kind of intimate collaboration between Shakespeare and Rowley that we see in *Merlin* is not wholly an anomaly in Shakespeare's art. *Merlin* differs from the two collaborations with Fletcher in some key respects— but then, the two Shakespeare-Fletcher plays differ from each other in important ways as well, as we have seen. (They show something of the range that Fletcher's efforts with other collaborators show. If we look at the Beaumont-Fletcher plays, we can find a work like *The Woman Hater* that is as strongly dominated by Beaumont as *Henry VIII* is by Shakespeare, and a work like *Cupid's Revenge* that is much nearer to an equal collaboration, in the manner of *Kinsmen*.) In each of these three late Shakespearean collaborations, the status of the play as a work of mixed authorship has been a barrier to the achievement of a full and accurate understanding—but in no case has this been more true than for *The Birth of Merlin*.

APPENDIX II

Francis Kirkman, Stationer

F RANCIS KIRKMAN was born in 1631 in London, the son of Francis Kirkman, blacksmith, and his wife Ellen; the parents raised their son in their own strict Calvinist faith.[1] The younger Francis was apprenticed to a scrivener, but was in the bookselling trade by the age of thirty. In one of his earliest publications, Webster and Rowley's *A Cure for a Cuckold* (1661), Kirkman printed an introduction, "The Stationer, to the Judicious Reader," in which he wrote this of himself:

> It was not long since I was onely a Book-Reader, and not a Book-seller, which Quality (my former Employment somewhat failing, and I being unwilling to be idle) I have now lately taken on me. It hath been my fancy and delight (e'er since I knew any thing) to converse with Books; and the pleasure I have taken in those of this nature, (viz. Plays) hath bin so extraordinary, that it hath bin much to my cost; for I have been (as we term it) a Gatherer of Plays for some years, and am confident I have more of several sorts than any man in England, Book-seller, or other: I can at any time shew 700 in number, which is within a small matter all that were ever printed.[2]

The details of Kirkman's career tend to confirm this self-portrait. From his earliest days as a stationer, Kirkman printed plays that were sometimes as much as a century old, plays that could have had only a very limited commercial potential in Restoration London. In his first year in business, for instance, he reprinted the hoary *Gammer Gurton's Needle*, and issued the first printed text of *Tom Tyler and his Wife*, both of which date from the early part of the reign of Elizabeth. These are more the choices of an enthusiast than of an opportunistic and unscrupulous businessman. Kirkman's involvement with the play lists of 1661 and 1671, and his connection with Gerard Langbaine, associate him with the earliest efforts to catalogue and study the achievements of the English Renaissance dramatists—something that is true for Kirkman more than for any other bookseller of his era.

Kirkman's output as a publisher extended far beyond the specific category of plays; he participated in most of the genres that were popular during the Restoration. He printed romances, sometimes translating and adapting French and Spanish originals personally. He was notably active as a publisher (and on occasion as an author) of bawdry, rogue literature, and frank pornography. (One of his early offerings of the latter was *The Presbyterian Lash, or Noctroff's Maid Whipt*, inspired by the contemporary scandal of Zachary Crofton, a clergyman with a taste for flagellation.) Kirkman's pornographic activities can be clucked at by those who are inclined to do so;[3] personally, I'm not inclined that way. Kirkman's mother wanted him to be a minister, and his father told him that the only books he need ever read were the Bible and *The Practice of Piety*; but Kirkman preferred stage plays and bawdry—choices with which I find myself in total sympathy. Thanks to Kirkman's choices and activities, we have at our disposal several interesting texts (of various types) that we might not otherwise possess.

All too often in the past, scholars and critics, when facing real or imagined difficulties in the historical record, have re-

treated into ad hominem accusations of incompetence or men-
dacity toward the individuals responsible for the problematical
evidence. In the last century, John Heminges and Henry Condell were often criticized for the supposedly terrible job they
did in putting together the First Folio. Kirkman's assignment
of *Cure for a Cuckold* to Webster and Rowley was once disputed on the grounds that Kirkman was "a liar";[4] many other examples could be given. Clearly, such charges are unsound and
specious. In cases in which the internal evidence of a play fails
to support (or overtly contradicts) an external attribution, that
attribution can be questioned (or rejected); but when the internal evidence confirms the external attribution, ad hominem
considerations cannot provide any legitimate justification for
refutation. This is as true for *The Birth of Merlin* as it is for *A
Cure for a Cuckold*.

THE
BIRTH
OF
MERLIN:

OR,

The Childe hath found his Father.

As it hath been several times Acted
with great Applause.

Written by *William Shakespear*, and
William Rowley.

Placere cupio.

LONDON: Printed by *Tho. Johnson* for *Francis Kirkman*, and
Henry Marsh, and are to be sold at the *Princes Arms* in
Chancery-Lane. 1 6 6 2.

Q	=	Quarto of 1662
T	=	Tyrrell, 1851
D	=	Delius, 1856
Molt.	=	Moltke, 1869
WP	=	Warnke and Proescholdt, 1887
pr. ed.	=	present editor

THE BIRTH OF MERLIN:

OR, THE CHILDE HATH FOUND HIS FATHER

Drammatis Personæ

The Scene *Brittain.*

Aurelius, King of *Brittain.*
Vortiger, King of ⟨*Welsh*⟩ *Brittain.*
Vter Pendragon the Prince, Brother to *Aurelius.*
Donobert, a Nobleman, and Father to *Constantia* and *Modestia.*
The Earl of *Gloster,* and Father to *Edwyn.*
Edoll, Earl of *Chester,* and General to King *Aurelius.*
Cador, Earl of *Cornwal,* and Suitor to *Constantia.*
Edwyn, Son to the Earl of *Gloster,* and Suitor to *Modestia.*
Toclio and *Oswald,* two Noblemen.
Merlin the Prophet.
Anselme the Hermit, after Bishop of *Winchester.*
Clown, brother to *Jone,* mother of *Merlin.*

Sir *Nichodemus Nothing,* a Courtier.
The Devil, father of *Merlin.*
Ostorius, the Saxon General.
Octa, a Saxon Nobleman.
Proximus, a Saxon Magician.
Two Bishops.
Two Saxon Lords.
Two of *Edols* Captains.
Two Gentlemen.
A little Antick Spirit.
Artesia, Sister to *Ostorius* the Saxon General.
Constantia ⎫
    and   ⎬ Daughters to *Donobert.*
Modestia ⎭
Jone Goe-too't, Mother of *Merlin.*
A Waiting-woman to *Artesia.*
Lucina, Queen of the Shades.

ACTUS I.

(SCENE I.)

A Room in the Castle of Lord Donobert.⟩

Enter Donobert, Gloster, Cador, Edwin, Constantia, and Modestia.

Cador. You teach me language, sir, as one that knows
The Debt of Love I owe unto her Vertues;
Wherein like a true Courtier I have fed
My self with hope of fair Success, and now
Attend your wisht consent to my long Suit. 5
Dono. Believe me, youthful Lord,
Time could not give an opportunity
More fitting your desires, always provided,
My Daughters love be suited with my Grant.
Cador. 'Tis the condition, sir, her Promise seal'd. 10
Dono. Ist so, *Constantia?*
Constan. I was content to give him words for oathes;
He swore so oft he lov'd me—
Dono. That thou believest him?
Const. He is a man, I hope. 15
Dono. That's in the trial, Girl.
Const. However, I am a woman, sir.
Dono. The Law's on thy side then: sha't have a Husband,

I, and a worthy one. Take her, brave *Cornwal,*
And make our happiness great as our wishes.
Cador. Sir, I thank you. 21
Glost. Double the fortunes of the day, my Lord,
And crown my wishes too: I have a son here,
Who in my absence would protest no less
Unto your other Daughter. 25
Dono. Ha, *Gloster,* is it so? what says Lord *Edwin?*
Will she protest as much to thee?
Edwin. Else must she want some of her Sisters faith, Sir.
Modesta. Of her credulity much rather, Sir:
My Lord, you are a Soldier, and methinks 30
The height of that Profession should diminish
All heat of Loves desires,
Being so late employ'd in blood and ruine.
Edwin. The more my Conscience tyes me to repair
The worlds losses in a new succession. 35
Modest. Necessity, it seems, ties your affections then,
And at that rate I would unwillingly
Be thrust upon you; a wife is a dish soon cloys, sir.
Edwin. Weak and diseased appetites it may.

The entire play, except the rhyming couplets, is printed as prose in Q: corr. D   Scene I. *etc. add. T*   2 her *WP:* their *Q*

20 your happiness *WP*

221

Modest. Most of your making have dull
    stomacks, sir.   40
Dono. If that be all, Girl, thou shalt quicken
    him;
Be kinde to him, *Modesta:* Noble *Edwin,*
Let it suffice, what's mine in her speaks
    yours ;
For her consent, let your fair suit go on,
She is a woman, sir, and will be won.   45
Edwin. You give me comfort, sir.

            Enter Toclio.
Dono.   Now, *Toclio?*
Toclio. The King, my honor'd Lords,
    requires your presence,
And calls a Councel for return of answer
Unto the parling enemy, whose Embassadors
Are on the way to Court.
Dono.   So suddenly?   50
Chester, it seems, has ply'd them hard at
    war.,
They sue so fast for peace, which by my advice
They ne're shall have, unless they leave the
    Realm.
Come, noble *Gloster,* let's attend the King.
It lies, sir, in your Son to do me pleasure, 55
And save the charges of a Wedding Dinner;
If you'l make haste to end your Love affairs,
One cost may give discharge to both my
    cares.   [*Exit Dono., Glost.*
Edwin. I'le do my best.
Cador. Now, *Toclio,* what stirring news at
    Court?   60
Toclio. Oh, my Lord, the Court's all fill'd
with rumor, the City with news, and the Coun-
try with wonder, and all the bells i'th' King-
dom must proclaim it, we have a new Holy-
day a coming.   65
Consta. A holy-day! for whom? for thee?
Toclio. Me, Madam! 'sfoot! I'de be loath
that any man should make a holy-day for me
yet:
In brief, 'tis thus: there's here arriv'd at
    Court,   70
Sent by the Earl of *Chester* to the King,
A man of rare esteem for holyness,
A reverent hermit, that by miracle
Not onely saved our army,
But without aid of man o'rethrew   75
The pagan Host, and with such wonder, sir,
As might confirm a Kingdom to his faith.
Edwin. This is strange news, indeed;
    where is he?
Toclio. In conference with the King, that
    much respects him.
Modest. Trust me, I long to see him.   80
        46 S. D. after 45 Q

Toclio. Faith, you will finde no great pleasure in him, for ought that I can see, Lady.
They say he is half a Prophet too: would he
could tell me any news of the lost Prince;
there's twenty Talents offer'd to him that finds
him.   86
Cador. Such news was breeding in the
    morning.
Toclio. And now it has birth and life, sir.
If fortune bless me, I'le once more search
those woods where then we lost him; I know
not yet what fate may follow me.   [*Exit.*
Cador. Fortune go with you, sir. Come,
    fair Mistriss,   92
Your Sister and Lord *Edwin* are in game,
And all their wits at stake to win the Set.
Consta. My sister has the hand yet; we had
    best leave them: 95
She will be out anon as well as I;
He wants but cunning to put in a Dye.
            [*Exit Cador, Constan.*
Edwin. You are a cunning Gamester,
    Madam,
Modest. It is a desperate Game, indeed,
    this Marriage,
Where there's no winning without loss to
    either.   100
Edwin. Why, what but your perfection,
    noble Lady,
Can bar the worthiness of this my suit?
If so you please I count my happiness
From difficult obtaining, you shall see
My duty and observance.   105
Modest. There shall be place to neither,
    noble sir;
I do beseech you, let this mild Reply
Give answer to your suit: for here I vow,
If e're I change my Virgin name, by you 109
It gains or looses.
Edwin.   My wishes have their crown.
Modest. Let them confine you then,
As to my promise you give faith and credence.
Edwin. In your command my willing
    absence speaks it.   [*Exit.*
Modest. Noble and vertuous: could I dream
    of Marriage,
I should affect thee, *Edwin.* Oh, my soul, 115
Here's something tells me that these best of
    creatures,
These models of the world, weak man and
    woman,
Should have their souls, their making, life,
    and being,
To some more excellent use: if what the
    sense
Calls pleasure were our ends, we might justly
    blame   120

222

Great natures wisdom, who rear'd a building
Of so much art and beauty to entertain
A guest so far incertain, so imperfect:
If onely speech distinguish us from beasts,
Who know no inequality of birth or place, 125
But still to fly from goodness: oh, how base
Were life at such a rate! No, no, that power
That gave to man his being, speech and wis-
dom,
Gave it for thankfulness. To him alone   129
That made me thus, may I whence truly know,
I'le pay to him, not man, the love I owe. [*Exit.*

(Scene II.

The British Court.)

*Flourish Cornets. Enter Aurelius King of
Brittain, Donobert, Gloster, Cador, Edwin,
Toclio, Oswold, and Attendants.*

Aurelius. No tiding of our brother yet?
'Tis strange,
So ne're the Court, and in our own Land too,
And yet no news of him: oh, this loss
Tempers the sweetness of our happy conquests
With much untimely sorrow.
Dono.   Royal sir, 5
His safety being unquestion'd should to time
Leave the redress of sorrow: were he dead,
Or taken by the foe, our fatal loss
Had wanted no quick Herald to disclose it.
Aurelius. That hope alone sustains me, 10
Nor will we be so ingrateful unto heaven
To question what we fear with what we enjoy.
Is answer of our message yet return'd
From that religious man, the holy Hermit,
Sent by the Earl of *Chester* to confirm us 15
In that miraculous act? For 'twas no less:
Our Army being in rout, nay, quite o'rethrown,
As *Chester* writes, even then this holy man,
Arm'd with his cross and staff, went smiling
on,
And boldly fronts the foe; at sight of whom 20
The *Saxons* stood amaz'd: for, to their seem-
ing,
Above the Hermit's head appear'd such
brightness,
Such clear and glorious beams, as if our men
March't all in fire; wherewith the *Pagans* fled,
And by our troops were all to death pursu'd.
Glost. 'Tis full of wonder, sir.   26
Aurel. Oh, *Gloster*, he's a jewel worth
a Kingdom.
Where's *Oswold* with his answer?
Oswold. 'Tis here, my Royal Lord.
Aurel. In writing? will he not sit with us?

Oswo. His Orizons perform'd, he bad me say,
He would attend with all submission.
Aurel. Proceed to councel then; and let
some give order,
The Embassadors being come to take our
answer,
They have admittance. *Oswold, Toclio,* 35
Be it your charge!—(*Exeunt Os. and Toclio.*)
And now, my Lords, observe
The holy councel of this reverend Hermit:
[*reads*] *As you respect your safety, limit not
That onely power that hath protected you;
Trust not an open enemy too far,*   40
*He's yet a looser, and knows you have won;
Mischiefs not ended are but then begun.*
Anselme the Hermit.
Dono. Powerful and pithie, which my
advice confirms:
No man leaves physick when his sickness
slakes,
But doubles the receipts: the word of Peace 45
Seems fair to blood-shot eyes, but being appli'd
With such a medicine as blinds all the sight
Argues desire of Cure, but not of Art.
Aurel. You argue from defects; if both the
name
And the condition of the Peace be one,   50
It is to be prefer'd, and in the offer,
Made by the *Saxon*, I see nought repugnant.
Glost. The time of Truce requir'd for thirty
days
Carries suspicion in it, since half that space
Will serve to strength their weakned Regi-
ment.   55
Cador. Who in less time will undertake to
free
Our Country from them?
Edwin.   Leave that unto our fortune.
Dono. Is not our bold and hopeful General
Still Master of the field, their Legions faln,
The rest intrencht for fear, half starv'd, and
wounded,   60
And shall we now give o're our fair advan-
tage?
'Fore heaven, my Lord, the danger is far more
In trusting to their words then to their weapons.

Enter Oswold.

Oswold. The Embassadors are come, sir.
Aurel.   Conduct them in.
We are resolv'd, my Lords, since policy fail'd
In the beginning, it shall have no hand   66
In the conclusion.
That heavenly power that hath so well begun

---

130 thence *D*   Scene II. *etc. add. T*   6 should]
you should *WP*   22 Hermit *Q*

36 *S. D. add. T*   48 not of *Q* : not knowledge of *T*
55 regiments *T.*   56 Who] We *WP*   62 'Fore *T* :
force *Q*

Their fatal overthrow, I know, can end it:
From which fair hope my self will give them
   answer.   70

*Flourish Cornets. Enter Artesia with the
    Saxon Lords.*

Dono. What's here? a woman Orator?
Aurel. Peace, *Donobert!*—Speak, what are
   you, Lady?
Artes. The sister of the *Saxon* General,
Warlike *Ostorius* the East *Anglese* King;
My name *Artesia,* who in terms of love   75
Brings peace and health to great *Aurelius,*
Wishing she may return as fair a present
As she makes tender of.
Aurel. The fairest present e're mine eyes
   were blest with!—
Command a chair there for this *Saxon*
   Beauty:—   80
Sit, Lady, we'l confer: your warlike brother
Sues for a peace, you say?
Artes. With endless love unto your State
   and Person.
Aurel. Ha's sent a moving Orator, believe
   me.—
What thinkst thou, *Donobert?*   85
Dono. Believe me, sir, were I but yong
   agen,
This gilded pill might take my stomack
   quickly.
Aurel. True, thou art old: how soon we do
   forget
Our own defects! Fair damsel,—oh, my
   tongue
Turns Traitor, and will betray my heart—
   sister to   90
Our enemy:—'sdeath, her beauty mazes me,
I cannot speak if I but look on her.—
What's that we did conclude?
Dono. This, Royal Lord—
Aurel.   Pish, thou canst not utter it:—
Fair'st of creatures, tell the King your Brother,
That we, in love—ha!—and honor to our
   Country,   96
Command his Armies to depart our Realm.
But if you please, fair soul—Lord *Donobert,*
Deliver you our pleasure.
Dono.   I shall, sir:
Lady, return, and certifie your brother— 100
Aurel. Thou art too blunt and rude! return
   so soon?
Fie, let her stay, and send some messenger
To certifie our pleasure.
Dono.   What meanes your Grace?
Aurel. To give her time of rest to her long
   Journey;

We would not willingly be thought uncivil. 105
Artes. Great King of *Brittain,* let it not
   seem strange,
To embrace the Princely Offers of a friend,
Whose vertues with thine own, in fairest merit,
Both States in Peace and Love may now inherit.
Aurel. She speakes of Love agen: 110
Sure, 'tis my fear, she knows I do not hate her.
Artes. Be, then, thy self, most great
   Aurelius,
And let not envy nor a deeper sin
In these thy Councellors deprive thy goodness
Of that fair honor we in seeking peace 115
Give first to thee, who never use to sue
But force our wishes. Yet, if this seem light,
Oh, let my sex, though worthless your respect,
Take the report of thy humanity,
Whose mild and vertuous life loud fame dis-
   playes,   120
As being o'recome by one so worthy praise.
Aurel. She has an Angels tongue.—Speak
   still.
Dono. This flattery is gross, sir; hear no
   more on't.—
Lady, these childish complements are needless;
You have your answer, and believe it, Madam,
His Grace, though yong, doth wear within his
   breast   126
Too grave a Councellor to be seduc't
By smoothing flattery or oyly words.
Artes. I come not, sir, to wooe him.
Dono. 'Twere folly, if you should; you
   must not wed him.   130
(*Aur.*) Shame take thy tongue! Being old
   and weak thy self,
Thou doat'st, and looking on thine own defects,
Speak'st what thou'dst wish in me. Do I com-
   mand
The deeds of others, mine own act not free?
Be pleas'd to smile or frown, we respect nei-
   ther: 135
My will and rule shall stand and fall together.
Most fair *Artesia,* see the King descends
To give thee welcome with these warlike
   Saxons,
And now on equal terms both sues and grants:
Instead of Truce, let a perpetual League 140
Seal our united bloods in holy marriage;
Send the East Angles King this happy news,
That thou with me hast made a League for
   ever,
And added to his state a friend and brother.
Speak, dearest Love, dare you confirm this
   Title?   145
Artes. I were no woman to deny a good

So high and noble to my fame and Country.
Aurel. Live, then, a Queen in *Brittain.*
Glost. He meanes to marry her.
Dono. Death! he shall marry the devil first!
Marry a *Pagan*, an Idolater?   151
Cador. He has won her quickly.
Edwin. She was woo'd afore she came, sure,
Or came of purpose to conclude the Match.
Aurel. Who dares oppose our will? My
Lord of *Gloster*,   155
Be you Embassador unto our Brother,
The Brother of our Queen *Artesia;*
Tell him for such our entertainment looks him,
Our marriage adding to the happiness
Of our intended joys; mans good or ill   160
In this like waves agree, come double still.

Enter Hermit.

Who's this? the Hermit? Welcome, my happiness!
Our Countries hope, most reverent holy man,
I wanted but thy blessing to make perfect
The infinite sum of my felicity.   165
Hermit. Alack, sweet Prince, that happiness is yonder,
Felicity and thou art far asunder;
This world can never give it.
Aurel. Thou art deceiv'd: see here what
I have found,
Beauty, Alliance, Peace, and strength of
Friends,   170
All in this all exceeding excellence:
The League's confirm'd.
Hermit. With whom, dear Lord?
Aurel. With the great Brother of this
Beauteous woman,
The Royal *Saxon* King
Hermit.   Oh, then I see,   175
And fear thou art too near thy misery.
What magick could so linck thee to this mischief?
By all the good that thou hast reapt by me,
Stand further from destruction.
Aurel. Speak as a man, and I shall hope to
obey thee.   180
Hermit. Idolaters, get hence! fond King,
let go:
Thou hug'st thy ruine and thy Countries woe.
Dono. Well spoke, old Father; too him,
bait him soundly.
Now, by heavens blest Lady, I can scarce keep
patience.
1. *Saxon Lord.* What devil is this?   185
2. *Saxon Lord.* That cursed Christian, by
whose hellish charmes
Our army was o'rethrown.

147 noble.a proposal to *T*   181 Idolatress *D*

Hermit. Why do you dally, sir? Oh, tempt
not heaven;
Warm not a serpent in your naked bosom:
Discharge them from your Court.
Aurel.   Thou speak'st like madness!
Command the frozen shepherd to the shade,
When he sits warm i'th' Sun; the fever sick
To add more heat unto his burning pain:
These may obey, 'tis less extremity   194
Then thou enjoynst to me. Cast but thine eye
Upon this beauty, do it, I'le forgive thee,
Though jealousie in others findes no pardon;
Then say thou dost not love; I shall then swear
Th'art immortal and no earthly man.
Oh, blame then my mortallity, not me.   200
Hermit. It is thy weakness brings thy
misery,
Unhappy Prince.
Aurel.   Be milder in thy doom.
Hermit. 'Tis you that must indure heavens
doom, which faln
Remember's just.
Artes. Thou shalt not live to see it.—How
fares my Lord?   205
If my poor presence breed dislike, great Prince,
I am no such neglected soul, will seek
To tie you to your word.
Aurel. My word, dear Love! may my
Religion,
Crown, State, and Kingdom fail, when I fail
thee.   210
Command Earl *Chester* to break up the camp
Without disturbance to our *Saxon* friends;
Send every hour swift posts to hasten on
The King her Brother, to conclude this League,
This endless happy Peace of Love and Marriage;
Till when provide for Revels, and give charge
That nought be wanting which ⟨may⟩ make
our Triumphs   217
Sportful and free to all. If such fair blood
Ingender ill, man must not look for good.
          [*Exit all but Hermit. Florish.*

Enter Modestia, reading in a book.

Modesta. How much the oft report of this
blest *Hermit*   220
Hath won on my desires; I must behold him:
And sure this should be he. Oh, the world's
folly,
Proud earth and dust, how low a price bears
goodness!
All that should make man absolute shines in
him.
Much reverent Sir, may I without offence   225
Give interruption to your holy thoughts?

198 love *D* : love me *Q* : love like me *T*   217 may
make *D* : make *Q* : will make *T*   219 men *T*

225

Hermit. What would you, Lady?
Modest. That which till now ne're found
a language in me:
I am in love.
   Her.   In Love? with. what?
   Modest.   With vertue.
   Her. There's no blame in that.   230
   Modest. Nay, sir, with you, with your
     Religious Life,
Your Vertue, Goodness, if there be a name
To express affection greater, that,
That would I learn and utter: Reverent Sir,
If there be any thing to bar my suit,   235
Be charitable and expose it; your prayers
Are the same Orizons which I will number.
Holy Sir,
Keep not instruction back from willingness,
Possess me of that knowledge leads you on 240
To this humility; for well I know,
Were greatness good, you would not live so
   low.
   Her. Are you a Virgin?
   Modest. Yes, Sir.
   Her. ˙ Your name?   245
   Modest. Modesta.
   Her. Your name and vertues meet, a
   Modest Virgin:
Live ever in the sanctimonious way
To Heaven and Happiness. There's goodness
   in you,
I must instruct you further. Come, look up,
Behold yon firmament: there sits a power, 251
Whose foot-stool is this earth. Oh, learn this
   lesson,
And practise it: he that will climb so high,
Must leave no joy beneath to move his eye.
                         [*Exit.*
   Modest. I apprehend you, sir: on Heaven
   I fix my love,   255
Earth gives us grief, our joys are all above;
For this was man in innocence naked born,
To show us wealth hinders our sweet return.
                         [*Exit.*

ACTUS II.

   (SCENE I.

   A Forest.)

Enter Clown and his Sister great with childe.

   Clown. Away, follow me no further, I am
none of thy brother. What, with Childe? great
with Childe, and knows not whose the Father
on't! I am asham'd to call thee Sister.
   Joan. Believe me, Brother, he was a Gentleman.   6

   Clown. Nay, I believe that; he gives arms,
and legs too, and has made you the Herald to
blaze 'em: but, *Joan, Joan,* sister *Joan,* can
you tell me his name that did it? how shall
we call my Cousin, your bastard, when we
have it?   12
   Joan. Alas, I know not the Gentlemans
   name, Brother.
I met him in these woods the last great
   hunting;
He was so kinde and proffer'd me so much,
As I had not the heart to ask him more.   16
   Clown. Not his name? why, this showes
your Country breeding now; had you been
brought up i'th' City, you'd have got a Father
first, and the childe afterwards: hast thou no
markes to know him by?   21
   Joan. He had most rich Attire, a fair Hat
and Feather, a gilt Sword, and most excellent
Hangers.
   Clown. Pox on his Hangers, would he had
bin gelt for his labor.   26
   Joan. Had you but heard him swear, you
would have thought—
   Clown. I, as you did; swearing and lying
goes together still. Did his Oathes get you
with Childe? we shall have a roaring Boy then,
yfaith. Well, sister, I must leave you.   32
   Joan. Dear Brother, stay, help me to finde
   him out,
I'le ask no further.
   Clown. 'Sfoot, who should I finde? who
should I ask for?   36
   Joan. Alas, I know not, he uses in these
   woods,
And these are witness of his oathes and promise.
   Clown. We are like to have a hot suit on't,
when our best witness's but a Knight a'th'
Post.   41
   Joan. Do but enquire this Forrest, I'le go
   with you;
Some happy fate may guide us till we meet him.
   Clown. Meet him? and what name shall
we have for him, when we meet him? 'Sfoot,
thou neither knowst him nor canst tell what
to call him. Was ever man tyr'd with such
a business, to have a sister got with childe,
and know not who did it? Well, you shall see
him, I'le do my best for you, Ile make Proclamation; if these Woods and Trees, as you
say, will bear any witness, let them answer.
Oh yes: If there be any man that wants a
name will come in for⸳conscience sake, and
acknowledge himself to be a Whore-Master,

233 that *Q* : than that word *D*   254 leave *Q* : let
T   Exit *om. T*   258 Exeunt *T*   Scene I. *etc.*
add. T   3 know *T*

11 call] name *D*   45 weet *Q*   53 Oh yes *Q* :
Oyes *D*

he shal have that laid to his charge in an hour, he shall not be rid on in an age; if he have Lands, he shall have an heir; if he have patience, he shall have a wife; if he have neither Lands nor patience, he shall have a whore. So ho, boy, so ho, so, so.   61

[*Within*] *Prince Vter.* So ho, boy, so ho, illo ho, illo ho.

Clown. Hark, hark, sister, there's one hollows to us; what a wicked world's this! a man cannot so soon name a whore, but a knave comes presently: and see where he is; stand close a while, sister.   68

Enter Prince Vter.

Prince. How like a voice that Eccho spake, but oh,
My thoughts are lost for ever in amazement.
Could I but meet a man to tell her beauties,
These trees would bend their tops to kiss the air
That from my lips should give her praises up.

Clown. He talks of a woman, sister.

Joan. This may be he, brother.   75

Clown. View him well; you see, he has a fair Sword, but his Hangers are faln.

Prince. Here did I see her first, here view her beauty: 78
Oh, had I known her name, I had been happy.

Clown. Sister, this is he, sure; he knows not thy name neither. A couple of wise fools yfaith, to get children, and know not one another.

Prince. You weeping leaves, upon whose tender cheeks   84
Doth stand a flood of tears at my complaint,
Who heard my vows and oathes—

Clown. Law, Law, he has been a great swearer too; tis he, sister.

Prince. For having overtook her;
As I have seen a forward blood-hound strip
The swifter of the cry, ready to seize   91
His wished hopes, upon the sudden view,
Struck with astonishment, at his arriv'd prey,
Instead of seizure stands at fearful bay;
Or like to *Marius* soldiers, who, o'retook,   95
The eye sight killing *Gorgon* at one look
Made everlasting stand: so fear'd my power,
Whose cloud aspir'd the Sun, dissolv'd a shower.
Pigmalion, then I tasted thy sad fate,
Whose Ivory picture and my fair were one:100
Our dotage past imagination.
I saw and felt desire—

Clown. Pox a your fingering! did he feel, sister?

Prince.   But enjoy'd not.
Oh fate, thou hadst thy days and nights to feed
On calm affection; one poor sight was all, 105
Converts my pleasure to perpetual thrall:
Imbracing thine, thou lostest breath and desire,
So I, relating mine, will here expire.
For here I vow to you mournful plants,
Who were the first made happy by her fame,
Never to part hence, till I know her name. 111

Clown. Give me thy hand, sister, *The Childe has found his Father.* This is he, sure; as I am a man, had I been a woman, these kinde words would have won me, I should have had a great belly too, that's certain. Well, I'le speak to him.—Most honest and fleshly minded Gentleman, give me your hand, sir.

Prince. Ha, what art thou, that thus rude and boldly darest
Take notice of a wretch so much ally'd   120
To misery as I am?

Clown. Nay, Sir, for our aliance, I shall be found to be a poor brother in Law of your worships: the Gentlewoman you spake on is my sister: you see what a clew she spreads; her name is *Joan Go-too't.* I am her elder, but she has been at it before me; 'tis a womans fault.—Pox a this bashfulness! come forward, *Jug,* prethee, speak to him.   129

Prince. Have you e're seen me, Lady?

Clown. Seen ye? ha, ha! It seems she has felt you too: here's a yong *Go-too't* a coming, sir; she is my sister; we all love to *Go-too't,* as well as your worship. She's a Maid yet, but you may make her a wife, when you please, sir.

Prince. I am amaz'd with wonder: Tell me, woman,   136
What sin have you committed worthy this?

Joan. Do you not know me, sir?

Prince. Know thee! as I do thunder, hell, and mischief;
Witch, scullion, hag!   140

Clown. I see he will marry her; he speaks so like a husband.

Prince. Death! I will cut their tongues out for this blasphemy.
Strumpet, villain, where have you ever seen me?

Clown. Speak for your self, with a pox to ye.   146

Prince. Slaves, Ile make you curse your selves for this temptation.

---

62 boy *T* : by *Q*   74 talk's *Q*   77 Hanger's *Q*
86 Who?] And *Q* : You *D*   91 swiftest *WP*   93 astonishment *Q*   95 whom *D*

103 not *T, etc.* : now *Q*   105 On *D* : Or *Q*   109 you *Q* : you, ye *T*   134 a] scarce a *conj. T*   137 you *Q* : I *conj. T*   140 scullion *D* : stallion *Q*

Joan. Oh, sir, if ever you did speak to me,
It was in smoother phrase, in fairer language.
Prince. Lightning consume me, if I ever
saw thee. 150
My rage o're flowes my blood, all patience flies
me. [*Beats her.*]
Clown. Hold, I beseech you, sir, I have
nothing to say to you.
Joan. Help, help! murder, murder! 154

Enter Toclio and Oswold.

Toclio. Make haste, Sir, this way the sound
came, it was a ⟨th'⟩ wood.
Oswold. See where she is, and the Prince,
the price of all our wishes.
Clown. The Prince, say ye? ha's made a
poor Subject of me, I am sure. 160
Toclio. Sweet Prince, noble *Vter,* speak,
how fare you, sir?
Oswold. Dear sir, recal your self; your fear-
ful absence
Hath won too much already on the grief
Of our sad King, from whom our laboring
search. 165
Hath had this fair success in meeting you.
Toclio. His silence and his looks argue
distraction.
Clown. Nay, he's mad, sure, he will not
acknowledge my sister, nor the childe neither.
Oswold. Let us entreat your Grace along
with us; 171
Your sight will bring new life to the King your
Brother.
Toclio. Will you go, sir?
Prince. Yes, any whether; guide me, all's
hell I see;
Man may change air, but not his misery. 175
[*Exit Prince, Toclio.*
Joan. Lend me one word with you, sir.
Clown. Well said, sister, he has a Feather,
and fair Hangers too, this may be he.
Oswold. What would you, fair one?
Joan. Sure, I have seen you in these woods
e're this. 180
Oswold. Trust me, never; I never saw this
place,
Till at this time my friend conducted me.
Joan. The more's my sorrow then.
Oswold. Would I could comfort you.
I am a Bachelor, but it seems you have 185
A husband, you have been fouly o'reshot else.
Clown. A womans fault, we are all subject
to go to't, sir.

Enter Toclio.

Toclio. Oswold, away; the Prince will not
stir a foot without you. 190

Oswold. I am coming. Farewel, woman.
Toclio. Prithee, make haste. ⟨*Exit Oswold.*⟩
Joan. Good sir, but one word with you,
e're you leave us.
Toclio. With me, fair soul? 195
Clown. Shee'l have a fling at him too; the
Childe must have a Father.
Joan. Have you ne'er seen me, sir?
Toclio. Seen thee? 'Sfoot, I have seen
many fair faces in my time: prithee, look up,
and do not weep so. Sure, pretty wanton, I
have seen this face before. 202
Joan. It is enough, though you ne're see
me more. [*sinks down.*
Toclio. 'Sfoot, she's faln: this place is
inchanted, sure; look to the woman, fellow.
[*Exit.*
Clown. Oh, she's dead, she's dead! As you
are a man, stay and help, sir.—*Joan, Joan,*
sister *Joan,* why, *Joan* Go too't, I say; will
you cast away your self, and your childe, and
me too? what do you mean, sister? 211
Joan. Oh, give me pardon, sir; 'twas too
much joy
Opprest my loving thoughts; I know you were
Too noble to deny me—ha! Where is he?
Clown. Who, the Gentleman? he's gone,
sister. 215
Joan. Oh! I am undone, then! Run, tell
him I did
But faint for joy; dear brother, haste; why dost
thou stay?
Oh, never cease, till he give answer to thee.
Clown. He: which he? what do you call
him, tro?
Joan. Unnatural brother, 220
Shew me the path he took; why dost thou dally?
Speak, oh, which way went he?
Clown. This way, that way, through the
bushes there.
Joan. Were it through fire, 225
The Journey's easie, winged with sweet desire.
[*Exit.*
Clown. Hey day, there's some hope of this
yet. Ile follow her for kindreds sake; if she
miss of her purpose now, she'l challenge all
she findes, I see; for if ever we meet with
a two-leg'd creature in the whole Kingdom,
the Childe shall have a Father, that's certain.
[*Exit.*

⟨SCENE II.

An Ante-chamber at the British Court.⟩
*Loud Musick. Enter two with the Sword and
Mace, Cador, Edwin, two Bishops,
Aurelius, Ostorius, leading Artesia*

Crown'd, Constancia, Modestia, Octa,
Proximus a Magician, Donobert, Gloster,
Oswold, Toclio; all pass over the Stage.
Manet Donobert, Gloster, Edwin, Cador.

Dono. Come, *Gloster,* I do not like this
  hasty Marriage.

Gloster. She was quickly wooed and won:
  not six days since
Arrived an enemy to sue for Peace,
And now crown'd Queen of *Brittain;* this is
  strange.

Dono. Her brother too made as quick speed
  in coming,   5
Leaving his *Saxons* and his starved Troops,
To take the advantage, whilst 'twas offer'd.
'Fore heaven, I fear the King's too credulous;
Our Army is discharg'd too.

Gloster. Yes, and our General commanded
  home.   10
Son *Edwin,* have you seen him since?

Edwin. He's come to Court, but will not
  view the presence,
Nor speak unto the King; he's so discontent
At this so strange aliance with the *Saxon,*
As nothing can perswade his patience.   15

Cador. You know his humor will indure
  no check,
No, if the King oppose it:
All crosses feeds both his spleen and his
  impatience;
Those affections are in him like powder,
Apt to inflame with every little spark,   20
And blow up all his reason.

Gloster. *Edol* of *Chester* is a noble Soldier.

Dono. So is he, by the Rood, ever most
  faithful
To the King and Kingdom, how e're his passions guide him.

Enter Edoll *with Captains.*

Cador. See where he comes, my Lord.   25

Omnes. Welcome to Court, brave Earl.

Edol. Do not deceive me by your flatteries:
Is not the Saxon here? the League confirm'd?
The Marriage ratifi'd? the Court divided
With Pagan Infidels, the least part Christians,
At least in their Commands? Oh, the gods! 31
It is a thought that takes away my sleep,
And dulls my senses so I scarcely know
  you:
Prepare my horses, Ile away to *Chester.*

Capt. What shall we do with our Companies, my Lord?   35

Edol. Keep them at home to increase
  Cuckolds,

And get some Cases for your Captainships;
Smooth up your brows, the wars has spoil'd
  your faces,
And few will now regard you.

Dono. Preserve your patience, Sir.   40

Edol. Preserve your Honors, Lords, your
  Countries Safety,
Your Lives and Lands from strangers. What
  black devil
Could so bewitch the King, so to discharge
A Royal Army in the height of conquest,
Nay, even already made victorious,   45
To give such credit to an enemy,
A starved foe, a stragling fugitive,
Beaten beneath our feet, so low dejected,
So servile, and so base, as hope of life
Had won them all to leave the Land for ever?

Dono. It was the Kings will.   51

Edol. It was your want of wisdom,
That should have laid before his tender youth
The dangers of a State, where forain Powers
Bandy for Soveraignty with Lawful Kings; 55
Who being setled once, to assure themselves,
Will never fail to seek the blood and life
Of all competitors.

Dono. Your words sound well, my Lord,
  and point at safety,
Both for the Realm and us; but why did you,
Within whose power it lay, as General,   61
With full Commission to dispose the war,
Lend ear to parly with the weakned foe?

Edol. Oh the good Gods!

Cador. And on that parly came this
  Embassie.   65

Edol. You will hear me?

Edwin. Your letters did declare it to the
  King,
Both of the Peace, and all Conditions
Brought by this *Saxon* Lady, whose fond love
Has thus bewitched him.   70

Edol. I will curse you all as black as hell,
Unless you hear me; your gross mistake would
  make
Wisdom her self run madding through the
  streets,
And quarrel with her shadow. Death!
Why kill'd ye not that woman?

Dono. Glost.   Oh, my Lord! 75

Edol. The great devil take me quick, had
  I been by,
And all the women of the world were barren,
She should have died, e're he had married her
On these conditions.

Cador. It is not reason that directs you thus.

Edol. Then have I none, for all I have
  directs me.   81

---

17 No] Not even *conj. WP*   18 both *Q* : but *D*
36 Cuckolds with *conj. WP*

48 low *T, etc.* : love *Q*   75 ye *Q* : you *D*

Never was man so palpably abus'd,
So basely marted, bought and sold to scorn.
My Honor, Fame, and hopeful Victories,
The loss of Time, Expences, Blood, and For-
   tunes,   85
All vanisht into nothing.
  Edwin. This rage is vain, my Lord:
What the King does nor they nor you can
  help.
  Edol. My Sword must fail me then.
  Cador. 'Gainst whom will you expose it?
  Edol. What's that to you? 'gainst all the
  devils in hell,   91
To guard my country.
  Edwin.   These are airy words.
  Edol. Sir, you tread too hard upon my
  patience.
  Edwin. I speak the duty of a Subjects faith,
And say agen, had you been here in presence,
What the King did, you had not dar'd to
  cross it.   96
  Edol. I will trample on his Life and Soul
  that says it.
  Cador. My Lord!
  Edwin.   Come, come.
  Edol.   Now, before heaven—
  Cador.   Dear sir!
  Edol. Not dare? thou liest beneath thy
  lungs.
  Gloster. No more, son Edwin.   100
  Edwin. I have done, sir; I take my leave.
  Edol. But thou shalt not, you shall take no
  leave of me, Sir.
  Dono. For wisdoms sake, my Lord —
  Edol. Sir, I'le leave him, and you, and all
  of you,
The Court and King, and let my Sword and
  friends   105
Shuffle for *Edols* safety: stay you here,
And hug the *Saxons,* till they cut your throats,
Or bring the Land to servile slavery.
Such yokes of baseness *Chester* must not suffer.
Go, and repent betimes these foul misdeeds,
For in this League all our whole Kingdom
  bleeds,   111
Which Ile prevent, or perish. [*Exit Edol,Capt.*
  Glost. See how his rage transports him!
  Cador. These passions set apart, a braver
  soldier
Breathes not i'th' world this day.   115
  Dono. I wish his own worth do not court
  his ruine.
The King must Rule, and we must learn to
  obay,
True vertue still directs the noble way.

  90 expose *Q* : oppose *D*   95 you *T, etc.* : your *Q*
  102 shall not *Q*   112 *S. D. after* 113 *Q*

⟨SCENE III.

Hall of state in the Palace.⟩

Loud Musick. Enter Aurelius,Artesia, Ostorius,
Octa, Proximus, Toclio, Oswold, Hermit.

  Aurel. Why is the Court so dull? me thinks,
  each room
And angle of our Palace should appear
Stuck full of objects fit for mirth and triumphs,
To show our high content. *Oswold,* fill wine!
Must we begin the Revels? Be it so, then! 5
Reach me the cup: Ile now begin a Health
To our lov'd Queen, the bright *Artesia,*
The Royal *Saxon* King, our warlike brother.
Go and command all the whole Court to
  pledge it.
Fill to the Hermit there! Most reverent
  Anselme,   10
Wee'l do thee Honor first, to pledge my Queen.
  Her. I drink no healths, great King, and if
  I did,
I would be loath to part with health to those
That have no power to give it back agen.
  Aurel. Mistake not, it is the argument of
  Love   15
And Duty to our Queen and us.
  Artes. But he ows none, it seems.
  Her. I do to vertue, Madam: temperate
  minds
Covets that health to drink, which nature
  gives
In every spring to man; he that doth hold 20
His body but a Tenement at will,
Bestows no cost, but to repair what's ill:
Yet if your healths or heat of Wine, fair
  Princes,
Could this old frame or these cras'd limbes
  restore,
Or keep out death or sickness, then fill more,
I'le make fresh way for appetite; if no, 26
On such a prodigal who would wealth bestow?
  Ostorius. He speaks not like a guest to
  grace a wedding.

Enter Toclio.

  Artes. No, sir, but like an envious imposter.
  Octa. A Christian slave, a Cinick.   30
  Ostor. What vertue could decline your
  Kingly spirit
To such respect of him whose magick spells
Met with your vanquisht Troops, and turn'd
  your Arms
To that necessity of fight, which, thro dis-
  pair

  Scene III. *etc. add. T*   *Scene II continued D*   8
and the *T*   34 which] when *D* through *WP*: the
Q : but for the *T*

Of any hope to stand but by his charms,   35
Had been defeated in a bloody conquest?
   Octa. 'Twas magick, hellbred magick did
    it, sir,
And that's a course, my Lord, which we
   esteem
In all our *Saxon* Wars unto the last
And lowest ebbe of servile treachery.   40
   Aurel. Sure, you are deceiv'd, it was the
   hand of heaven
That in his vertue gave us victory.
Is there a power in man that can strike fear
Thorough a general camp, or create spirits
In recreant bosoms above present sense?   45
   Ostor. To blind the sense there may, with
   apparition
Of well arm'd troops within themselves are air,
Form'd into humane shapes, and such that day
Were by that Sorcerer rais'd to cross our
   fortunes.
   Aurel. There is a law tells us that words
   want force   50
To make deeds void; examples must be shown
By instances alike, e're I believe it.
   Ostor. 'Tis easily perform'd, believe me, sir:
Propose your own desires, and give but way
To what our Magick here shall straight per-
   form,   55
And then let his or our deserts be censur'd.
   Aurel. We could not wish a greater
   happiness
Then what this satisfaction brings with it.
Let him proceed, fair brother.
   Ostor.   He shall, sir.
Come, learned *Proximus,* this task be thine:
Let thy great charms confound the opinion 61
This Christian by his spells hath falsly won.
   Prox. Great King, propound your wishes,
   then:
What persons, of what State, what numbers, or
   how arm'd,
Please your own thoughts; they shall appear
before you.   65
   Aurel. Strange art! What thinkst thou,
   reverent *Hermit?*
   Her. Let him go on, sir.
   Aurel. Wilt thou behold his cunning?
   Her. Right gladly, sir; it will be my joy to
   tell,
That I was here to laugh at him and hell.   70
   Aurel. I like thy confidence.
   Artes. His sawcy impudence!   Proceed to
   th'trial.
   Prox. Speak your desires my Lord, and be
   it place't
In any angle underneath the Moon,

47 within *Q* (=*which within*): which in *T*
811663

The center of the Earth, the Sea, the Air,   75
The region of the fire, nay, hell it self,
And I'le present it.
   Aurel. Wee'l have no sight so fearful, onely
   this:
If all thy art can reach it, show me here   79
The two great Champions of the *Trojan* War,
Achilles and brave *Hector,* our great Ancestor,
Both in their warlike habits, Armor, Shields,
And Weapons then in use for fight.
   Prox. 'Tis done, my Lord, command a halt
   and silence,
As each man will respect his life or danger. 85
Armel, Plesgeth!

            Enter Spirits.
   Spirits. Quid vis?
   Prox. Attend me.
   Aurel. The Apparition comes; on our dis-
   pleasure,
Let all keep place and silence.   90
       [Within Drums beat Marches.

Enter Proximus, *bringing in* Hector, *attir'd*
   and arm'd after the Trojan manner, with
   Target, Sword, and Battel-ax, a Trumpet
   before him, and a Spirit in flame colours
   with a Torch; at the other door Achilles
   with his Spear and Falchon, a Trumpet,
   and a Spirit in black before him; Trumpets
   sound alarm, and they manage their wea-
   pons to begin the Fight: and after some
   Charges, the Hermit steps between them,
   at which seeming amaz'd the spirits
   tremble. Thunder within.

   Prox. What means this stay, bright *Armel,*
   Plesgeth?
Why fear you and fall back?
Renew the Alarms, and enforce the Combat,
Or hell or darkness circles you for ever.
   Arm. We dare not.   95
   Prox. Ha!
   Plesgeth. Our charms are all dissolv'd:
   Armel, away!
'Tis worse then hell to us, whilest here we
   stay.   *[Exit all.*
   Her. What! at a Non-plus, sir? command
   them back, for shame.
   Prox. What power o're-aws my Spells?
   Return, you Hell-hounds!   100
Armel, Plesgeth, double damnation seize you!
By all the Infernal powers, the prince of devils
Is in this Hermits habit: what else could force
My Spirits quake or tremble thus?
   Her. Weak argument to hide your want of
   skill: 105

S. D. Enter Spirit *Q*   *S. D.* tremble] and tremble *Q*

Does the devil fear the devil, or war with hell?
They have not been acquainted long, it seems.
Know, mis-believing Pagan, even that Power,
That overthrew your Forces, still lets you see,
He onely can controul both hell and thee. 110
Prox. Disgrace and mischief! Ile enforce new charms,
New spells, and spirits rais'd from the low Abyss
Of hells unbottom'd depths.
Aurel.   We have enough, sir;
Give o're your charms, wee'l finde some other time
To praise your Art. I dare not but acknowledge 115
That heavenly Power my heart stands witness to:
Be not dismaid, my Lords, at this disaster,
Nor thou, my fairest Queen: we'l change the Scene
To some more pleasing sports. Lead to your Chamber. 119
How 'ere in this thy pleasures finde a cross,
Our joy's too fixed here to suffer loss.
Toclio. Which I shall adde to, sir, with news I bring:
The Prince, your Brother, lives.
Aurel. Ha!
Toclio. And comes to grace this high and heaven-knit Marriage. 125
Aurel. Why dost thou flatter me, to make me think
Such happiness attends me?

Enter Prince Uter and Oswold.

Toclio. His presence speaks my truth, sir.
Dono. Force me, 'tis he: look, *Gloster.*
Glost. A blessing beyond hope, sir. 130
Aurel. Ha! 'tis he: welcome, my second Comfort.
Artesia, Dearest Love, it is my Brother,
My Princely Brother, all my Kingdoms hope:
Oh, give him welcome, as thou lov'st my health.
Artes. You have so free a welcome, sir, from me, 135
As this your presence has such power, I swear,
O're me, a stranger, that I must forget
My Countrey, Name, and Friends, and count this place
My Joy and Birth-right.
Prince. 'Tis she! 'tis she, I swear! oh, ye good gods, 'tis she! 140
That face within those woods where first I saw her,
Captived my senses, and thus many moneths
Bar'd me from all society of men.

How came she to this place, 144
Brother *Aurelius?* Speak that Angels name,
Her heaven-blest name, oh, speak it quickly, Sir.
Aurel. It is *Artesia,* the Royal Saxon Princess.
Prince. A woman, and no Deity, no feigned shape,
To mock the reason of admiring sense,
On whom a hope as low as mine may live, 150
Love, and enjoy, dear Brother, may it not?
Aurel. She is all the Good or Vertue thou canst name,
My Wife, my Queen.
Prince. Ha! your wife!
Artes. Which you shall finde, sir, if that time and fortune 155
May make my love but worthy of your tryal.
Prince. Oh!
Aurel. What troubles you, dear Brother?
Why with so strange and fixt an eye dost thou
Behold my Joys? 160
Artes. You are not well, sir.
Prince. Yes, yes. — Oh, you immortal powers,
Why has poor man so many entrances
For sorrow to creep in at, when our sense
Is much too weak to hold his happiness? 165
Oh, say, I was born deaf: and let your silence
Confirm in me the knowing my defect;
At least be charitable to conceal my sin,
For hearing is no less in me, dear Brother.
Aurel. No more! 170
I see thou art a Rival in the Joys
Of my high Bliss. Come, my *Artesia;*
The Day's most prais'd when 'tis ecclipst by Night,
Great Good must have as great Ill opposite.
Prince. Stay, hear but a word; yet now I think on't, 175
This is your Wedding-night, and were it mine,
I should be angry with least loss of time.
Artes. Envy speaks no such words, has no such looks.
Prince. Sweet rest unto you both. 179
Aurel. Lights to our Nuptial Chamber.
Artes. Could you speak so,
I would not fear how much my grief did grow.
Aurel. Lights to our Chamber; on, on, set on!   [*Exeunt. Manet Prince.*
Prince. ' Could you speak so,
I would not fear how much my griefs did grow.'
Those were her very words; sure, I am waking:
She wrung me by the hand, and spake them to me 186

119 your *Q* : our *WP*   120 Force *Q* : 'Fore *T, etc.*   184 grief *D, etc.*

232

With a most passionate affection.
Perhaps she loves, and now repents her choice,
In marriage with my brother. Oh, fond man,
How darest thou trust thy Traitors thoughts,
   thus to   190
Betray thy self? 'twas but a waking dream
Wherein thou madest thy wishes speak, not
   her,
In which thy foolish hopes strives to prolong
A wretched being. So sickly children play
With health lov'd toys, which for a time delay,
But do not cure the fit. Be, then, a man, 196
Meet that destruction which thou canst not flie.
From not to live, make it thy best to die,
And call her now, whom thou didst hope to wed,
Thy brothers wife: thou art too nere a kin, 200
And such an act above all name's a sin
Not to be blotted out; heaven pardon me!
She's banisht from my bosom now for ever.
To lowest ebbes men justly hope a flood;
When vice grows barren, all desires are good.

Enter Waiting Gentlewoman with a Jewel.

Gent. The noble Prince, I take it, sir? 206
Prince. You speak me what I should be,
   Lady.
Gent. Know, by that name, sir, Queen
   Artesia greets you.
Prince. Alas, good vertue, how is she mis-
   taken!
Gent. Commending her affection in this
   Jewel, sir.   210
Prince. She binds my service to her: ha!
   a Jewel; 'tis
A fair one, trust me, and methinks, it much
Resembles something I have seen with her.
Gen. It is an artificial crab, Sir.
Prince. A creature that goes backward. 215
Gent. True, from the way it looks.
Prince. There is no moral in it aludes to
   her self?
Gent. 'Tis your construction gives you that,
   sir;
She's a woman.
Prince. And, like this, may use her legs
   and eyes   220
Two several ways.
Gent.   Just like the Sea-crab,
Which on the Mussel prayes, whilst he bills
   at a stone..
Prince. Pretty in troth. Prithee, tell me,
   art thou honest?
Gent. I hope I seem no other, sir.
Prince. And those that seem so are some-
   times bad enough.   225

Gent. If they will accuse themselves for
   want of witness,
Let them, I am not so foolish.
Prince.   I see th'art wise.
Come, speak me truly: what is the greatest sin?
Gent. That which man never acted; what
   has been done
Is as the least, common to all as one.   230
Prince. Dost think thy Lady is of thy
   opinion?
Gent. She's a bad Scholar else; I have
   brought her up,
And she dares owe me still.
Prince. I, 'tis a fault in greatness, they dare
   owe
Many, e're they pay one. But darest thou
Expose thy scholar to my examining?   236
Gent. Yes, in good troth, sir, and pray put
   her to't too;
'Tis a hard lesson, if she answer it not.
Prince. Thou know'st the hardest?
Gent. As far as a woman may, sir.   240
Prince. I commend thy plainness.
When wilt thou bring me to thy Lady?
Gent. Next opportunity I attend you, sir.
Prince. Thanks, take this, and commend
   me to her.
Gent. Think of your Sea-crab, sir, I pray.
                 [*Exit.*
Prince. Oh, by any means, Lady.—   246
What should all this tend to?
If it be Love or Lust that thus incites her,
The sin is horrid and incestuous;
If to betray my life, what hopes she by it? 250
Yes, it may be a practice 'twixt themselves,
To expel the *Brittains* and ensure the State
Through our destructions; all this may be
Valid, with a deeper reach in villany
Then all my thoughts can guess at; — however,
I will confer with her, and if I finde   256
Lust hath given Life to Envy in her minde,
I may prevent the danger: so men wise
By the same step by which they fell, may rise.
Vices are Vertues, if so thought and seen, 260
And Trees with foulest roots branch soonest
   green.   [*Exit.*

ACT 3.

SCENE I.

⟨*Before the Palace of King Aurelius.*⟩
Enter Clown and his Sister.

Clown. Come, sister, thou that art all fool,
all mad-woman.

---

190 traitorous *T, etc.*   198 best *Q* : hest *D*   200
ne're *Q*   254 Valid *Q*: Veil'd *D*   *S. D. Before etc. add. T*
   1 that *om. T*

233

Joan. Prithee, have patience, we are now at Court.   4

Clown. At Court! ha, ha, that proves thy madness: was there ever any woman in thy taking travel'd to Court for a husband? 'Slid, 'tis enough for them to get children, and the City to keep 'em, and the Countrey to finde Nurses: every thing must be done in his due place, sister.   11

Joan. Be but content a while; for, sure, I know
This Journey will be happy. Oh, dear brother,
This night my sweet Friend came to comfort me;
I saw him and embrac't him in mine arms. 15

Clown. Why did you not hold him, and call me to help you?

Joan. Alas, I thought I had been with him still,
But when I wak't —   19

Clown. Ah! pox of all Loger-heads, then you were but in a Dream all this while, and we may still go look him. Well, since we are come to Court, cast your Cats eyes about you, and either finde him out you dreamt on, or some other, for Ile trouble my self no further.   25

Ent⟨er⟩ Dono⟨bert⟩, Cador, Edw⟨in⟩ & Toclio.

See, see, here comes more Courtiers; look about you; come, pray, view 'em all well; the old man has none of the marks about him, the other have both Swords and Feathers: what thinkest thou of that tall yong Gentleman?

Joan. He much resembles him; but, sure, my friend,   31
Brother, was not so high of stature.

Clown. Oh, beast, wast thou got a childe with a short thing too?

Dono. Come, come, Ile hear no more on't: Go, Lord *Edwin,*   35
Tell her, this day her sister shall be married
To *Cador,* Earl of *Cornwall;* so shall she
To thee, brave *Edwin,* if she'l have my blessing.

Edwin. She is addicted to a single Life,
She will not hear of Marriage.   40

Dono. Tush, fear it not: go you from me to her,
Use your best skill, my Lord, and if you fail,
I have a trick shall do it: haste, haste about it.

Edwin. Sir, I am gone;   44
My hope is in your help more then my own.

Dono. And worthy *Toclio,* to your care I must
Commend this business

20 A pox *T, etc.*   22 look for him *T*   29 both *Q* : but *D*   33 got a *Q* : got with *T*

For Lights and Musick, and what else is needful.

Toclio. I shall, my Lord.   49

Clown. We would intreat a word, sir. Come forward, sister. [*Ex. Dono., Toc., Cador.*

Edwin. What lackst thou, fellow?

Clown. I lack a father for a childe, sir.

Edwin. How! a God-father?   54

Clown. No, sir, we mean the own father: it may be you, sir, for any thing we know; I think the childe is like you.

Edwin. Like me! prithee, where is it?

Clown. Nay, 'tis not born yet, sir, 'tis forth coming, you see; the childe must have a father: what do you think of my sister?   61

Edwin. Why, I think if she ne're had husband, she's a whore, and thou a fool. Farewell.   [*Exit.*

Clown. I thank you, sir. Well, pull up thy heart, sister; if there be any Law i'th' Court, this fellow shall father it, 'cause he uses me so scurvily. There's a great Wedding towards, they say; we'l amongst them for a husband for thee.   70

Enter Sir Nicodemus *with a Letter.*

If we miss there, Ile have another bout with him that abus'd me. See! look, there comes another Hat and Feather, this should be a close Letcher, he's reading of a Love-letter.

Sir Nic. Earl *Cador's* Marriage, and a Masque to grace it.   75
So, so.
This night shall make me famous for Presentments.—
How now, what are you?

Clown. A couple of *Great Brittains* you may see by our bellies, sir.   80

Sir Nic. And what of this, sir?

Clown. Why, thus the matter stands, sir: There's one of your Courtiers Hunting Nags has made a Gap through another mans Inclosure. Now, sir, here's the question, who should be at charge of a Fur-bush to stop it?

Sir Nic. Ha, ha, this is out of my element: the Law must end it.   88

Clown. Your Worship says well; for, surely, I think some Lawyer had a hand in the business, we have such a troublesom Issue.

Sir Nic. But what's thy business with me now?

Clown. Nay, sir, the business is done already, you may see by my sisters belly.   95

Sir Nic. Oh, now I finde thee: this Gentlewoman, it seems, has been humbled.

Clown. As low as the ground would give her leave, sir, and your Worship knows this:

234

though there be many fathers without children, yet to have a childe without a father were most unnatural.   102

Sir Nic. That s true, ifaith, I never heard of a childe yet that e're begot his father.

Clown. Why, true, you say wisely, sir.

Sir Nic. And therefore I conclude, that he that got the childe is without all question the father of it.

Clown. I, now you come to the matter, sir; and our suit is to your Worship for the discovery of this father.   111

Sir Nic. Why, lives he in the Court here?

Joan. Yes, sir, and I desire but Marriage.

Sir Nic. And does the knave refuse it? Come, come, be merry, wench; he shall marry thee, and keep the childe too, if my Knighthood can do any thing. I am bound by mine Orders to help distressed Ladies, and can there be a greater injury to a woman with childe, then to lack a father for't? I am asham'd of your simpleness: Come, come, give me a Courtiers Fee for my pains, and Ile be thy Advocate my self, and justice shall be found; nay, Ile sue the Law for it; but give me my Fee first.   125

Clown. If all the money I have i'th world will do it, you shall have it, sir.

Sir Nic. An Angel does it.

Clown. Nay, there's two, for your better eye sight, sir.   130

Sir Nic. Why, well said! Give me thy hand, wench, Ile teach thee a trick for all this, shall get a father for thy childe presently, and this it is, mark now: You meet a man, as you meet me now, thou claimest Marriage of me, and layest the childe to my charge; I deny it: push, that's nothing, hold thy Claim fast, thy words carries it, and no Law can withstand it. 138

Clown. Ist possible?

Sir Nic. Past all opposition; her own word carries it: let her challenge any man, the childe shall call him Father; there's a trick for your money now.   143

Clown. Troth, Sir, we thank you, we'l make use of your trick, and go no further to seek the childe a Father, for we challenge you, Sir: sister, lay it to him, he shall marry thee, I shall have a worshipful old man to my brother. 148

Sir Nic. Ha, ha, I like thy pleasantness.

Joan. Nay, indeed, Sir, I do challenge you.

Clown. You think we jest, sir?

Sir Nic. I, by my troth, do I. I like thy wit, yfaith: thou shalt live at Court with me;

didst never here of *Nicodemus Nothing?* I am the man.   155

Clown. Nothing? 'slid, we are out agen: thou wast never got with childe with nothing, sure.

Joan. I know not what to say.   159

Sir Nic. Never grieve, wench, show me the man, and process shall fly out.

Clown. 'Tis enough for us to finde the children, we look that you should finde the Father, and therefore either do us justice, or we'l stand to our first challenge.   165

Sir Nic. Would you have justice without an Adversary? unless you can show me the man, I can do you no good in it.

Clown. Why, then I hope you'l do us no harm, sir; you'l restore my money.   170

Sir Nic. What, my Fee? marry, Law forbid it!

Finde out the party, and you shall have justice, Your fault clos'd up, and all shall be amended, The Childe, his Father, and the Law (def-) ended.   [*Exit.*

Clown. Well, he has deserv'd his Fee, indeed, for he has brought our suit to a quick end, I promise you, and yet the Childe has never a Father; nor we have no more mony to seek after him. A shame of all lecherous placcats! now you look like a Cat had newly kitten'd; what will you do now, tro? Follow me no further, lest I beat your brains out.   182

Joan. Impose upon me any punishment, Rather then leave me now.

Clown. Well, I think I am bewitcht with thee; I cannot finde in my heart to forsake her. There was never sister would have abus'd a poor brother as thou hast done; I am even pin'd away with fretting, there's nothing but flesh and bones about me. Well, and I had my money agen, it were some comfort. Hark, sister, [*Thunder*] does it not thunder? 192

Joan. Oh yes, most fearfully: What shall we do, brother?

Clown. Marry, e'ene get some shelter, e're the storm catch us: away, let's away, I prithee.

Enter the Devil in mans habit, richly attir'd, his feet and his head horrid.

Joan. Ha, 'tis he! Stay, brother, dear brother, stay.   196

Clown. What's the matter now?

Joan. My love, my friend is come; yonder he goes.

---

121 your *om. D*   130 eye *om T*.   136 push] pish *T, etc.*   137 word *D*   146 the childe *om. T*   168 do you *Q* : do *T*   172-3 Finde .. clos'd up *om. D*   174 child find his *D*   Law] Law-suit *WP* defended *pr. ed.* : ended *Q, etc.*   178 we have no *Q*: have we *T* : we have on *D*   185 bewitch *Q*

Clown. Where, where? show me where;
I'le stop him, if the devil be not in him.   200
Joan. Look there, look yonder!
Oh, dear friend, pity my distress,
For heaven and goodness, do but speak to me.
Devil. She calls me, and yet drives me
headlong from her.   204
Poor mortal, thou and I are much uneven,
Thou must not speak of goodness nor of
heaven,
If I confer with thee; but be of comfort:
Whilst men do breath, and *Brittains* name
be known,
The fatal fruit thou bear'st within thy womb
Shall here be famous till the day of doom.   210
Clown. 'Slid, who's that talks so? I can
see no body.
Joan. Then art thou blind or mad. See
where he goes,
And beckons me to come; oh, lead me forth,
I'le follow thee in spight of fear or death.[*Exit.*
Clown. Oh brave! she'l run to the devil for
a husband; she's stark mad, sure, and talks to
a shaddow, for I could see no substance: well,
I'le after her; the childe was got by chance,
and the father must be found at all adventure.
[*Exit.*

⟨SCENE II.
The Porch of a Church.⟩
Enter Hermit, Modesta, and Edwin.

Modesta. Oh, reverent sir, by you my heart
hath reacht
At the large hopes of holy Piety,
And for this I craved your company,
Here in your sight religiously to vow
My chaste thoughts up to heaven, and make
you now   5
The witness of my faith.
Her. Angels assist thy hopes.
Edwin. What meanes my Love? thou art
my promis'd wife.
Modest. To part with willingly what friends
and life
Can make no good assurance of.   10
Edwin. Oh, finde remorse, fair soul, to
love and merit,
And yet recant thy vow.
Modest. Never:
This world and I are parted now for ever.
Her. To finde the way to bliss, oh, happy
woman,   15
Th'ast learn'd the hardest Lesson well, I see.
Now show thy fortitude and constancy:
Let these thy friends thy sad departure weep,

209 fruit] print *D*   Scene II. *etc. add. T*   3 I]
have I *D*

Thou shalt but loose the wealth thou could'st
not keep.
My contemplation calls me, I must leave ye.
Edwin. O, reverent Sir, perswade not her
to leave me.   21
Her. My Lord, I do not, nor to cease to
love ye;
I onely pray her faith may fixed stand;
Marriage was blest, I know, with heavens own
hand.   [*Exit.*
Edwin. You hear him, Lady, 'tis not a
virgins state,   25
But sanctity of life, must make you happy.
Modest. Good sir, you say you love me;
gentle *Edwin,*
Even by that love I do beseech you, leave me.
Edwin. Think of your fathers tears, your
weeping friends,
Whom cruel grief makes pale and bloodless
for you.   30
Modest. Would I were dead to all.
Edwin. Why do you weep?
Modest. Oh, who would live to see
How men with care and cost seek misery?
Edwin. Why do you seek it then? What
joy, what pleasure
Can give you comfort in a single life?   35
Modest. The contemplation of a happy
death,
Which is to me so pleasing that I think
No torture could divert me: What's this world,
Wherein you'd have me walk, but a sad
passage
To a dread Judgement-Seat, from whence
even now   40
We are but bail'd, upon our good abearing,
Till that great Sessions come, when Death, the
Cryer,
Will surely summon us and all to appear,
To plead us guilty or our bail to clear?   44
What musick's this?   [*Soft Musick.*

*Enter two Bishops, Donobert, Gloster, Cador,
Constancia, Oswold, Toclio.*
Edwin. Oh, now resolve, and think upon
my love!
This sounds the Marriage of your beauteous
sister,
Vertuous *Constancia,* with the noble *Cador.*
Look, and behold this pleasure.
Modest. Cover me with night,   50
It is a vanity not worth the sight.
Dono. See, see, she's yonder.
Pass on, son *Cador,* Daughter *Constancia,*
I beseech you all, unless she first move speech,
Salute her not.—*Edwin,* what good success?

S. D. Bishops, Edwin, Donobert *Q*

236

Edwin. Nothing as yet, unless this object
  take her.   56
Dono. See, see, her eye is fixt upon her
  sister;
Seem careless all, and take no notice of her: —
On afore there; come, my *Constancia.*
Modest. Not speak to me, nor dain to cast
  an eye,   60
To look on my despised poverty?
I must be more charitable;—pray, stay,
  Lady,
Are not you she whom I did once call sister?
Constan. I did acknowledge such a name
  to one,
Whilst she was worthy of it, in whose folly, 65
Since you neglect your fame and friends
  together,
In you I drown'd a sisters name for ever.
Modest. Your looks did speak no less.
Glost. It now begins to work, this sight has
  moved her.
Dono. I knew this trick would take, or
  nothing.   70
Modest. Though you disdain in me a sisters
  name,
Yet charity, me thinks, should be so strong
To instruct e're you reject. I am a wretch,
Even follies instance, who perhaps have er'd,
Not having known the goodness bears so high
And fair a show in you; which being exprest,
I may recant this low despised life,   77
And please those friends whom I mov'd to
  grief.
Cador. She is coming, yfaith; be merry,
  Edwin.
Consta. Since you desire instruction, you
  shall have it.   80
What ist should make you thus desire to live
Vow'd to a single life?
Modest. Because I know I cannot flie from
  death.
Oh, my good sister, I beseech you, hear me:
This world is but a Masque, catching weak
  eyes   85
With what is not our selves but our disguise,
A Vizard that falls off, the Dance being done,
And leaves Deaths Glass for all to look upon;
Our best happiness here lasts but a night,
Whose burning Tapers makes false Ware seem
  right.   90
Who knows not this, and will not now provide
Some better shift before his shame be spy'd,
And knowing this vain world at last will leave
  him,
Shake off these robes that help but to deceive
  him?

70 knew *T*: know *Q*   78 mov'd *Q*: have mov'd *D*

Const. Her words are powerful, I am
  amaz'd to hear her!   95
Dono. Her soul's inchanted with infected
  Spells.
Leave her, best Girl; for now in thee
Ile seek the fruits of Age, Posterity.—
Out o' my sight! sure, I was half asleep
Or drunk, when I begot thee.   100
Const. Good sir, forbear. What say you to
  that, sister?
The joy of children, a blest Mothers Name!
Oh, who without much grief can loose such
  Fame?
Modest. Who can enjoy it without sorrow
  rather?
And that most certain where the joy's unsure,
Seeing the fruit that we beget endure   106
So many miseries, that oft we pray
The Heavens to shut up their afflicted day;
At best we do but bring forth Heirs to die,
And fill the Coffins of our enemy.   110
Const. Oh, my soul!
Dono.   Hear her no more, *Constancia,*
She's sure bewitcht with Error; leave her,
  Girl.
Const. Then must I leave all goodness, sir:
  away,
Stand off, I say.
Dono. How's this?   115
Const. I have no father, friend, no husband
  now;
All are but borrowed robes, in which we
  masque
To waste and spend the time, when all our Life
Is but one good betwixt two Ague-days,
Which from the first e're we have time to
  praise,   120
A second Fever takes us: Oh, my best sister,
My souls eternal friend, forgive the rashness
Of my distemper'd tongue; for how could she,
Knew not her self, know thy felicity.
From which worlds cannot how remove me?
Dono. Art thou mad too, fond woman?
  what's thy meaning?   126
Const. To seek eternal happiness in heaven,
Which all this world affords not.
Cador. Think of thy Vow, thou art my
  promis'd Wife.
Const. Pray, trouble me no further.
Omnes.   Strange alteration! 130
Cador. Why do you stand at gaze, you
  sacred Priests?
You holy men, be equal to the Gods,
And consummate my Marriage with this
  woman.
Bishop. Her self gives barr, my Lord, to
  your desires

237

And our performance; 'tis against the Law 135
And Orders of the Church to force a Marriage.
  Cador. How am I wrong'd! Was this your
    trick, my Lord?
  Dono. I am abus'd past sufferance;
Grief and amazement strive which Sense of
    mine
Shall loose her being first. Yet let me call thee
    Daughter.   140
  Cador. Me, Wife.
  Const. Your words are air, you speak of
    want to wealth,
And wish her sickness, newly rais'd to health.
  Dono. Bewitched Girls, tempt not an old
    mans fury,   144
That hath no strength to uphold his feeble age,
But what your sights give life to: oh, beware,
And do not make me curse you.
  [*Kneel.*] *Modest.* Dear father,
Here at your feet we kneel, grant us but this,
That, in your sight and hearing, the good
    Hermit   150
May plead our Cause; which, if it shall not
    give
Such satisfaction as your Age desires,
We will submit to you.
  Const.   You gave us life;
Save not our bodies, but our souls, from death.
  Dono. This gives some comfort yet: Rise
    with my blessings. —   155
Have patience, noble *Cador*, worthy *Edwin;*
Send for the Hermit that we may confer.
For, sure, Religion tyes you not to leave
Your careful Father thus; if so it be,
Take you content, and give all grief to me.
                                      [*Exeunt.*

                 (Scene III.
            A cave in the Forest.)
    Thunder and Lightning; Enter Devil.

  Devil. Mix light and darkness; earth and
    heaven dissolve,
Be of one piece agen, and turn to *Chaos;*
Break all your works, you powers, and spoil
    the world,
Or, if you will maintain earth still, give way
And life to this abortive birth now coming,   5
Whose fame shall add unto your Oracles.
Lucina, Hecate, dreadful Queen of Night,
Bright *Proserpine,* be pleas'd for *Ceres* love,
From *Stigian* darkness summon up the Fates,
And in a moment bring them quickly hither,
Lest death do vent her birth and her together.
                                      [*Thunder.*
Assist, you spirits of infernal deeps,   12

Squint ey'd *Erictho,* midnight *Incubus,*
Rise, rise to aid this birth prodigious.

       Enter Lucina and the three Fates.

Thanks, *Hecate;* hail, sister to the Gods!   15
There lies your way, haste with the Fates, and
    help,
Give quick dispatch unto her laboring throws,
To bring this mixture of infernal seed
To humane being;   [*Exit Fates.*
And to beguil her pains, till back you come, 20
Anticks shall dance and Musick fill the room. —
                                       [*Dance.*
  Devil. Thanks, Queen of Shades.
  Lucina. Farewel, great servant to th'in-
    fernal King.
In honor of this childe, the Fates shall bring
All their assisting powers of Knowledge, Arts,
Learning, Wisdom, all the hidden parts   26
Of all-admiring Prophecy, to fore-see
The event of times to come: his Art shall
    stand
A wall of brass to guard the *Brittain* Land.
Even from this minute, all his Arts appears 30
Manlike in Judgement, Person, State, and
    years.
Upon his brest the Fates have fixt his name,
And since his birth place was this forrest here,
They now have nam'd him *Merlin Silvester.*
  Devil. And *Merlins* name in *Brittany* shall
    live,   35
Whilst men inhabit here or Fates can give
Power to amazing wonder; envy shall weep,
And mischief sit and shake her ebbone wings,
Whilst all the world of *Merlins* magick sings.
                                        [*Exit.*

                 (Scene IV.
              The Forest.)
             Enter Clown.

  Clown. Well, I wonder how my poor sister
does, after all this thundering; I think she's
dead, for I can hear no tidings of her. These
woods yields small comfort for her; I could
meet nothing but a swinherds wife, keeping
hogs by the Forestside, but neither she nor
none of her sowes would stir a foot to help us;
indeed, I think she durst not trust her self
amongst the trees with me, for I must needs
confess I offer'd some kindness to her. Well,
I would fain know what's become of my sister:
if she have brought me a yong Cousin, his
face may be a picture to finde his Father by.
So oh! sister *Joan, Joan Go-too't,* where art
thou?   15

148 *S. D.* Kneel *printed as part of text Q*   160 you
Q : your *WP*   Scene III. *etc. add. T*

14 *S. D. after* 13 *Q*   26 Learning, and wisdom *D*
35 Britany *D* : Brittain *Q*   Scene IV. *etc. add. T*

(Within) *Joan.* Here, here, brother, stay
but a while, I come to thee.
  Clown. O brave! she's alive still, I know
her voice; she speaks, and speaks cherfully,
methinks. How now, what Moon-calf has
she got with her?   21

   Enter Joan and Merlin with a Book.

  Joan. Come, my dear *Merlin,* why dost
   thou fix thine eye
So deeply on that book?
  Merlin.   To sound the depth
Of Arts, of Learning, Wisdom, Knowledge.
  Joan. Oh, my dear, dear son,   25
Those studies fits thee when thou art a man.
  Merlin. Why, mother, I can be but half
a man at best,
And that is your mortality; the rest
In me is spirit; 'tis not meat, nor time,
That gives this growth and bigness; no, my
   years   30
Shall be more strange then yet my birth
   appears.
Look, mother, there's my Uncle.
  Joan. How doest thou know him, son? thou
never saw'st him.   34
  Merlin. Yet I know him, and know the
pains he has taken for ye, to finde out my
Father.—Give me your hand, good Uncle.
  Clown. Ha, ha, I'de laugh at that, yfaith.
Do you know me, sir?   39
  Merlin. Yes, by the same token that
even now you kist the swinherds-wife i'th'
woods, and would have done more, if she
would have let you, Uncle.   43
  Clown. A witch, a witch, a witch, sister:
rid him out of your company, he is either
a witch or a conjurer; he could never have
known this else.   47
  Joan. Pray, love him, brother, he is my son.
  Clown. Ha, ha, this is worse then all the
rest, yfaith; by his beard he is more like your
husband. Let me see, is your great belly gone?
  Joan. Yes, and this the happy fruit. 52
  Clown. What, this Hartichoke? A Childe
born with a beard on his face?
  Merlin. Yes, and strong legs to go, and
teeth to eat.   56
  Clown. You can nurse up your self, then?
There's some charges sav'd for Soap and
Caudle. 'Slid, I have heard of some that has
been born with teeth, but never none with
such a talking tongue before.   61
  Joan. Come, come, you must use him
kindly, brother;

Did you but know his worth, you would make
  much of him.
  Clown. Make much of a Moncky? This is
worse then *Tom Thumb,* that let a fart in his
Mothers belly; a Childe to speak, eat, and go
the first hour of his birth; nay, such a Baby
as had need of a Barber before he was born
too; why, sister, this is monstrous, and shames
all our kindred.   70
  Joan. That thus 'gainst nature and our
   common births
He comes thus furnisht to salute the world,
Is power of Fates, and gift of his great father.
  Clown. Why, of what profession is your
father, sir?   75
  Merlin. He keeps a Hot-house i'th' Low
Countries; will you see him, sir?
  Clown. See him? why, sister, has the childe
found his father?   79
  Mer. Yes, and Ile fetch him, Uncle. [*Exit.*
  Clown. Do not Uncle me, till I know your
kindred: for my conscience, some Baboon
begot thee.—Surely, thou art horribly deceiv'd,
sister, this Urchin cannot be of thy breeding;
I shall be asham'd to call him cousin, though
his father be a Gentleman.   86

   Enter Merlin and Devil.

  Merlin. Now, my kinde Uncle, see:
The Childe has found his Father, this is he.
  Clown. The devil it is; ha, ha, is this your
sweet-heart, sister? have we run through the
Countrey, haunted the City, and examin'd the
Court to finde out a Gallant with a Hat and
Feather, and a silken Sword, and golden
Hangers, and do you now bring me to a Raga-
muffin with a face like a Frying-pan? 95
  Joan. Fie, brother, you mistake, behold
him better.
  Clown. How's this? do you juggle with me,
or are mine eyes matches? Hat and Feather,
Sword, and Hangers, and all! this is a Gallant
indeed, sister; this has all the marks of him
we look for.   102
  Devil. And you have found him now, sir:
Give me your hand, I now must call you
brother.
  Clown. Not till you have married my sister,
for all this while she's but your whore, sir.
  Devil. Thou art too plain, Ile satisfie that
   wrong   107
To her, and thee, and all, with liberal hand:
Come, why art thou fearful?
  Clown. Nay, I am not afraid, and you were
the devil, sir.   111

---

35 Yet *Q* : Yes *D*   59 caudle *D* : Candle *Q*   82 for *Q* : fore *T*

Devil. Thou needst not; keep with thy
sister still,
And Ile supply your wants, you shall lack
nothing
That gold and wealth can purchase.   114
Clown. Thank you, brother: we have gone
many a weary step to finde you; you may be
a husband for a Lady, for you are far fetcht
and dear bought, I assure you. Pray, how
should I call your son, my cousin here?
Devil. His name is *Merlin.*   120
Clown. Merlin? Your hand, cousin *Merlin;*
for your fathers sake I accept you to my
kindred: if you grow in all things as your
Beard does, you will be talkt on. By your
Mothers side, cousin, you come of the *Go-too'ts,
Suffolk* bred, but our standing house is at
Hocklye i'th' Hole, and *Layton-buzzard.* For
your father, no doubt you may from him claim
Titles of Worship, but I cannot describe it;
I think his Ancestors came first from *Hell-bree*
in *Wales,* cousin.   131
Devil. No matter whence we do derive our
Name:
All *Brittany* shall ring of *Merlin's* fame,
And wonder at his acts. Go hence to *Wales,*
There live a while; there *Vortiger* the King
Builds Castles and strong Holds, which cannot
stand,   136
Unless supported by yong *Merlins* hand.
There shall thy fame begin: Wars are a
breeding;
The Saxons practise Treason, yet unseen,
Which shortly shall break out.—Fair Love,
farewell;   140
Dear son and brother, here must I leave you
all,
Yet still I will be near at *Merlins* call. [*Exit.*
Merl. Will you go, Uncle?
Clown. Yes, Ile follow you, cousin.—Well,
I do most horribly begin to suspect my kindred;
this brother in law of mine is the Devil, sure,
and though he hide his horns with his Hat and
Feather, I spi'd his cloven foot for all his
cunning.   [*Exit.*

⟨SCENE V.
The British Court.⟩
Enter Ostorius, Octa, and Proximus.

Ostor. Come, come, time calls our close
Complots to action.
Go, *Proximus* with winged speed flie hence,
Hye thee to *Wales:* salute great *Vortiger*
With these our Letters; bid the King to arms,
Tell him we have new friends, more Forces
landed   5

In *Norfolk* and *Northumberland;* bid him
Make haste to meet us; if he keep his word,
Wee'l part the Realm between us.
Octa. Bend all thine Art to quit that late
disgrace
The Christian Hermit gave thee; make thy
revenge   10
Both sure and home.
Prox.   That thought, sir, spurs me on,
Till I have wrought their swift destruction.
[*Exit.*
Ostor. Go, then, and prosper. *Octa,* be
vigilant:
Speak, are the Forts possest? the Guards made
sure?
Revolve, I pray, on how large consequence   15
The bare event and sequel of our hopes
Joyntly consists, that have embark't our lives
Upon the hazzard of the least miscarriage.
Octa. All's sure: the Queen your sister hath
contrived
The cunning Plot so sure, as at an instant   20
The Brothers shall be both surpriz'd and taken.
Ostor. And both shall die; yet one a while
must live,
Till we by him have gather'd strength and
power
To meet bold *Edol,* their stern General,
That now, contrary to the Kings command,   25
Hath re-united all his cashier'd Troops,
And this way beats his drums to threaten us.
Octa. Then our Plot's discover'd.
Ostor. Come, th'art a fool, his Army and
his life
Is given unto us: where is the Queen my sister?
Octa. In conference with the Prince.   31
Ostor. Bring the Guards nearer, all is fair
and good;
Their Conference, I hope, shall end in blood.
[*Exeunt.*

⟨SCENE VI.
A Room in the Palace.⟩
Enter Prince and Artesia.

Artes. Come, come, you do but flatter;
What you term Love is but a Dream of blood,
Wakes with enjoying, and with open eyes
Forgot, contemn'd, and lost.
Prince. I must be wary, her words are
dangerous.—   5
True, we'l speak of Love no more, then.
Artes. Nay, if you will, you may;
'Tis but in jest, and yet so children play
With fiery flames, and covet what is bright,
But, feeling his effects, abhor the light.   10

Pleasure is like a Building, the more high,
The narrower still it grows; Cedars do dye
Soonest at top.
   Prince.   How does your instance suit?
   Artes.   From Art and Nature to make sure
      the root,   15
And lay a fast foundation, e're I try
The incertain Changes of a wavering Skie.
Make your example thus.—You have a kiss,—
Was it not pleasing?
   Prince.   Above all name to express it.
   Artes.   Yet now the pleasure's gone,   20
And you have lost your joys possession.
   Prince.   Yet when you please, this flood
      may ebb again.
   Artes.   But where it never ebbs, there runs
      the main.
   Prince.   Who can attain such hopes?
   Artes.   Ile show the way to it, give you   25
A taste once more of what you may enjoy.
                            [*Kiss.*
   Prince.   Impudent whore!—
I were more false than Atheism can be,
Should I not call this high felicity.
   Artes.   If I should trust your faith, alas,
      I fear,   30
You soon would change belief.
   Prince.   I would covet Martyrdom to make't
      confirm'd.
   Artes.   Give me your hand on that you'l
      keep your word?
   Prince.   I will.
   Artes.   Enough: Help, husband, king
      Aurelius, help!   35
Rescue betraid *Artesia!*
   Prince.   Nay, then 'tis I that am betraid,
      I see;
Yet with thy blood Ile end thy Treachery.
   Artes.   How now! what troubles you? Is
      this you, sir,
That but even now would suffer Martyrdom 40
To win your hopes, and is there now such
      terror
In names of men to fright you? nay, then I see
What mettle you are made on.
   Prince.   Ha! was it but tryal? then I ask
      your pardon:
What a dull slave was I to be so fearful!—   45
Ile trust her now no more, yet try the utmost.—
I am resolved, no brother, no man breath-
      ing,
Were he my bloods begetter, should withhold
Me from your love; I'd leap into his bosom,
And from his brest pull forth that happiness 50
Heaven had reserved in you for my enjoying.

14 instance *T, etc.*: instanced *Q*   25 you *WP*:
me *Q*

   Artes.   I, now you speak a Lover like a
      Prince!—
Treason, treason!
   Prince.   Agen?
   Artes.   Help, Saxon Princes: Treason!   55

      Enter Ostorius, Octa &c.

   Ostor.   Rescue the Queen: strike down the
      Villain.

Enter Edoll, Aurelius, Donobert, Cador, Edwin,
   Toclio, Oswold, at the other Door.
   Edol.   Call in the Guards: the Prince in
      danger!
Fall back, dear Sir, my brest shall buckler you.
   Aurel.   Beat down their weapons!
   Edol.   Slave, wert thou made of brass, my
      sword shall bite thee.   ·   60
   Aurel.   Withdraw, on pain of death: where
      is the Traitor?
   Artes.   Oh, save your life, my Lord; let it
      suffice,
My beauty forc't mine own captivity.
   Aurel.   Who did attempt to wrong thee?
   Prince.   Hear me, Sir.
   Aurel.   Oh, my sad soul! was't thou?   65
   Artes.   Oh, do not stand to speak; one
      minutes stay
Prevents a second speech for ever.
   Aurel.   Make our Guards strong:
My dear *Artesia,* let us know thy wrongs
And our own dangers.   70
   Artes.   The Prince your brother, with these
      Brittain Lords,
Have all agreed to take me hence by force
And marry me to him.
   Prince.   The Devil shall wed thee first:
Thy baseness and thy lust confound and rot
      thee!   75
   Artes.   He courted me even now, and in
      mine ear
Sham'd not to plead his most dishonest love,
And their attempts to seize your sacred person,
Either to shut you up within some prison,
Or, which is worse, I fear, to murther you. 80
   Omnes Brittains.   'Tis all as false as hell.
   Edol.   And as foul as she is.
   Artes.   You know me, Sir?
   Edol.   Yes, Deadly Sin, we know you,
And shall discover all your villany.
   Aurel.   Chester, forbear!   85
   Ostor.   Their treasons, sir, are plain:
Why are their Souldiers lodg'd so near the
      Court?
   Octa.   Nay, why came he in arms so sud-
      denly?

66 stand *Q*: stay *T*   81 all as *om. T*

Edol. You fleering Anticks, do not wake my fury.

Octa. Fury!   90

Edol. Ratsbane, do not urge me.

Artes. Good sir, keep farther from them.

Prince Oh, my sick heart!

She is a witch by nature, devil by art.

Aurel. Bite thine own slanderous tongue; 'tis thou art false.   95

I have observ'd your passions long ere this.

Ostor Stand on your guard, my Lord, we are your friends,

And all our Force is yours.

Edol. To spoil and rob the Kingdom.

Aurel.   Sir, be silent.

Edol. Silent! how long? till Doomsday? shall I stand by,   100

And hear mine Honor blasted with foul Treason,

The State half lost, and your life endanger'd, Yet be silent?

Artes. Yes, my blunt Lord, unless you speak your Treasons.

Sir, let your Guards, as Traitors, seize them all, And then let tortures and devulsive racks 106

Force a Confession from them.

Edol. Wilde-fire and Brimstone eat thee! Hear me, sir.

Aurel. Sir, Ile not hear you.

Edol.   But you shall. Not hear me! Were the worlds Monarch, *Cesar,* living, he Should hear me.   111

I tell you, Sir, these serpents have betraid Your Life and Kingdom: does not every day Bring tidings of more swarms of lowsie slaves,

The offal fugitives of barren *Germany,*   115

That land upon our Coasts, and by our neglect Settle in *Norfolk* and *Northumberland?*

Ostor. They come as Aids and Safeguards to the King.

Octa. Has he not need, when *Vortiger's* in arms,

And you raise Powers, 'tis thought, to joyn with him?   120

Edol. Peace, you pernicious Rat.

Dono.   Prithee, forbear.

Edol. Away! suffer a gilded rascal, A low-bred despicable creeper, an insulting Toad,

To spit his poison'd venome in my face!

Octa. Sir, sir!   125

Edol. Do not reply, you Cur; for, by the Gods,

Tho' the Kings presence guard thee, I shall break all patience,

And, like a Lion rous'd to spoil, shall run Foul-mouth'd upon thee, and devour thee quick.—   129

Speak, sir: will you forsake these scorpions, Or stay till they have stung you to the heart?

Aurel. Y'are traitors all. This is our wife, our Queen:

Brother *Ostorius,* troop your *Saxons* up, We'l hence to *Winchester,* ⟨and⟩ raise more powers,   134

To man with strength the Castle *Camilot.*— Go hence, false men, joyn you with *Vortiger,* The murderer of our brother *Constantine :* We'l hunt both him and you with dreadful vengance.

Since *Brittain* fails, we'l trust to forrain friends,

And guard our person from your traitorous ends.   140

[*Exeunt Aurel., Ostor., Octa, Artes., Toc., Osw.*

Edwin. He's sure bewitcht.

Glost.   What counsel now for safety?

Dono. Onely this, sir: with all the speed we can,

Preserve the person of the King and Kingdom.

Cador. Which to effect, 'tis best march hence to *Wales,*

And set on *Vortiger* before he joyn   145

His Forces with the *Saxons.*

Edwin. On, then, with speed for *Wales* and *Vortiger!*

That tempest once o'reblown, we come, *Ostorius,*   148

To meet thy traiterous *Saxons,* thee and them, That with advantage thus have won the King, To back your factions and to work our ruines. This, by the Gods and my good Sword, I'le set

In bloody lines upon thy Burgonet. [*Exeunt.*

ACT 4.

SCENE I.

⟨*Before a Ruined Castle in Wales.*⟩

Enter Clown, Merlin, and a little antick Spirit.

Mer. How now, Uncle? why do you search your pockets so? Do you miss any thing?

Clown. Ha! Cousin *Merlin,* I hope your beard does not overgrow your honesty; I pray, remember, you are made up of sisters thread; I am your mothers brother, whosoever was your father.   7

102-3 *One line D*   102 and *om. WP*   103 Yet]
And yet *WP*   114 slaves] knaves *T*   116 and]
and have *T*   117 Settle *pr. ed.* : Settled *Q, etc.*

134 and *add.* Molt., *WP*   141 bewitch *Q*   S. D.
Before *etc. add. T*   5 of] of my *D*

Merlin. Why, wherein can you task my duty, Uncle?

Clown. Your self or your page it must be, I have kept no other company, since your mother bound your head to my Protectorship; I do feel a fault of one side; either it was that Sparrowhawk, or a Cast of *Merlins,* for I finde a Covy of Cardecu's sprung out of my pocket.

Merlin. Why, do you want any money, Uncle? Sirrah, had you any from him?   17

Clown. Deny it not, for my pockets are witness against you.

Spirit. Yes, I had, to teach you better wit to look to it.   21

Clown. Pray, use your fingers better, and my wit may serve as it is, sir.

Merlin. Well, restore it.

Spirit. There it is.   25

Clown. I, there's some honesty in this; 'twas a token from your invisible Father, Cousin, which I would not have to go invisibly from me agen.

Mer. Well, you are sure you have it now, Uncle?   31

Clown. Yes, and mean to keep it now from your pages filching fingers too.

Spirit. If you have it so sure, pray show it me agen.   35

Clown. Yes, my little juggler, I dare show it. Ha, cleanly conveyance agen! ye have no invisible fingers, have ye? 'Tis gone, certainly.

Spirit. Why, sir, I toucht you not.   40

Mer. Why, look you, Uncle, I have it now: how ill do you look to it! here, keep it safer.

Clown. Ha, ha, this is fine, yfaith. I must keep some other company, if you have these slights of hand.   45

Merlin. Come, come, Uncle, 'tis all my Art, which shall not offend you, sir, onely I give you a taste of it to show you sport.

Clown. Oh, but 'tis ill jesting with a mans pocket, tho'. But I am glad to see you cunning, Cousin, for now will I warrant thee a living till thou diest. You have heard the news in *Wales* here?   53

Mer. Uncle, let me prevent your care and counsel,
'Twill give you better knowledge of my cunning.
You would prefer me now, in hope of gain,
To *Vortiger,* King of the Welch *Brittains,*
To whom are all the Artists summon'd now,
That seeks the secrets of futurity: 59
The Bards, the Druids, Wizards, Conjurers,

Not an Auraspex with his whisling spells,
No Capnomanster with his musty fumes,
No Witch or Juggler, but is thither sent,
To calculate the strange and fear'd event
Of his prodigious Castle, now in building,   65
Where all the labors of the painful day
Are ruin'd still i'th' night, and to this place
You would have me go.   68

Clown. Well, if thy mother were not my sister, I would say she was a witch that begot thee; but this is thy father, not thy mother wit. Thou hast taken my tale into thy mouth, and spake my thoughts before me; therefore away, shuffle thy self amongst the Conjurers, and be a made man before thou comest to age.   75

Mer. Nay, but stay, Uncle, you overslip my dangers:
The Prophecies and all the cunning Wizards
Have certifi'd the King that this his Castle
Can never stand, till the foundation's laid
With Mortar temper'd with the fatal blood   80
Of such a childe whose father was no mortal.

Clown. What's this to thee? If the devil were thy father, was not thy mother born at *Carmarden?* Diggon for that, then; and then it must be a childes blood, and who will take thee for a childe with such a beard of thy face? Is there not diggon for that too, Cousin?   87

Merlin. I must not go: lend me your ear a while,
I'le give you reasons to the contrary.

Enter two Gentlemen.

1. *Gentle.* Sure, this is an endless piece of work the King has sent us about!   91

2. *Gentle.* Kings may do it, man; the like has been done to finde out the Unicorn.

1. *Gentle.* Which will be sooner found, I think, then this fiend begotten childe we seek for.   96

2. *Gentle.* Pox of those Conjurers that would speak of such a one, and yet all their cunning could not tell us where to finde him.

1. *Gentle.* In *Wales* they say assuredly he lives; come, let's enquire further.   101

Mer. Uncle, your perswasions must not prevail with me: I know mine enemies better then you do.

Clown. I say, th'art a bastard then, if thou disobey thine Uncle: was not *Joan Go-too't,* thy mother, my sister? If the devil were thy father, what kin art thou to any man alive

15 Covy] *Some copies of* Q *appear to read* Cony   50
you Q : your D, *etc.*

61 Aurasper Q : Aruspex T, *etc.*   62 Capuomanster Q : Capnomancer T, *etc.*   65 his] this T   71 thee T, *etc.* : this Q   73 spoke my words D   100 say] said T

but Bailys and Brokers? and they are but brothers in Law to thee neither.   110
1. *Gentle.* How's this? I think we shall speed here.
2. *Gentle.* I, and unlook't for too: go ne're and listen to them.   114
Clown. Hast thou a beard to hide it? wil't thou show thy self a childe? wil't thou have more hair then wit? Wil't thou deny thy mother, because no body knows thy father? Or shall thine Uncle be an ass?   119
1. *Gentle.* Bless ye, friend: pray, what call you this small Gentlemans name?
Clown. Small, sir? a small man may be a great Gentleman; his father may be of an ancient house, for ought we know, sir.   124
2. *Gentle.* Why? do you not know his father?
Clown. No, nor you neither, I think, unless the devil be in ye.
1. *Gentle.* What is his name, sir?
Clown. His name is my Cousin, sir, his education is my sisters son, but his maners are his own.   131
Merlin. Why ask ye, Gentlemen? my name is *Merlin.*
Clown. Yes, and a Goshawk was his father, for ought we know; for I am sure his mother was a Wind-sucker.   136
2. *Gentle.* He has a mother, then?
Clown. As sure as I have a sister, sir.
1. *Gentle.* But his father you leave doubtful.
Clown. Well, Sir, as wise men as you doubt whether he had a father or no?   141
1. *Gentle.* Sure, this is he we seek for.
2. *Gent.* I think no less: and, sir, we let you know
The King hath sent for you.
Clown. The more childe he; and he had bin rul'd by me,   145
He should have gone before he was sent for.
1. *Gent.* May we not see his mother?
Clown. Yes, and feel her too, if you anger her; a devilish thing, I can tell ye, she has been. Ile go fetch her to ye.   [*Exit.*
2. *Gent.* Sir, it were fit you did resolve for speed,   151
You must unto the King.
Mer.   My Service, sir,
Shall need no strict command, it shall obey
Most peaceably; but needless 'tis to fetch
What is brought home: my journey may be staid,   155
The King is coming hither
With the same quest you bore before him; hark,

115-16 Wilt then show *D*

This drum will tell ye.
     [*Within* Drums beat a low March.
1. *Gent.* This is some cunning indeed, sir.
Florish. Enter *Vortiger, reading a letter,*
Proximus, with Drum and Soldiers, &c.
Vorti. Still in our eye your message,
Proximus,   160
We keep to spur our speed:
Ostorius and *Octa* we shall salute
With succor against Prince *Vter* and *Aurelius,*
Whom now we hear incamps at *Winchester.*
There's nothing interrupts our way so much
As doth the erection of this fatal Castle,   166
That spite of all our Art and daily labor,
The night still ruines.
Prox. As erst I did affirm, still I maintain,
The fiend begotten childe must be found out,
Whose blood gives strength to the foundation;
It cannot stand else.

     Enter *Clown and Joan, Merlin.*

Vorti.   Ha! Is't so?   172
Then, *Proximus,* by this intelligence
He should be found: speak, is this he you tell of?
Clown. Yes, Sir, and I his Uncle, and she his mother.   176
Vorti. And who is his father?
Clown. Why, she, his mother, can best tell you that, and yet I think the childe be wise enough, for he has found his father.   180
Vort. Woman, is this thy son?
Joan. It is, my Lord.
Vor. What was his father? Or where lives he?
Merl. Mother, speak freely and unastonisht;   184
That which you dar'd to act, dread not to name.
Joan. In which I shall betray my sin and shame.
But since it must be so, then know, great King,
All that my self yet knows of him is this:
In pride of blood and beauty I did live,   189
My glass the Altar was, my face the Idol;
Such was my peevish love unto my self,
That I did hate all other; such disdain
Was in my scornful eye that I suppos'd
No mortal creature worthy to enjoy me.
Thus with the Peacock I beheld my train,   195
But never saw the blackness of my feet;
Oft have I chid the winds for breathing on me,
And curst the Sun, fearing to blast my beauty.
In midst of this most leaprous disease,
A seeming fair yong man appear'd unto me,

164 encamp'd *D*   166 fatal *Q*: famous *T*   172
S. D. Joan, joining Merlin *WP*

In all things suiting my aspiring pride,   201
And with him brought along a conquering
     power,
To which my frailty yielded; from whose
     embraces
This issue came; what more he is, I know
     not.   204
Vorti. Some *Incubus* or Spirit of the night
Begot him then, for, sure, no mortal did it.
     Mer. No matter who, my Lord; leave
     further quest,
Since 'tis as hurtful as unnecessary
More to enquire: Go to the cause, my Lord,
Why you have sought me thus?   210
Vorti. I doubt not but thou knowst; yet, to
     be plain,
I sought thee for thy blood.
     Mer. By whose direction?
     Prox. By mine;
My Art infalable instructed me,   215
Upon thy blood must the foundation rise
Of the Kings building; it cannot stand else.
     Mer. Hast thou such leisure to enquire my
     Fate,
And let thine own hang careless over thee?
Knowst thou what pendelous mischief roofs
     thy head,   220
How fatal, and how sudden?
     Prox. Pish!
Bearded abortive, thou foretel my danger!
My Lord, he trifles to delay his own.
     Mer. No, I yield my self: and here before
     the King   225
Make good thine Augury, as I shall mine.
If thy fate fall not, thou hast spoke all truth,
And let my blood satisfie the Kings desires:
If thou thy self wilt write thine Epitaph,
Dispatch it quickly, there's not a minutes
     time   230
'Twixt thee and thy death.
     Prox. Ha, ha, ha!
          [*A stone falls and kills Proximus.*
     Mer. I, so thou mayest die laughing.
     Vorti. Ha! This is above admiration: look,
is he dead?   235
     Clown. Yes, sir, here's brains to make morter
on, if you'l use them. Cousin *Merlin,* there's
no more of this stone fruit ready to fall, is
there? I pray, give your Uncle a little fair
warning.   240
     Mer. Remove that shape of death. And
     now, my Lord,
For clear satisfaction of your doubts,
Merlin will show the fatal cause that keeps

Your Castle down and hinders your proceed-
     ings.
Stand there, and by an apparition see   245
The labor and end of all your destiny.
Mother and Uncle, you must be absent.
     Clown. Is your father coming, Cousin?
     Mer. Nay, you must be gone.   249
     Joan. Come, you'l offend him, brother.
     Clown. I would fain see my Brother i'law;
if you were married, I might lawfully call him
so.   ⟨*Exeunt Joan and Clown.*⟩ *Merlin
          strikes his wand. Thunder and
          Lightning; two Dragons appear, a
          White and a Red; they fight a while,
          and pause.*
     Vor. What means this stay?
     Mer. Be not amaz'd, my Lord, for on the
     victory,   255
Of loss or gain, as these two Champions ends,
Your fate, your life, and kingdom all depends;
Therefore observe it well.
     Vor. I shall: heaven be auspicious to us.
          [*Thunder: The two Dragons fight
          agen, and the White Dragon drives
          off the Red.*
     Vor. The conquest is on the white Dragons
     part.   260
Now, *Merlin,* faithfully expound the meaning.
     Mer. Your Grace must then not be offended
     with me.
     Vor. It is the weakest part I found in thee,
To doubt of me so slightly. Shall I blame
My prophet that foretells me of my dangers?
Thy cunning I approve most excellent.   266
     Mer. Then know, my Lord, there is a
     dampish Cave,
The nightly habitation of these Dragons,
Vaulted beneath where you would build your
     Castle,
Whose enmity and nightly combats there   270
Maintain a constant ruine of your labors.
To make it more plain, the Dragons, then,
Your self betoken and the *Saxon* King;
The vanquisht Red is, sir, your dreadful
     Emblem.
     Vort. Oh, my fate!   275
     Mer. Nay, you must hear with patience,
     Royal sir.
You slew the lawful King *Constantius:*
'Twas a red deed, your Crown his blood did
     cement.
The English *Saxon,* first brought in by you
For aid against *Constantius* brethren,   280

244 your Castle *T, etc.* your fatal Castle *Q*   246
and the end *WP*   *S. D.* Exeunt .. Clown *add. T*
space *T*   231 Betwixt *WP*   *S. D. after* 231 *Q*
254 stay] play *conj. Elze*   263 Is it *D*   found]
242-3 *End* show, down *D : corr. pr. ed.*   found *T*   271 our labour *T*

Is the white horror who now, knit together,
Have driven and shut you up in these wilde
    mountains;
And though they now seek to unite with
    friendship,
It is to wound your bosom, not embrace it,
And with an utter extirpation   285
To rout the *Brittains* out, and plant the
    English.
Seek for your safety, Sir, and spend no time
To build the(e) airy Castles; for Prince *Vter*,
Armed with vengeance for his brothers blood,
Is hard upon you. If you mistrust me,   290
And to my words crave witness, sir, then
    know,
Here comes a messenger to tell you so.
                    [*Exit Mer.*

Enter Messenger.

Messen. My Lord! Prince *Vter!*
Vort. And who else, sir?
Messen. *Edol,* the great General.   295
Vort. The great Devil! they are coming to
    meet us?
Messen. With a full power, my Lord.
Vort.   With a full vengeance,
They mean to meet us; so! we are ready
To their confront. At full march, double
    footing,
We'l loose no ground, nor shall their numbers
    fright us: 300
If it be Fate, it cannot be withstood;
We got our Crown so, be it lost in blood.
                    [*Exeunt.*
                (Scene II.
    Open Country in Wales.)
*Enter Prince Vter, Edol, Cador, Edwin, Toclio,
    with Drum and Soldiers.*

Prince. Stay, and advice; hold, drum!
Edol. Beat, slave! why do you pause?
Why make a stand? where are our enemies?
Or do you mean we fight amongst our selves?
Prince. Nay, noble *Edol,*   5
Let us here take counsel, it cannot hurt,
It is the surest Garison to safety.
Edol. Fie on such slow delays! so fearful
    men,
That are to pass over a flowing river,
Stand on the bank to parly of the danger, 10
Till the tide rise, and then be swallowed.
Is not the King in field?
    Cador. Proud *Vortiger,* the Trator, is in
    field.

Edwin. The Murderer and Usurper.
Edol. Let him be the devil, so I may fight
    with him.   15
For heavens love, sir, march on! Oh, my
    patience!
Will you delay, untill the *Saxons* come
To aid his party?   [*A Tucket.*
Prince. There's no such fear: prithee, be
    calm a while.   19
Hark! it seems by this, he comes or sends to us.
Edol. If it be for parly, I will drown the
    summons,
If all our drums and hoarseness choke me not.

Enter Captain.

Prince. Nay, prithee, hear.—From whence
    art thou?
Cap. From the King *Vortiger,*
Edol. Traitor, there's none such: Alarum,
    drum; strike, slave,   25
Or, by mine honor, I will break thy head,
And beat thy drums heads both about thine
    ears.
Prince. Hold, noble *Edol,*
Let's hear what Articles he can inforce.
Edol. What articles or what conditions 30
Can you expect to value half your wrong,
Unless he kill himself by thousand tortures,
And send his carcase to appease your ven-
    geance
For the foul murder of *Constantius,*
And that's not a tenth part neither.   35
Prince. 'Tis true,
My brothers blood is crying to me now;
I do applaud thy counsel: hence, be gone!—
                    [*Exit Capt.*
We'l hear no parly now but by our swords.
Edol. And those shall speak home in death
    killing words: 40
Alarum to the fight; sound, sound the
    Alarum.   [*Exeunt.*

                (Scene III.
    A Field of Battle.)

*Alarum.   Enter Edol, driving all Vortigers
    Force before him, then Exit. Enter Prince
    Vter pursuing Vortiger.*

Vort. Dost follow me?
Prince.   Yes, to thy death I will.
Vort. Stay, be advis'd;
I would not be the onely fall of Princes,
I slew thy brother.

289 To rout *Q*: Drive *T*   288 thee *pr. ed.*: the *Q,*
etc.   291 craves *Q*   299 confront as full *Q*: *corr.*
D   Scene II. *etc. add. T*   11 then *Q*: they *T*

16–17 *End* on, delay *WP*: *corr. pr. ed.*   22 me
repeated Q   27 drums heads *Q*: drumsticks *D*
38 appaud *Q*   thy] your *T*   counsels *D*   Scene III.
etc. add. T   1 thy *Q*: the *T*   3 I *Q*: It *D*

Prince. Thou didst, black Traitor,   5
And in that vengeance I pursue thee.
Vort. Take mercy for thy self, and flie my
  sword,
Save thine own life as satisfaction,
Which here I give thee for thy brothers death.
Prince. Give what's thine own: a Traitors
  heart and head,   10
That's all thou art right Lord of. The King-
  dom
Which thou usurp'st, thou most unhappy
  Tyrant,
Is leaving thee; the Saxons which thou
  broughtst
To back thy usurpations, are grown great,
And where they seat themselves, do hourly
  seek   15
To blot the Records of old *Brute* and *Brittains*
From memory of men, calling themselves
Hingest-men, and *Hingest-land,* that no more
The *Brittain* name be known: all this by thee,
Thou base destroyer of thy Native Countrey.

Enter Edol.

Edol. What, stand you talking?   [*Fight.*
Prince. Hold, *Edol.*
Ed. Hold out, my sword,
And listen not to King or Princes word; 24
There's work enough abroad, this task is mine.
                                  [*Alarum.*
Prince. Prosper thy Valour, as thy Vertues
  shine.   [*Exeunt.*

⟨Scene IV.

Another Part of the Field of Battle.⟩

Enter Cador and Edwin.

Cador. Bright Victory her self fights on our
  part,
And, buckled in a golden Beaver, rides
Triumphantly before us.
Edw. Justice is with her,
Who ever takes the true and rightful cause. 5
Let us not lag behinde them.

Enter Prince.

Cador. Here comes the Prince. How goes
  our fortunes, Sir?
Prince. Hopeful and fair, brave *Cador.*
Proud *Vortiger,* beat down by *Edols* sword,
Was rescu'd by the following multitudes, 10
And now for safety's fled unto a Castle
Here standing on the hill: but I have sent

A cry of hounds as violent as hunger,
To break his stony walls; or, if they fail,
We'l send in wilde fire to dislodge him thence,
Or burn them all with flaming violence.   16
                                  [*Exeunt.*

⟨Scene V.

Another Part of the Field.⟩

Blazing Star appears.

*Florish Tromp. Enter Prince Vter, Edol,
Cador, Edwin, Toclio, with Drum and
Soldiers.*

Prin. Look, *Edol:*
Still this fiery exalation shoots
His frightful horrors on th'amazed world;
See, in the beam that's 'bout his flaming
  ring,
A Dragons head appears, from out whose
  mouth   5
Two flaming flakes of fire stretch East and
  West.
Edol. And see, from forth the body of the
  Star
Seven smaller blazing streams directly point
On this affrighted kingdom.
Cador. 'Tis a dreadful Meteor.   10
Edwin. And doth portend strange fears.
Prince. This is no Crown of Peace; this
  angry fire
Hath something more to burn then *Vortiger;*
If it alone were pointed at his fall,
It would pull in his blasing Piramids   15
And be appeas'd, for *Vortiger* is dead.
Edol. These never come without their large
  effects.
Prince. The will of heaven be done! our
  sorrow's this,
We want a mistick *Pithon* to expound
This fiery Oracle.
Cador.   Oh no, my Lord,   20
You have the best that ever *Brittain* bred;
And durst I prophecy of your Prophet, sir,
None like him shall succeed him.
Prince. You mean *Merlin?*
Cador. True, sir, wonderous *Merlin;*   25
He met us in the way, and did foretell
The fortunes of this day successful to us.
Edwin. He's sure about the Camp; send
  for him, sir.
Cador. He told the bloody *Vortiger* his
  fate,
And truely too, and if I could give faith 30
To any Wizards skill, it should be *Merlin.*

5 *Ends* didst *WP*   7 flie] flec *T*   18 and Brittain
Hingest-land *WP*   21 *S. D.* Fight *printed as part*
of Edol's speech D   Scene IV. *D: no new scene T*
Another *etc. add. WP*

Scene V] Scene IV *etc. T*   *S. D.* with *repeated Q*
1–2 *One line D: corr. Elze*   4 that's *T:* that *Q*   6
flakes *Q:* snakes *T*   15 his *Q:* its *T*

811663   377   E e

Enter Merlin and Clown.

Cador. And see, my Lord, as if to satisfie
Your Highness pleasure, *Merlin* is come.
Prince. See,
The Comet's in his eye, disturb him not.   35
Edol. With what a piercing judgement he
beholds it!
Mer. Whither will Heaven and Fate trans-
late this Kingdom?
What revolutions, rise and fall of Nations
Is figur'd yonder in that Star, that sings
The change of *Brittians* State and death of
Kings?   40
Ha! He's dead already; how swiftly mischief
creeps!
Thy fatal end, sweet Prince, even *Merlin*
weeps.
Prince. He does foresee some evil, his
action shows it,   43
For, e're he does expound, he weeps the story.
Edol. There's another weeps too. Sirrah,
dost thou understand what thou lamentst for?
Clown. No, sir, I am his Uncle, and weep
because my Cousin weeps; flesh and blood
cannot forbear.
Prince. Gentle *Merlin,* speak thy prophetick
knowledge   50
In explanation of this fiery horror,
From which we gather from thy mournful
tears
Much sorrow and disaster in it.
Mer. 'Tis true,
Fair Prince, but you must hear the rest with
patience.   55
Prince. I vow I will, tho' it portend my
ruine.
Mer. There's no such fear.
This brought the fiery fall of *Vortiger,*
And yet not him alone: this day is faln
A King more good, the glory of our Land,   60
The milde and gentle, sweet *Aurelius.*
Prince. Our brother!
Edwin. Forefend it heaven!
Mer. He at his Palace Royal, sir,   64
At *Winchester,* this day is dead and poison'd.
Cador. By whom? Or what means, *Merlin?*
Mer. By the Traiterous Saxons.
Edol. I ever fear'd as much: that devil
Ostorius
And the damn'd witch *Artesia,* sure, has done it.
Prince. Poison'd! oh, look further, gentle
Merlin,   70

Behold the Star agen, and do but finde
Revenge for me, though it cost thousand lives,
And mine the foremost.
Mer. Comfort your self, the heavens have
given it fully:
All the portentious ills to you is told.   75
Now hear a happy story, sir, from me
To you and to your fair posterity.
Clown. Me thinks, I see something like
a peel'd Onion; it makes me weep agen.   79
Mer. Be silent, Uncle, you'l be forc't else.
Clown. Can you not finde in the Star, Cousin,
whether I can hold my tongue or no?
Edol. Yes, I must cut it out.
Clown. Phu, you speak without book, sir,
my Cousin *Merlin* knows.   85
Mer. True, I must tie it up. Now speak
your pleasure, Uncle.
Clown. Hum, hum, hum, hum.
Mer. So, so.—
Now observe, my Lord, and there behold,   90
Above yon flame-hair'd beam that upward
shoots,
Appears a Dragons head, out of whose mouth
Two streaming lights point their flame-fea-
ther'd darts
Contrary ways, yet both shall have their aims:
Again behold, from the ignifirent body   95
Seven splendant and illustrious rays are spred,
All speaking Heralds to this *Brittain* Isle,
And thus they are expounded: The Dragons
head
Is the Herogliphick that figures out   99
Your Princely self, that here must reign a King;
Those by-form'd fires that from the Dragons
mouth
Shoot East and West, emblem two Royal babes,
Which shall proceed from you, a son and
daughter.
Her pointed constellation, Northwest bending,
Crowns Her a Queen in *Ireland,* of whom first
springs   105
That Kingdoms Title to the *Brittain* Kings.
Clown. Hum, hum, hum.
Mer. But of your Son thus Fate and *Merlin*
tells:
All after times shall fill their Chronicles
With fame of his renown, whose warlike
sword   110
Shall pass through fertile *France* and *Germany;*
Nor shall his conquering foot be forc't to
stand,
Till *Romes* Imperial Wreath hath crown'd his
Fame

32-3 *Three lines* D, *div. after* Lord, pleasure : *corr.*
pr. ed.   40 State *Q* : fate *T*   52 By which *Molt.*
56 *Prefix* Mer *Q*   59 him] his *conj. Elze*   66
what] by what *T*

79 Oinon *Q*   84 Phu *Q* : O, ha *D*   95 ignifirent
Q : ignisirent *T* : igniferous *D*   104 bending *Q* :
tending *D*   112 conquering *T, etc.* : conjuring *Q*

With Monarch of the West, from whose seven
hills,
With Conquest and contributory Kings,   115
He back returns to inlarge the *Brittain* bounds,
His Heraldry adorn'd with thirteen Crowns.
Clown. Hum, hum, hum.
Mer. He to the world shall add another
Worthy,
And, as a Loadstone, for his prowess draw 120
A train of Marshal Lovers to his Court:
It shall be then the best of Knight-hoods
honor,
At *Winchester* to fill his Castle Hall,
And at his Royal Table sit and feast   124
In warlike orders, all their arms round hurl'd,
As if they meant to circumscribe the world.
[*he touches the Clowns mouth with his wand.*
Clown. Hum, hum, hum: oh, that I could
speak a little!
Mer. I know your mind, Uncle; agen be
silent.   [*strikes agen.*
Prince. Thou speakst of wonders, *Merlin;*
prithee, go on,
Declare at full this Constellation.   130
Mer. Those seven beams pointing down-
ward, sir, betoken
The troubles of this Land, which then shall
meet
With other Fate: War and Dissension strives
To make division, till seven Kings agree
To draw this Kingdom to a Hepterchy.   135
Prince. Thine art hath made such proof
that we believe
Thy words authentical: be ever neer us,
My Prophet and the Guide of all my actions.
Mer. My service shall be faithful to your
person,
And all my studies for my Countries safety. 140
Clown. Hum, hum, hum.
Mer. Come, you are releast, sir.
Clown. Cousin, pray, help me to my tongue
agen; you do not mean I shall be dumb still,
I hope?   145
Mer. Why, hast thou not thy tongue?
Clown. Ha! yes, I feel it now, I was so long
dumb, I could not well tell whether I spake
or no.
Prince. Is't thy advice we presently pur-
sue   149
The bloody *Saxons,* that have slain my brother?
Mer. With your best speed, my Lord;
Prosperity will keep you company.
Cador. Take, then, your Title with you,
Royal Prince,
'Twill adde unto our strength: *Long live King
Uter!*   155

153 you *Q* : your *T*

Edol. Put the Addition to't that Heaven
hath given you:
The DRAGON is your Emblem, bear it bravely,
And so live long and ever happy, styl'd
Vter-Pendragon, lawful King of *Brittain.*
Prince. Thanks, *Edol,* we imbrace the
name and title,   160
And in our Sheild and Standard shall the figure
Of a Red Dragon still be born before us,
To fright the bloody Saxons. Oh, my *Aurelius,*
Sweet rest thy soul; let thy disturbed spirit
Expect reveng'e; think what it would, it hath:
The Dragon's coming in his fiery wrath.   166
                    [*Exeunt.*

ACT 5.

SCENE I.

⟨*A barren Waste, a huge Rock appearing.*⟩
Thunder, then Musick.
Enter Joan fearfully, the Devil following her.

Joan. Hence, thou black horror! is thy
lustful fire
Kindled agen? Not thy loud throated thunder
Nor thy adulterate infernal Musick
Shall e're bewitch me more: oh, too too
much
Is past already.   5
Devil. Why dost thou fly me?
I come a Lover to thee, to imbrace
And gently twine thy body in mine arms.
Joan. Out, thou Hell-hound!
Devil. What hound so e're I be,   10
Fawning and sporting as I would with thee,
Why should I not be stroakt and plaid withal?
Will't thou not thank the Lion might devour
thee,
If he shall let thee pass?
Joan. Yes, thou art he;
Free me, and Ile thank thee.
Devil. Why, whither wouldst?
I am at home with thee, thou art mine own,
Have we not charge of family together?   17
Where is your son?
Joan. Oh, darkness cover me!
Devil. There is a pride which thou hast
won by me,
The mother of a fame, shall never die.   20
Kings shall have need of written Chronicles
To keep their names alive, but *Merlin* none;
Ages to ages shall like *Sabalists*
Report the wonders of his name and glory,
While there are tongues and times to tell his
story.   25
Joan. Oh, rot my memory before my flesh,

158 live long *T* : long live *Q*   S. D. A barren *etc.*
add. *T*   23 Sabalists *Q* : satellites *D*

Let him be called some hell or earth-bred
   monster,
That ne're had hapless woman for a mother!
Sweet death, deliver me! Hence from my sight:
Why shouldst thou now appear? I had no
   pride   30
Nor lustful thought about me, to conjure
And call thee to my ruine, when as at first
Thy cursed person became visible.
Devil. I am the same I was.
Joan.   But I am chang'd.
Devil. Agen Ile change thee to the same
   thou wert,   35
To quench my lust.—Come forth, by thunder
   led,
My Coajutors in the spoils of mortals. [*Thunder.*

Enter Spirit.

Claspe in your Ebon arms that prize of mine,
Mount her as high as palled *Hecate;*
And on this rock Ile stand to cast up fumes 40
And darkness o're the blew fac'd firmament:
From *Brittain* and from *Merlin* Ile remove her.
They ne're shall meet agen.
Joan. Help me some saving hand,
If not too late, I cry: let mercy come!   45

Enter Merlin.

Mer. Stay, you black slaves of night, let
   loose your hold,
Set her down safe, or by th'infernal Stix,
Ile binde you up with exorcisms so strong,
That all the black pentagoron of hell   49
Shall ne're release you. Save your selves and
   vanish!   [*Exit Spirit.*
Devil. Ha! What's he?
Mer. The Childe has found his Father. Do
   you not know me?
Devil. Merlin!
Joan. Oh, help me, gentle son.
Mer. Fear not, they shall not hurt you. 55
Devil. Relievest thou her to disobey thy
   father?
Mer. Obedience is no lesson in your school;
Nature and kind to her commands my duty;
The part that you begot was against kinde,
So all I ow to you is to be unkind.   60
Devil. Ile blast thee, slave, to death, and
   on this rock
Stick thee ⟨as⟩ an eternal Monument.
Mer. Ha, ha, thy powers too weak; what
   art thou, devil,
But an inferior lustful *Incubus,*
Taking advantage of the wanton flesh,   65

Wherewith thou dost beguile the ignorant?
Put off the form of thy humanity,
And cral upon thy speckled belly, serpent,
Or Ile unclasp the jaws of *Achoron,*
And fix thee ever in the local fire.   70
Devil. Traitor to hell! curse that I e're
   begot thee!
Mer. Thou didst beget thy scourge: storm
   not, nor stir;
The power of *Merlins* Art is all confirm'd
In the Fates decretals. Ile ransack hell,
And make thy masters bow unto my spells. 75
Thou first shall taste it.—
        [*Thunder and Lightning in the Rock.*
*Tenibrarum princeps, devitiarum & infirorum
Deus, hunc Incubum in ignis eterni abisum
accipite, aut in hoc carcere tenebroso in sempe-
ternum astringere mando.*   80
        [*the Rock incloses him.*
Sol there beget earthquakes or some noisom
   damps,
For never shalt thou touch a woman more.—
How chear you, mother?
Joan. Oh, now my son is my deliverer, 84
Yet I must name him with my deepest sorrow.
        [*Alarum afar off.*
Mer. Take comfort now: past times are
   ne're recal'd;
I did foresee your mischief, and prevent it.
Hark, how the sounds of war now call me
   hence
To aid *Pendragon* that in battail stands
Against the Saxons, from whose aid   90
Merlin must not be absent. Leave this
   soyl,
And Ile conduct you to a place retir'd,
Which I by art have rais'd, call'd *Merlins
Bower.*
There shall you dwell with solitary sighs,
With grones and passions your companions,
To weep away this flesh you have offended
   with,   96
And leave all bare unto your aierial soul:
And when you die, I will erect a Monument
Upon the verdant Plains of *Salisbury,*
No King shall have so high a sepulchre,   100
With pendulous stones that I will hang by
   art,
Where neither Lime nor Morter shalbe us'd,
A dark *Enigma* to the memory,
For none shall have the power to number
   them,—
A place that I will hollow for your rest,   105

28 a] his *T*   36 quench to *Q*   *S. D.* Spirits *D,*
etc.   50 your] you *Q*   *S. D.* Exeunt Spirits *D,*
etc.   62 an *Q* : as an *D*

75 master *T*   spell *D*   76 shalt *T, etc.*   77
princeps *conj.* Elze : precis *Q*   81 some *om. D*
103 the *Q* : thy *T* : men's *conj.* WP   105 hollow *Q* :
hallow *T, etc.*

Where no Night-hag shall walk, nor Ware-
wolf tread,
Where *Merlins* Mother shall be sepulcher'd.
                        [*Exeunt.*

⟨Scene II.
The British Camp.⟩
Enter Donobert, Gloster, and Hermit.

Dono. Sincerely, *Gloster,* I have told you
all:
My Daughters are both vow'd to Single Life,
And this day gone unto the Nunnery,
Though I begot them to another end,
And fairly promis'd them in Marriage,   5
One to Earl *Cador,* t'other to your son,
My worthy friend, the Earl of *Gloster.*
Those lost, I am lost: they are lost, all's
lost.
Answer me this, then: Ist a sin to marry?
Hermit. Oh no, my Lord.   10
Dono. Go to, then, Ile go no further with
you;
I perswade you to no ill; perswade you, then,
That I perswade you well.
Gloster. 'Twill be a good Office in you, sir.

Enter Cador and Edwin.

Dono. Which since they thus neglect,   15
My memory shall lose them now for ever.—
See, see, the Noble Lords, their promis'd Hus-
bands!
Had Fate so pleas'd, you might have call'd me
Father.
Edwin. Those hopes are past, my Lord;
for even this minute
We saw them both enter the Monastery,   20
Secluded from the world and men for ever.
Cador. 'Tis both our griefs we cannot, Sir:
But from the King take you the Times joy
from us:
The Saxon King *Ostorius* slain and *Octa* fled,
That Woman-fury, Queen *Artesia,*   25
Is fast in hold, and forc't to re-deliver
London and *Winchester* (which she had for-
tifi'd)
To Princely *Vter,* lately styl'd *Pendragon,*
Who now triumphantly is marching hither
To be invested with the *Brittain* Crown.   30
Dono. The joy of this shall banish from
my breast
All thought that I was Father to two Children,
Two stubborn Daughters, that have left me
thus.
Let my old arms embrace, and call you Sons,

Scene II. *etc. add. T*   3 unto] into *T*   19 even
Q : ever *T*   23 you the] the *conj.* WP   30
British *T*

For, by the Honor of my Fathers House,   35
I'le part my estate most equally betwixt you.
Edwin, Cador. Sir y'are most noble!

*Flor. Tromp. Enter Edol with Drum and
Colours, Oswold bearing the Standard,
Toclio the Sheild, with the Red Dragon
pictur'd in'em, two Bishops with the
Crown, Prince Vter, Merlin, Artesia
bound, Guard, and Clown.*

Prince. Set up our Sheild and Standard,
noble Soldiers.
We have firm hope that, tho' our Dragon
sleep,
Merlin will us and our fair Kingdom keep.   40
Clown. As his Uncle lives, I warrant you.
Glost. Happy Restorer of the *Brittains* fame,
Uprising Sun, let us salute thy glory:
Ride in a day perpetual about us,
And no night be in thy thrones zodiack.   45
Why do we stay to binde those Princely browes
With this Imperial Honor?
Prince.   Stay, noble *Gloster :*
That monster first must be expel'd our eye,
Or we shall take no joy in it.
Dono. If that be hindrance, give her quick
Judgement,   50
And send her hence to death; she has long
deserv'd it.
Edol. Let my Sentence stand for all: take
her hence,
And stake her carcase in the burning Sun,
Till it be parcht and dry, and then fley off
Her wicked skin, and stuff the pelt with straw
To be shown up and down at Fairs and
Markets: 56
Two pence a piece to see so foul a Monster
Will be a fair Monopoly, and worth the
begging.
Artes. Ha, ha, ha!
Edol. Dost laugh, *Erictho?*
Artes.   Yes, at thy poor invention.
Is there no better torture-monger?   61
Dono. Burn her to dust.
Artes. That's a *Phœnix* death, and glorious.
Edol. I, that's too good for her.
Prince. Alive she shall be buried, circled
in a wall.   65
Thou murdress of a King, there starve to
death.
Artes. Then Ile starve death when he comes
for his prey,
And i'th' mean time Ile live upon your curses.
Edol. I, 'tis diet good enough; away with
her.

39 firm *Q* : fair *T*   58 will *Q* : 'Twill *WP* and
. . . begging *om. T*   69 'tis diet *Q* : it is *D*

Artes. With joy, my best of wishes is
  before;   70
Thy brother's poison'd, but I wanted more.
                                          [*Exit.*
Prince. Why does our Prophet *Merlin*
  stand apart,
Sadly observing these our Ceremonies,
And not applaud our joys with thy hid know-
  ledge?
Let thy divining Art now satisfie   75
Some part of my desires; for well I know,
'Tis in thy power to show the full event,
That shall both end our Reign and Chronicle.
Speak, learned *Merlin,* and resolve my fears,
Whether by war we shal expel the Saxons, 80
Or govern what we hold with beauteous peace
In *Wales* and *Brittain?*
Mer. Long happiness attend *Pendragons*
  Reign!
What Heaven decrees, fate hath no power to
  alter:
The Saxons, sir, will keep the ground they have,
And by supplying numbers still increase, 86
Till *Brittain* be no more. So please your
  Grace,
I will in visible apparitions
Present you Prophecies which shall concern
Succeeding Princes which my Art shall raise,
Till men shall call these times the latter days.
Prince. Do it, my *Merlin,*   92
And Crown me with much joy and wonder.

86 incease *Q*

*Merlin strikes. Hoeboys. Enter a King in
Armour, his Sheild quarter'd with thirteen
Crowns. At the other door enter divers
Princes who present their Crowns to him
at his feet, and do him homage; then enters
Death and strikes him; he, growing sick,
Crowns Constantine. Exeunt.*

Mer. This King, my Lord, presents your
  Royal Son,
Who in his prime of years shall be so fortunate,
That thirteen several Princes shall present 96
Their several Crowns unto him, and all Kings
  else
Shall so admire his fame and victories,
That they shall all be glad,
Either through fear or love, to do him homage;
But death (who neither favors the weak nor
  valliant)   101
In the middest of all his glories soon shall
  seize him,
Scarcely permitting him to appoint one
In all his purchased Kingdoms to succeed him.
Prince. Thanks to our Prophet   105
For this so wish'd for satisfaction;
And hereby now we learn that always Fate
Must be observ'd, what ever that decree:
All future times shall still record this Story,
Of *Merlin's* learned worth and *Arthur's* glory.
                                   [*Exeunt Omnes.*

FINIS.

97 to him *T*   101 favours neither *T*

THE BIRTH OF MERLIN

ACT I

i. 2. *her*: *their* is just possible, as Cador may mean courteously to include Donobert's other daughter.

35. *worlds*: two syllables.

43. *speaks yours*: 'declares itself in your favour'.

45. A common saying; cf. *Titus Andronicus*, II. i. 82, 83.

67–9. An allusion to the practice of declaring holidays in honour of the dead.

130. *may I whence truly know*: 'if I may keep in mind the true end of my creation.'

ii. 6, 7. 'The fact that his safety is unquestioned should make the healing of your grief a mere matter of time.' The *you* interpolated by WP is not needed.

55. *strength*: a verb.

56, 57. WP propose to give this speech to Aurelius.

87. *take my stomack*: 'excite my appetite'; not, as WP explain, 'take away my appetite.'

119–21. WP have probably found the correct interpretation of these lines. 120 should be regarded as parenthetical, and 121 taken in immediate connexion with *report of thy humanity* in 119. 'Let me because of my sex take back with me the news of your mercy (already a well-known attribute of yours) reporting that our conqueror is so worthy of praise.'

158. 'Tell him our prospective hospitality regards him as such (i. e. our brother).'

160, 161. The syntax is confused, but the meaning is: 'man's fortune, whether good or bad, resembles waves in this that it never comes singly'. Cf. *Hamlet*, IV. v. 78, 79, for the sense.

197. 'Though my jealousy will not pardon any one else for doing so.'

198. If the *me* of the quarto is to be retained after *love*, it must be understood as an 'ethical dative'. Cf. Abbott, *Sh. Gr.* § 220.

207. *will*: 'as will'.

ACT II

i. 40, 41. *Knight a'th Post*: said by WP to be a slang name for professional false witnesses.

53. *Oh yes*: 'Oyez'; cf. *Oldcastle*, I. i. 9, &c.

95–8. *who*, &c.: 'whom, once overtaken, the eyesight killing Gorgon with a single look made to stand still everlastingly: even so my might, abashed like a cloud which had aspired to cloak the sun, dissolved into a mere shower (of rain or tears).' WP try unsuccessfully to explain the allusions.

104. *thou*: the antecedent is *Pigmalion* in 99, *Oh fate* being a mere exclamation.

134. *a Maid*: Tyrrell proposed unnecessarily *scarce a maid*.

137. *you*: Tyrrell's conjecture of *I* may be correct and is adopted by WP, but the text has a satisfactory meaning as it stands.

157. *a* stands here apparently for *a'th*.

ii. 90. *expose*: 'unsheathe'.

iii. 34. The text of Q is obviously corrupt, and the most satisfactory emendation seems to be that of WP. which we have adopted. We must assume that the MS. had some such abbreviated form of *through* as *thro'* or *thr'*.

198. *best*: used substantively, 'best prospect.' This word seems genuine, but the line as a whole is certainly obscure and may be corrupt.

ACT III

i. 174. The line is certainly corrupt as it stands. I have no confidence in any of the emendations so far proposed.

209. *fruit*: D's reading *print* does not appear in his prefatory list of emendations and is probably only an uncorrected typographical error.

ii. 160. *you*, the quarto reading, is certainly correct, being contrasted with *me* at the end of the line.

iv. 117, 118. Cf. *Yorkshire Tragedy*, I. 82, 83.

vi. 3. 'Which wakes as soon as it has satisfied its desire and with open eyes is forgot,' &c.

14. *instance suit*: this emendation is claimed by Delius, but it had been silently introduced into the text by Tyrrell five years before.

83. *Deadly Sin*: a reminiscence of the moral interlude.

ACT IV

i. 14. *Cast*: the clown plays on two meanings of the word: (1) 'a number of birds' (N.E.D. s. v. 14), and (2) 'a trick' (N.E.D. s. v. 24).

15. *Covy*: WP give the quarto reading as *Cony*, but the Malone copy in the Bodleian certainly has *Covy*.

Cardecu: 'Quart d'ecu.'

257. *Of*: the modern English, as WP explain, would be *On*.

iii. 3. *fall*: 'cause of falling', 'slayer'; cf. N.E.D. s. v. *Fall* sb.[1] 17.

v. 79. *agen*: a mere intensive; cf. Abbott, *Sh. Gr.* § 27.

114. *With Monarch*: 'with the title of monarch'; cf. *Faire Em*, v. i. 35.

ACT V

i. 23. *Sabalists*: Delius quotes the quarto reading incorrectly as *Satalists* and conjectures *satellites*—a most feeble emendation. It is by no means certain that *Sabalists* is wrong, though no editor has been able to explain it. If we must have an emendation, I would suggest *Fabulists*, 'story tellers.' In case the author of the MS. from which Q was printed used a small initial the two words would have been almost identical in appearance.

77. *princeps* : WP ·retain the quarto reading *precis*, which they explain as a cabalistic epithet of God. Du Cange, however, recognizes no such word.

ii. 12. *persuade you, then* : ' persuade yourselves (be convinced), then.'

30. *Brittain* : used as an adjective ; cf. Abbott, *Sh. Gr.* § 22.

94. *presents* : ' represents '.

31. E.H.C. Oliphant, "How Not to Play the Game of Parallels," *Journal of English and Germanic Philology* 28 (1929), p. 14; quoted in: Eric Rasmussen, "Shakespeare's Hand in *The Second Maiden's Tragedy*," *Shakespeare Quarterly* 40 (1989), p. 19.

CHAPTER II

1. Rowley, of course, is not the only Elizabethan/Jacobean dramatist to write fat-clown roles; Shakespeare's Falstaff, and Lodam in Shirley's *The Wedding*, both come to mind, and there may well be other relevant instances. If, however, we were to insist that these fat-clown parts of Rowley's are not indicative of his authorship because they are not unique to him, we would be perpetrating a major distortion and misrepresentation of the relevant materials for the sake of an arbitrary regulation. The part of the Clown in *Merlin* shows various specific common features with the fat-clown parts in Rowley's plays, as noted in Chapter IV.

2. S. Schoenbaum, *Middleton's Tragedies, A Critical Study* (New York, Columbia University Press, 1955), p. 47.

3. Richard Levin, *The Multiple Plot in English Renaissance Drama* (Chicago, University of Chicago Press, 1971), pp. 3-4, 34-48.

4. S. Schoenbaum, *Middleton's Tragedies*, p. 57.

5. Richard Levin, *The Multiple Plot*, pp. 66-75; *A Fair Quarrel*, edited by R.V. Holdsworth (London, Ernest Benn, New Mermaid edition, 1974), pp. xxi-xxxix.

6. Dorothy M. Farr, *Thomas Middleton and the Drama of Realism* (New York, Barnes & Noble, 1973), p. 4

7. Alfred Harbage, *Shakespeare and the Rival Traditions* (New York, MacMillan, 1952), pp. 25ff.

8. Dewar M. Robb, "The Canon of William Rowley's Plays," *Modern Language Review* 45 (1950), pp. 129-41.

9. *A Fair Quarrel*, II,ii,35; see Holdsworth's New Mermaid edition, p. 43.

10. D.M. Robb, "The Canon of Rowley's Plays," p. 132.

11. C.W. Stork, editor, *William Rowley, His All's Lost by Lust and A Shoemaker a Gentleman* (Philadelphia, Publications of the University of Pennsylvania, 1910), pp. 159-60.

12. Cyrus Hoy, "Shares 5," *SB* 13 (1960), p. 82.

13. William Rowley, *A Critical Old-Spelling Edition of A Match at Midnight*, edited by Stephen Blase Young (New York, Garland, 1980), pp. 22-37.

14. This is not to imply that "Nicholas Nemo" was original with or unique to Rowley; ibid., pp. 242-3. In addition to the precedents cited by Young, note "Nicholas Nebulo" in *The Family of Love*, IV,iii,52, in a portion of that play that Lake assigns to Dekker; *The Canon of Middleton's Plays*, p. 99.

15. In *Match at Midnight*, II,iii,144-6, Ancient Young calls Captain Carvegut and Lieutenant Bottom:

> Foule food that lyes all day undisgested,
> Upon the queasie stomack of some Taverne,
> And are spewed out at midnight.

This type of imagery runs throughout *Wit at Several Weapons*; for two examples from that play, see note 3 to Chapter III.

16. S. Schoenbaum, *Internal Evidence*, pp. 156 and 229. C.J. Sisson discovered and published the records in question; see his *Lost Plays of Shakespeare's Age* (Cambridge, Cambridge University Press, 1936).

17. Terence P. Logan and Denzell S. Smith, editors, *The Later Jacobean and Caroline Dramatists: A Survey and Bibliography of Recent Studies in English Renaissance Drama* (Lincoln, University of Nebraska Press, 1978), p. 66.

18. David Lake, *The Canon of Middleton's Plays*, pp. 215-30.

19. Norman A. Brittin, *Thomas Middleton* (New York, Twayne, 1972), p. 97.

20. David Lake, *The Canon of Middleton's Plays*, p. 229. It is worth noting that of these three textual features in *Witch* thought to be indicative of Rowley's contribution, only one, the "'um" for "'em" (V,i,87), is in the comic subplot most commonly assigned to Rowley. The two instances of "tush" (III,ii,46, III,iii,9) are found in the speeches of Frank Thorney and Susan Carter, characters often given to Ford. This would seem to support Anthony Harris' opinion, quoted in Chapter I, about the inapplicability of such a schematic breakdown of individual shares in a collaborative work.

21. It may be worthwhile to remember the "&c." from the title page of *The Witch of Edmonton*. Consider: in Henslowe's Diary there are records of payments to Day, Hathway, Wentworth Smith, and "the other poet" for the play *The Black Dog of Newgate* (1602). We cannot identify this "other poet"—but we should not therefore assume that he did not exist. Similarly, the "etc." from *Witch* might well be an honest indicator of one or more other hands.

22. William Rowley, *A Critical Old-Spelling Edition of William Rowley's A New Wonder, a Woman Never Vexed*, edited by Trudi Laura Darby (New York, Garland, 1988), pp. 6-18.

23. David Lake, *The Canon of Middleton's Plays*, pp. 206-14.

24. A few more words about Rowley's canon: we have mentioned *The Thracian Wonder* as a false attribution to Webster and Rowley—so holds the consensus judgment. Yet there are suggestions of Rowley's hand in the play, especially, as one might suspect, in the clown's part. The clown character Muscod has a father whom he treats with disrespect (F2v) and a sister who is one of the love interests in the play. Muscod also possesses a desire for social advancement—"I have a foolish desire to be a Lord" (G2v)—in all these respects resembling Rowley's Bustopha and Jaques. Some of the specific features cited as Rowleian in Chapter IV of this study have parallels in Muscod's speeches: "I shall pine" and "Lets fill our bellies" (both D1), "so ho, ho boys" (G4v), and "Wilde-geese ... Woodcocks" (G4) and "Ring-tale" (H1). Some of Muscod's textual preferences are compatible with Rowley's usage pattern, like "S'nails" and "t'other" (both B3).

I suspect that a reasonable case might be made for Rowley's participation in the authorship of *Thracian Wonder*—though I have hesitated to make the attempt in this volume; I wanted to avoid the appearance of "stacking the deck," by suggesting that another of Kirkman's disputed attributions has overlooked validity. For that reason, this study accepts the standard verdict rejecting the attribution of *Thracian Wonder* to Webster and Rowley—a rejection that seems clearly correct as far as Webster is concerned. (Other stylistic and textual features in the play suggest that if Rowley is present, he could not be the sole author; at this point, I have no idea who his collaborator might have been. The date of authorship often assigned to *Thracian Wonder*, ca. 1599, is plainly too early, given the play's obvious debts to *The Winter's Tale* and *The Tempest*—far beyond what derivation from common sources and the shared pastoral idiom can account for. A post-*Tempest* date would place *Thracian Wonder* within the time span of Rowley's playwriting career.)

CHAPTER III

1. Cyrus Hoy, "Shares 1," *SB* 8 (1956); see Erdman and Fogel, *Evidence for Authorship*, p. 210.

2. Cyrus Hoy, "Shares 7," *SB* 15 (1962), p. 72.

3. David Lake, *The Canon of Middleton's Plays*, pp. 211-13. Lake prefers the view that "Rowley for once has adopted a Middletonian oath" to the alternative explanation of more intimate collaboration—though *Wit at Several Weapons* has features that point to a closer interrelationship of the two writers' shares than Lake allows. Compare these two passages:

> ... if these two fellows might be bought and sodden, and *boil'd to a jelly*, and eaten fasting every morning, I do not think but a man should find strange things in his stomach.

That is from *Wit*, I,ii; this is from IV,i—

> ... you had need of Cordials,
> Some rich Electuary, made of a Son and Heir,
> An elder brother, in a Cullis, whole,
> 'Tmust be some wealthy Gregory, *boyl'd to a Jelly*,
> That must restore you to a state of new Gowns,
> French ruffs, and mutable head-tires.

If we accept Lake's division of authorship in *Wit*, we must suppose that the first excerpt was written by Rowley, the second by Middleton. I find it far more plausible to think that the two passages were written by one partner (Middleton) rather than both. Examples like this make me believe ever more firmly that textual evidence is less certain and absolute than many scholars allow, and that it needs to be supplemented and confirmed with other forms of evidence for sound conclusions to be reached.

This very striking type of food-and-eating imagery, in which people become dishes to be consumed, occurs throughout *Wit at Several Weapons*, and suggests Middleton more than Rowley. We might assume that there was a fair amount of mixed authorship involved in the composition of the play, and that the occasional intrusion of Middletonian features into Rowleian scenes are traces of Middleton's hand. But we cannot be sure—and that is an important point. Lake's recognition of the possibility that Rowley might vary his usual textual preferences on occasion is prudent and reasonable—and has obvious relevance to the study of *Merlin*.

4. S. Schoenbaum, *Internal Evidence*, p. 131.

5. For Rowley's textual preferences, see David Lake, *The Canon of Middleton's Plays*, pp. 199-205 and 244ff.

6. "I'th'" appears in I,i,63, I,ii,192, II,i,19, II,ii,115, III,i,66 and 126, III,iv,41 and 76 and 127, IV,i,67, and V,ii,68; "on't" occurs at I,ii,123, II,i,4 and 39, II,iii,175, and III,i,35.

7. *The Riverside Shakespeare*, p. 506 n. 104.

8. C.F. Tucker Brooke, *The Shakespeare Apocrypha*, pp. xlv-xlvi.

9. Donald Foster, review of *William Shakespeare and The Birth of Merlin* and Eric Sams' *Shakespeare's Lost Play, Edmund Ironside*, *Shakespeare Quarterly* 39 (1988), p. 119.

10. The one partial exception is not a play but a masque, *The World Tossed at Tennis*; textual evidence shows that Rowley wrote the first 470 lines and Middleton the rest. Simplicity, the clown character, appears in both portions. Yet this raises another key difficulty that practitioners of textual analysis often neglect: does the textual profile of *World Tossed* mean that Rowley composed the first half of the masque and Middleton the second—or merely that Rowley wrote the first half down on paper, and Middleton the second? A dominance of a given writer's textual profile in a given body of text may reflect a scribal function as well as an authorial function. This helps to explain cases in which textual and stylistic evidence diverge (see n. 3 above, and Appendix I). There is at least one feature in Middleton's portion of *World Tossed*, the "bag and baggage" pun in line 609, that hints at some input by Rowley (Stork, p. 41).

11. Fred Allison Howe, "The Authorship of *The Birth of Merlin*," *Modern Philology* 4 (1906), pp. 193-205.

CHAPTER IV

1. David Frost, *School of Shakespeare*, p. 257.

2. Anthony Harris makes some fascinating observations about the generally overlooked (or denied) demonic aspects of Prospero's magic—aspects that have relevance to *The Birth of Merlin*; see his *Night's Black Agents*, pp. 129-48. Though Cerimon does not actually perform magic in *Pericles*, he does represent a magus figure as the term is used by Frances Yates; see *Majesty and Magic in Shakespeare's Last Plays*, p. 88.

3. Anthony Harris has pertinent points about the stage effects in this play; see *Night's Black Agents*, pp. 155-6.

4. Richard Levin, *The Multiple Plot in English Renaissance Drama*, p. 55.

5. David Young, *The Heart's Forest: A Study of Shakespeare's Pastoral Plays* (New Haven, Yale University Press, 1972), p. 78.

6. I agree with the viewpoint that maintains that the Hymen who appears in V,ii of *As You Like It* is the "real" Hymen, not a forester or shepherd dressed up by Rosalind as a mythological figure in a masque. See Edward I. Berry's "Rosalynde and Rosalind," *Shakespeare Quarterly* 31 (1980), pp. 42-52.

7. David Frost, *School of Shakespeare*, pp. 209-45.

8. See Trudi Laura Darby's edition of *New Wonder*, p. 40.

9. Ibid., pp. 96 and 191.

10. Caroline Spurgeon, *Shakespeare's Imagery and What It Tells Us* (Cambridge, Cambridge University Press, 1935), pp. 101-10.

11. It is not necessary for us to consider sympathetic animal imagery unique to Shakespeare to use it as a legitimate identifying feature. My own sense of the literature is that if we look long enough and hard enough, we are likely to find something, somewhere, that is at least somewhat similar to any supposedly unique feature. In the present instance, we can note that in John Day's *The Isle of Gulls*, II,ii, Violetta and Hippolita have speeches expressing sympathy for the hunted deer, at least somewhat comparable to what we find in Shakespeare (the passage in question does not exploit animal imagery—the sympathetic sentiments are simply expressed in

conversation). It is accurate to say that sympathetic animal imagery is typical of Shakespeare, and rare-to-nonexistent in the works
of most of his contemporaries. (John Day is an interesting figure
in reference to Shakespeare; see n. 14 below.)

12. If, that is, we accept Stork's emendation of the corrupt quarto
    text; see p. 238 of Stork's edition of *Shoemaker*.

13. This device, of a crab-shaped jewel as love token, is not original
    with Shakespeare; it derives from Sir Philip Sidney's *Arcadia*,
    where Musidorus gives such a jewel to Mopsa. A reader disposed
    to cavil might wonder why this feature would not constitute one
    datum of internal evidence showing that Sidney wrote *Merlin*; I
    would concede that it might, *if* the play had been published under
    Sidney's name and *if* it contained hundreds of other indications of
    his authorship. In practice, drawing distinctions between autho-
    rial and non-authorial connections and commonalities is not in-
    surmountably difficult.

14. I note a few parallels between *Merlin* and some of the earlier scenes
    of *Pericles* that are not universally associated with Shakespeare. I
    believe that Shakespeare's hand can be shown to be present in
    these early scenes, intermixed with the contribution of one or
    more other writers. Most likely John Day is one—see F.D. Hoeni-
    ger's "How Significant are Textual Parallels? A New Author for
    Pericles?" *Shakespeare Quarterly* 11 (1960), pp. 27-38.

15. See Holdsworth's New Mermaid edition of *Fair Quarrel*, p. 5 n. 5,
    p. 48 n. 120.

16. It may be worth noting that we have cited two points of contact
    between Proximus' death scene here in *Merlin* and Clarence's
    death scene, I,iv, in *Richard III*—"Had you such leisure in the
    time of death" (34) and "restore a purse" (140). Both scenes offer
    heavily occultified murders as prelude to greater violence. Other
    of the Shakespearean parallels in *Merlin* that are cited only in pass-
    ing have this kind of contexual dimension; to trace all of them in
    detail would distend this study with minor features, to a point at
    which even the most interested and committed reader might be
    numbed into indifference. I can only ask the reader to remain
    aware that any study such as this must be partial and limited, and
    that there is much more that could be said about Shakespeare's
    hand in *Merlin*.

17. Caroline Spurgeon, *Shakespeare's Imagery*, pp. 91-6.

18. Ibid., pp. 21-3.

19. Frances A. Yates, *Theatre of the World* (Boston, Routledge & Kegan Paul, 1969), pp. 176-85.

20. Robert J. Fehrenbach, Lea Ann Boone, and Mario A. Di Cesare, editors, *A Concordance to the Plays, Poems, and Translations of Christopher Marlowe* (Ithaca, NY, Cornell University Press, 1982).

21. Stephen L. Bates and Sidney D. Orr, editors, *A Concordance to the Poems of Ben Jonson* (Athens, OH, Ohio University Press, 1978).

22. Charles G. Osgood, editor, *A Concordance to the Poems of Edmund Spenser* (Washington, DC, Carnegie Institution, 1915).

23. Homer C. Combs and Zay Rusk Sullens, editors, *A Concordance to the English Poems of John Donne* (Chicago, Packard, 1940).

24. Eric Rasmussen, "Shakespeare's Hand in *The Second Maiden's Tragedy*," *Shakespeare Quarterly* 40 (1989), p. 18.

25. R.W. Dent, *Proverbial Language in English Drama Exclusive of Shakespeare, 1495-1616* (Berkeley, University of California Press, 1984), pp. 574, 662-3.

CHAPTER V

1. MacDonald P. Jackson, *Studies in Attribution: Middleton and Shakespeare* (Salzburg, Austria, Salzburg Jacobean Studies 79, Salzburg Studies in English Literature, 1979), pp. 80-93, 202-5.

2. Trudi Laura Darby, editor, *New Wonder*, p. 17.

3. Totals for "and" and "a" in *Merlin* are for the entire text excluding the stage directions. The words were counted as they occur in their modern senses, i.e. omitting instances in which "and" means "if" in modern usage (III,i,190; III,iv,110; IV,i,144), in which "a" means "in" or "on" or "of" (II,i,156), and in which "a" would be a hyphenated prefix in modern punctuation ("a coming," II,i,132; "a breeding," III,iv,138-9). Editorial emendations (III,vi,134) were also omitted.

4. F.E. Halliday, *Shakespeare Companion*, pp. 350-1.

5. Alfred Hart, *Shakespeare and the Homilies, and Other Pieces of Re-*

search into the Elizabethan Drama (New York, AMS Press reprint, 1971), pp. 219-41.

6. Ibid., pp. 242-56.

7. Eric Sams, *Shakespeare's Lost Play, Edmund Ironside* (London, Fourth Estate, 1985), pp. 339-56.

8. The list is not, and is not meant to be, complete and exhaustive. Proper names are omitted, even when they constitute unusual coinages that might argue for inclusion (i.e. "Hingest-men, and Hingest-land," IV,iii,18). Hyphenated compounds are treated as current usage dictates, i.e. "eyesight-killing" rather than the text's "eye sight killing"; some possible compounds have not been included ("Phoenix death," V,ii,63, for example); some terms that the text treats as compounds but modern usage doesn't have also been omitted ("shepherds-wife," III,iv,41). Choosing among word forms is problematical in some cases; one might wonder why the list contains "obtaining" and "examining," but not "supplying" and "permitting" (V,ii,86 and 103), none of which is present verbatim in the Shakespeare canon. I have tried to craft a list that gives a fair representation of the play's varied vocabulary without going to extremes or grabbing every possible inclusion. I have made judgments on individual words that other individuals might not reach in the same way, based on particular usages. Thus, the use of "obtaining" as a gerund, and the odd form "tiding" (if it is not a printer's error) seemed distinctive enough to me to merit mention. Depending on how rigorously or leniently one wishes to distinguish between separate word forms, this list could be expanded or contracted. I've attempted to steer a middle course between the extremes.

9. Walter Whiter, *A Specimen of a Commentary on Shakespeare*, edited by Alan Over and Mary Bell (London, Methuen, 1967).

10. Edward Armstrong, *Shakespeare's Imagination* (Lincoln, University of Nebraska Press, 1963), pp. 203-17. This is the revised edition of Armstrong's 1946 original, and contains an expanded and very useful discussion of applications of image-cluster study in authorship questions.

11. Kenneth Muir, *Shakespeare as Collaborator* (New York, Barnes & Noble, 1960), pp. 14-26; Moody E. Prior, "Imagery as a Test of Authorship," *Shakespeare Quarterly* 6 (1955), pp. 381-6.

12. Eric Sams, *Shakespeare's Lost Play*, pp. 249-79. E.B. Everitt, in his earlier studies of this play's authorship, also used image clusters as evidence.

13. Edward Armstrong, *Shakespeare's Imagination*, pp. 25ff. and 198ff.

14. S. Schoenbaum, *Internal Evidence*, pp. 188-9.

15. One delightful example: Shakespeare's hand in *Kinsmen* was once disputed with the view that the imagery in the opening scene is "too consistently brilliant" to be his (! ! !)—see Armstrong, *Shakespeare's Imagination*, p. 203.

16. C.F. Tucker Brooke, *The Shakespeare Apocrypha*, p. xliii.

17. Edward Armstrong, *Shakespeare's Imagination*, p. 204.

18. Ibid., pp. 213-14.

19. Kenneth Muir, *Shakespeare as Collaborator*, p. 22.

20. Ibid., pp. 118-20.

21. Ibid., p. 120.

22. Edward Armstrong, *Shakespeare's Imagination*, pp. 208-9.

23. Ibid., pp. 100-3.

24. Paul A. Cantor, "Shakespeare's *The Tempest*: The Wise Man as Hero," *Shakespeare Quarterly* 31 (1980), pp. 71-3. As noted in Chapter IV, the phrase "borrowed robes" occurs both in *Merlin*, III,ii,117 and in *MacBeth*, I,iii,109.

CHAPTER VI

1. Robert Grudon, *Mighty Opposites: Shakespeare and Renaissance Contrariety* (Berkeley, University of California Press, 1979).

2. Edward Armstrong, *Shakespeare's Imagination*, pp. 107ff.

3. Exactly how does music provoke good to harm? Shakespeare, in this couplet, may be referring to the theory that certain types of music have the power to provoke violent reactions in listeners; see Frances A. Yates, *Astraea: The Imperial Theme in the Sixteenth Century* (Boston, Routledge & Kegan Paul, 1975), pp. 151-65. If this is so, the couplet would stand as one sign of Shakespeare's interest in the esoteric intellectual and artistic movements allied to

the Renaissance Hermetist and Neoplatonist philosophy that is the subject of several of Frances Yates' works.

4. Frances A. Yates, *Majesty and Magic in Shakespeare's Last Plays: A New Approach to Cymbeline, Henry VIII and The Tempest* (Boulder, CO, Shambhala, 1978), pp. 17-35. Originally published as *Shakespeare's Last Plays: A New Approach* (Boston, Routledge & Kegan Paul, 1975).

5. Frances A. Yates, *Theatre of the World*, pp. 1-41, 190-7; *The Rosicrucian Enlightenment* (Boston, Routledge & Kegan Paul, 1972), pp. 30-40ff.

6. Frances A. Yates, *Astraea*, pp. 29-130.

7. Frances A. Yates, *Majesty and Magic*, pp. 109-24.

8. Ibid., pp. 30 and 54-5.

9. C.F. Tucker Brooke, *Shakespeare Apocrypha*, p. xlvi.

10. Frances A. Yates, *Rosicrucian Enlightenment*, pp. 1-29.

11. Fredson Bowers, general editor, *The Dramatic Works in the Beaumont and Fletcher Canon*, Vol. II (Cambridge, Cambridge University Press, 1970), pp. 569-73, 692-5.

12. The lineation for *Cupid's Revenge* refers to the edition cited in note 11 above; other editions vary the Act-Scene division (I,v in Bowers is I,iv elsewhere).

13. William Wells, "*The Birth of Merlin*," *Modern Language Review* 16 (1921), pp. 129-37; E.H.C. Oliphant, *The Plays of Beaumont and Fletcher* (New Haven, CT, Yale University Press, 1927; New York, Phaeton Press reprint, 1970), pp. 402-14.

14. Cyrus Hoy, "Shares 3," *SB* 11 (1958), pp. 90-1. In Hoy's authorship division of *Cupid's Revenge*, Beaumont wrote I,i and iii, II,i-ii and iv-v, III,i-ii, IV,i and v, and V,i; Fletcher wrote I,ii and iv, II,iii and vi, III,iii-iv, IV,ii-iv, and V,ii-iii. (Hoy's I,iv is Bowers' I,v.)

15. For the shared "Ha!" see p. 977 of *The Riverside Shakespeare*. The quotation from *When You See Me You Know Me* derives from the Tudor Facsimile Texts reprint of the 1613 quarto (AMS Press, New York, 1913).

16. S. Schoenbaum, *Shakespeare's Lives* (New York, Oxford University Press, 1970), pp. 126-35 et seq.

17. Ibid., p. 120.

18. The imaginer in question is Peter Alexander; see A.C. Partridge, *Orthography in Shakespeare and Elizabethan Drama* (Lincoln, University of Nebraska Press, 1964), p. 142. It is not my intent to ridicule Alexander, widely admired for his scholarship; and having imagined Shakespeare at Stonehenge, I am hardly in a position to criticize others' imaginative leaps. Yet we do need to keep our imaginations from blocking advances in our understanding of the subject at hand; the clear evidence of Shakespeare's hand in *Merlin* takes precedence over the "received wisdom" about Shakespeare's retirement.

19. S. Schoenbaum, *Shakespeare's Lives*, pp. 42-3.

20. Ibid., p. 43.

21. The King's Men were acting a play called *Cardenio* in 1613; on Sept. 9, 1653, Humphrey Moseley registered the play as the work of Shakespeare and Fletcher. The play has not survived in its original form, though Theobald's *Double Falsehood* is supposed to have been based on it (F.E. Halliday, *Shakespeare Companion*, pp. 83-4). The alleged connection between *Cardenio* and *Double Falsehood* has often been dismissed—though Oliphant has some interesting observations on the subject in his *Beaumont and Fletcher*, pp. 282-302. I see no good reason for skepticism about the actual existence of *Cardenio* as a Shakespeare-Fletcher work; it conforms to what we know about their collaboration.

22. In the same Stationers Register entry that mentions *Cardenio* (see n. 21 above), Humphrey Moseley registered a *Henry I* and a *Henry II* as by Shakespeare and Davenport. Seven years later, on June 29, 1660, Moseley registered three plays: "The History of King Stephen. Duke Humphrey, A Tragedy. Iphis & Iantha, or a marriage without a man, a Comedy. By Will: Shakespeare" (F.E. Halliday, *Shakespeare Companion*, p. 325). Commentators have been almost universally skeptical about these entries. Yet is such skepticism really warranted? Given the high rate of nonsurvival among English Renaissance plays, it seems virtually inevitable that *some* Shakespearean and partially Shakespearean works have been lost. (Personally, I find the idea of a Shakespearean *Iphis and Iantha* fascinating.) Concerning Davenport, we can note that he was roughly of the same generation as Fletcher and Rowley, and seems to fit with Shakespeare's tendency to collaborate with younger

men; indeed, Davenport is thought to have been born ca. 1590, so that any collaboration between the two men would have to have occurred relatively late in Shakespeare's career. And if Shakespeare returned to his long-disused history-play format for *Henry VIII*, he might well have collaborated on a *Henry I* and *Henry II* as well.

CHAPTER VII

1. S. Schoenbaum, *Internal Evidence*, p. 261.

2. D.M. McKeithan, "Shakespearian Echoes in the Florimel Plot of Fletcher and Rowley's *The Maid in the Mill*," *Philological Quarterly* 17 (1938), pp. 396-8.

3. Una Ellis-Fermor, *"The Two Noble Kinsmen,"* in *Shakespeare the Dramatist*, edited by Kenneth Muir (New York, Barnes & Noble, 1961).

4. Kenneth Muir, *Shakespeare as Collaborator*, pp. 109-12.

5. F.E. Halliday, *Shakespeare Companion*, pp. 53-4, 306, 507.

6. S. Schoenbaum, *Shakespeare's Lives*, pp. 212-31.

7. Gary Taylor, "Shakespeare's New Poem," *The New York Times Book Review*, Dec. 15, 1985. (See also the new Oxford edition of the "Complete Works," edited by Taylor and Stanley Wells.)

8. Eric Rasmussen, "Shakespeare's Hand in *The Second Maiden's Tragedy*," *Shakespeare Quarterly* 40 (1989), pp. 1-26.

9. Eliot Slater, *The Problem of The Reign of King Edward III: A Statistical Approach* (Cambridge, Cambridge University Press, 1988).

10. Donald Foster, *Elegy by W.S.: A Study in Attribution* (Newark, DE, University of Delaware Press, 1989).

11. Ibid., p. 234.

APPENDIX I

1. A.C. Partridge, *Orthography in Shakespeare and Elizabethan Drama* (Lincoln, University of Nebraska Press, 1964), p. 148. The literature on *Henry VIII* is of course enormous; Erdman and Fogel give a useful summary in *Evidence for Authorship*, pp. 457-78.

272 THE BIRTH OF MERLIN

2. Philip Edwards has written of Fletcher's works, "Even the sympathetic reader finds them bizarre, perplexing, and unattractive . . . They do little to explain the human condition; their comment on contemporary society is trifling; their psychology and politics are often (not always) jejune; identification with the characters is a superhuman effort." And this, from a man who admires Fletcher's art and wishes his plays more widely read! See "The Danger Not the Death: The Art of John Fletcher," in *Jacobean Theatre*, p. 160. For the abundant differences between Shakespeare's and Fletcher's textual habits, see the citation of Erdman and Fogel in note 1 above.

3. Cyrus Hoy, "Shares 7," *SB* 15 (1962), pp. 76-90.

4. Michael J.B. Allen and Kenneth Muir, editors, *Shakespeare's Plays in Quarto* (Berkeley, University of California Press, 1981), pp. 58-9.

5. Regarding Shakespeare's tendency to repeat himself in any given play, note that "opinion crowns" and "whiles others" occur twice in *Troilus*, as do "tread upon," "desires access to you," and "glad to receive" in *Measure*, "breathe a while," "so far afoot," and "great name" in *1 Henry IV*, "battles join'd," "latest gasp," "both wind and tide," "For well I wot," "linger thus," and "in hope he'll prove a widower shortly" in *3 Henry VI*, etc. etc.—dozens and scores of examples can be added to the list, from virtually every Shakespearean play.

6. See *Henry VIII*, I,iv,27 and 28; II,i,43, 53, and 143; II,iv,18; III,i,92; III,ii,306; and V,iv,14. We might also note II,ii,8-9, which, though it concludes a prose speech, is effectively a line of verse with a "sir" tacked onto its end.

7. See *The Two Noble Kinsmen*, II,ii,1, 117, and 203; II,iii,45, 63, and 68; II,iv,16; II,v,37, 51, 53, and 64; III,iii,31; III,iv,1; III,vi,35, 45, 69, 210, and 301; IV,i,44, 51, 65, and 76; IV,ii,72 and 151; V,i,33; and V,ii,57 and 108. Yet the many examples of Fletcher's solo works demonstrate that if these scenes in *Kinsmen* were truly written by Fletcher alone, such sixth-stress lines would be even more common.

8. For a useful summary of the critical literature on *Kinsmen*, see Erdman and Fogel's *Evidence for Authorship*, pp. 486-94.

APPENDIX II

1. The material on Francis Kirkman is drawn from several standard sources—not all of which agree on details. The *Dictionary of National Biography*, for instance, gives the year of his birth as 1632.

2. *The Complete Works of John Webster*, edited by F.L. Lucas (London, 1927; New York, Gordian Press, 1966), Vol. 3, p. 29.

3. In his overview of seventeenth-century pornography, *Unfit for Modest Ears* (Totowa, NJ, Rowman and Littlefield, 1979), Roger Thompson has a number of harsh things to say about Kirkman; see pp. 72-4, 80-2, 207, 211. I find it hard to share Thompson's indignation; given the repressive authoritarian culture of the time, my sympathies tend to run in the opposite direction. The explosion of pornography in the middle of the seventeenth century certainly appears to have been, in large part, a reaction to the extreme constraints of Puritanism; Kirkman's involvement in publishing pornography can be seen as mirroring that reaction on a personal level (Thompson, pp. 81, 197-8, 211-15).

4. See Lucas' *Webster*, Vol. 3, p. 10.

Bibliography

PRIMARY WORKS: EDITIONS CITED

Shakespeare
The Riverside Shakespeare, G. Blakemore Evans, textual editor. Boston, Houghton Mifflin, 1974.

William Rowley
Rowley's works have never been collected; quotations from and line citations to his works in this study refer to the following editions of individual plays:

The Spanish Gipsie and All's Lost by Lust, edited by Edgar C. Morris. Boston, D.C. Heath & Co., 1908. (For *All's Lost by Lust*.)

William Rowley, his All's Lost by Lust and A Shoemaker a Gentleman, edited by C.W. Stork. Philadelphia, Publications of the University of Pennsylvania, 1910. (For *A Shoemaker a Gentleman*.)

A Critical, Old-Spelling Edition of William Rowley's A New Wonder, a Woman Never Vexed, edited by Trudi Laura Darby. New York, Garland Publishing, 1988.

A Critical Old-Spelling Edition of A Match at Midnight, edited by Stephen Blase Young. New York, Garland Publishing, 1980.

The Witch of Edmonton, with a commentary by Simon Trussler, and notes by Jacqui Russell. London, Methuen, 1983.

The Changeling, edited by George W. Williams. Lincoln, University of Nebraska Press, 1966.

A Fair Quarrel, edited by R.V. Holdsworth. London, Ernest Benn, 1974.

Modern editions of a number of Rowley's works are available only in the collected editions of the works of his collaborators:

A Cure for a Cuckold in F.L. Lucas' edition of *The Complete Works of John Webster* (London, 1927; New York, Gordian Press, 1966)

The World Tossed at Tennis in A.H. Bullen's edition of *The Works of Thomas Middleton* (London, 1885-6; New York, AMS Press, 1964), etc. *Quotations from and line citations to these works refer to these standard editions.*

Beaumont and Fletcher

The Dramatic Works in the Beaumont and Fletcher Canon, Vol. II, Fredson Bowers, general editor. Cambridge, Cambridge University Press, 1970. (For *Cupid's Revenge.*)

The Works of Francis Beaumont and John Fletcher, Variorum Edition, A.H. Bullen, general editor. London, George Bell & Sons, 1905.

The Works of Francis Beaumont and John Fletcher, edited by Arnold Glover. Cambridge, Cambridge University Press, 1905.

Samuel Rowley

When You See Me You Know Me, Tudor Facsimile Texts series, 106. New York, AMS Press, 1913.

The Shakespeare Apocrypha

The Shakespeare Apocrypha, edited by C.F. Tucker Brooke, Oxford, Oxford University Press, 1908.

SECONDARY WORKS

Albright, Evelyn May. *Dramatic Publication in England, 1580-1640.* New York, Gordian Press, 1971.

Allen, Michael J.B., and Kenneth Muir, editors. *Shakespeare's Plays in Quarto.* Berkeley, University of California Press, 1981.

Armstrong, Edward A. *Shakespeare's Imagination.* Lincoln, University of Nebraska Press, 1963.

Bald, R.C. "*The Booke of Sir Thomas More* and Its Problems." *Shakespeare Survey* 2 (1949), pp. 44-65.

Bates, Stephen L., and Sidney D. Orr, editors. *A Concordance to the Poems of Ben Jonson*. Athens, Ohio University Press, 1978.

Bentley, Gerald Eades. *The Jacobean and Caroline Stage*. Oxford, Clarendon Press, 1941-68.

Berry, Edward I. "Rosalynde and Rosalind." *Shakespeare Quarterly* 31 (1980), pp. 42-52.

Brittin, Norman A. *Thomas Middleton*. New York, Twayne, 1972.

Campbell, O.J., and E.G. Quinn, editors. *The Reader's Encyclopedia of Shakespeare*. New York, Crowell, 1966.

Cantor, Paul A. "Shakespeare's *The Tempest*: the Wise Man as Hero." *Shakespeare Quarterly* 31 (1980), pp. 64-75.

Combs, Homer C., and Zay Rusk Sullens, editors. *A Concordance to the English Poems of John Donne*. Chicago, Packard, 1940.

Dent, R.W. *Proverbial Language in English Drama Exclusive of Shakespeare, 1495-1616*. Berkeley, University of California Press, 1984.

Edwards, Philip. "The Danger not the Death: The Art of John Fletcher." *Jacobean Theatre*. J.R. Brown and Bernard Harris, editors. New York, Capricorn, 1967, pp. 159-78.

Ellis-Fermor, Una. *Shakespeare the Dramatist*. Kenneth Muir, editor. New York, Barnes & Noble, 1961.

Erdman, David V., and Ephim G. Fogel, editors. *Evidence for Authorship: Essays on Problems of Attribution*. Ithaca, NY, Cornell University Press, 1966.

Farr, Dorothy M. *Thomas Middleton and the Drama of Realism*. New York, Barnes & Noble, 1973.

Fehrenbach, Robert J., Lea Ann Boone, and Mario A. Di Cesare, editors. *A Concordance to the Plays, Poems, and Translations of Christopher Marlowe*. Ithaca, NY, Cornell University Press, 1982.

Foster, Donald W. *Elegy by W.S.: A Study in Attribution*. Newark, DE, University of Delaware Press, 1989.

Foster, Donald W. "'Shall I Die' Post Mortem: Defining Shakespeare." *Shakespeare Quarterly* 38 (1987), pp. 58-77.

Foster, Donald W. Untitled review of *William Shakespeare and The*

Birth of Merlin and Eric Sams' *Shakespeare's Lost Play: Edmund Iron-side*. *Shakespeare Quarterly* 39 (1988), pp. 118-23.

Frost, David L. *The School of Shakespeare*. Cambridge, Cambridge University Press, 1968.

Grudon, Robert. *Mighty Opposites: Shakespeare and Renaissance Contrariety*. Berkeley, University of California Press, 1979.

Halliday, F.E. *A Shakespeare Companion 1564-1964*. Baltimore, Penguin, 1964.

Harbage, Alfred. *Shakespeare and the Rival Traditions*. New York, MacMillan, 1952.

Harris, Anthony. *Night's Black Agents: Witchcraft and Magic in Seventeenth-Century English Drama*. Manchester, Manchester University Press, 1980.

Hoeniger, F.D. "How Significant are Textual Parallels? A New Author for *Pericles?*" *Shakespeare Quarterly* 11 (1960), pp. 27-38.

Hope, Charles. "The Real Leonardo." *The New York Review of Books*, Vol. 36, No. 13, August 17, 1989, pp. 16-18.

Howe, F.A. "The Authorship of *The Birth of Merlin*." *Modern Philology* 4 (1906), pp. 193-205.

Hoy, Cyrus. "The Shares of Fletcher and His Collaborators in the Beaumont and Fletcher Canon," Parts 1-7. *Studies in Bibliography* 8 (1956), pp. 129-46; 9 (1957), pp. 143-62; 11 (1958), pp. 85-106; 12 (1959), pp. 91-116; 13 (1960), pp. 77-108; 14 (1961), pp. 45-67; and 15 (1962), pp. 71-90.

Jackson, MacDonald P. *Studies in Attribution: Middleton and Shakespeare*. Salzburg, Austria, Salzburg Jacobean Studies 79, Salzburg Studies in English Literature, 1979.

Lake, David J. *The Canon of Thomas Middleton's Plays*. Cambridge, Cambridge University Press, 1975.

Langbaine, Gerard. *An Account of the English Dramatic Poets*. London, 1691.

Levin, Richard. *The Multiple Plot in English Renaissance Drama*. Chicago, University of Chicago Press, 1971.

Logan, Terence P., and Denzell S. Smith, editors. *The Popular School: A Survey and Bibliography of Recent Studies in English Renaissance Drama*. Lincoln, University of Nebraska Press, 1975.

Logan, Terence P., and Denzell S. Smith, editors. *The Later Jacobean and Caroline Dramatists: A Survey and Bibliography of Recent Studies in English Renaissance Drama*. Lincoln, University of Nebraska Press, 1978.

McKeithan, D.M. "Shakespearian Echoes in the Florimel Plot of Fletcher and Rowley's *The Maid in the Mill.*" *Philological Quarterly* 17 (1938), pp. 396-8.

Muir, Kenneth. *Shakespeare as Collaborator*. New York, Barnes & Noble, 1960.

Oliphant, E.H.C. *The Plays of Beaumont and Fletcher*. New Haven, Yale University Press, 1927.

Osgood, Charles G., editor. *A Concordance to the Poems of Edmund Spenser*. Washington, DC, Carnegie Institution, 1915.

Partridge, A.C. *Orthography in Shakespeare and Elizabethan Drama*. Lincoln, University of Nebraska Press, 1964.

Rasmussen, Eric. "Shakespeare's Hand in *The Second Maiden's Tragedy.*" *Shakespeare Quarterly* 40 (1989), pp. 1-26.

Reed, Robert R., Jr. *The Occult on the Tudor and Stuart Stage*. Boston, Christopher Publishing House, 1965.

Robb, Dewar M. "The Canon of William Rowley's Plays." *Modern Language Review* 45 (1950), pp. 129-41.

Sams, Eric. *Shakespeare's Lost Play: Edmund Ironside*. London, Fourth Estate, 1985.

Schoenbaum, Samuel. *Internal Evidence and Elizabethan Dramatic Authorship*. Evanston, IL, Northwestern University Press, 1966.

Schoenbaum, Samuel. *Middleton's Tragedies: A Critical Study*. New York, Columbia University Press, 1955.

Schoenbaum, Samuel. *Shakespeare's Lives*. Oxford, Oxford University Press, 1970.

Schoenbaum, Samuel. *William Shakespeare, A Compact Documentary Life*. Oxford, Oxford University Press, 1977.

Simons, Arthur. "Middleton and Rowley." *The Cambridge History of English Literature*. A.W. Ward and A.R. Waller, editors. Cambridge, Cambridge University Press, 1969.

Slater, Eliot, *The Problem of The Reign of King Edward III: A Statistical Approach*. Cambridge, Cambridge University Press, 1988.

Spevack, Marvin. *The Harvard Concordance to Shakespeare*. Cambridge, MA, Harvard University Press, 1973.

Spurgeon, Caroline. *Shakespeare's Imagery and What It Tells Us*. Cambridge, Cambridge University Press, 1935.

Taylor, Gary. "Shakespeare's New Poem." *The New York Times Book Review*, Dec. 15, 1985.

Thompson, Roger. *Unfit for Modest Ears*. Totowa, NJ, Rowman and Littlefield, 1979.

Wells, William. "*The Birth of Merlin*." *Modern Language Review* 16 (1921), pp. 129-37.

Whiter, Walter. *A Specimen of a Commentary on Shakespeare*. Alan Over and Mary Bell, editors. London, Methuen, 1967.

Yates, Frances A. *Astraea: The Imperial Theme in the Sixteenth Century*. Boston, Routledge & Kegan Paul, 1975.

Yates, Frances A. *Majesty and Magic in Shakespeare's Last Plays: A New Approach to Cymbeline, Henry VIII, and The Tempest*. Boulder, CO, Shambhala, 1978.

Yates, Frances A. *The Rosicrucian Enlightenment*. Boston, Routledge & Kegan Paul, 1972.

Yates, Frances A. *Theatre of the World*. Boston, Routledge & Kegan Paul, 1969.

Young, David. *The Heart's Forest: A Study of Shakespeare's Pastoral Plays*. New Haven, CT, Yale University Press, 1972.

Index

208
Textual preferences, 44-9, 188, 198-9
Vocabulary, 135-40
Works—
Antony and Cleopatra, 62, 70, 80, 84, 99, 100, 103, 111, 117, 120, 126, 168, 190, 192, 197, 207
All's Well That Ends Well, 49, 61-2, 74, 96-7, 103, 111, 118, 120, 123, 146, 196
As You Like It, 55, 57, 61, 74, 81, 92, 104, 106, 121, 123, 170, 190, 194, 196, 203, 210, 212
Cardenio, 7, 173, 185, 270 n.21
Comedy of Errors, The, 21, 72, 80, 95, 102, 123, 173, 188, 203, 208
Coriolanus, 70, 73, 99, 100, 114, 119, 120, 122, 144, 157, 171, 202-3, 205, 207, 210, 212
Cymbeline, 20, 32-3, 54-5, 57-8, 61-2, 68-71, 84-5, 90-1, 96, 101, 103, 107, 113, 119-21, 123, 144, 149, 150, 153-4, 163-4, 195-7, 203, 207-8, 213
Edmund Ironside, 135, 140, 182
Edward III, 135, 140, 182-3
Funeral Elegy, A, 21, 182
Hamlet, 8, 48, 52, 64, 71, 80, 88, 91, 99, 102, 104, 106, 114, 125, 144, 192, 196, 202, 211-12
1 Henry IV, 34, 58, 65, 71, 80, 84, 89, 107, 112, 114, 117,

119, 122, 139, 144, 156, 189, 196-7, 204, 211
2 Henry IV, 49, 50, 83, 98, 92, 98-9, 102, 105, 107, 114, 119, 139, 146, 191, 195-6, 206, 211, 213
Henry V, 48, 50, 52, 61, 64, 71-2, 78-9, 85, 100, 103, 107, 109, 114, 118-19, 139, 144, 156, 170, 202-3, 206-7
1 Henry VI, 6, 63, 72-3, 78, 80, 83-4, 85-6, 89, 90, 95-6, 98-9, 106, 113-14, 119, 125, 151-2, 170-1, 173, 193-6, 201-2, 205
2 Henry VI, 6, 70-2, 90, 95, 104-8, 110, 114, 118, 126-7, 150, 154, 156, 193, 196, 199-202, 206-7, 211
3 Henry VI, 6, 72-3, 80, 82, 84, 90, 99, 100, 105, 108, 110, 113, 118, 126, 139, 194, 201-2, 207
Henry VIII, 2, 7, 9, 19, 45, 55, 62, 65, 71, 80, 84, 90-2, 99, 101, 104, 107-8, 112, 117, 119, 121, 163-4, 167-8, 172, 185-208, 213
Julius Caesar, 74, 80, 89, 95, 103-4, 108, 111, 114, 116-18, 120, 125, 157, 195, 203, 212
King John, 63-5, 71, 85-6, 89, 100, 107, 111, 114, 116, 118-19, 123, 126, 147-8, 171, 188, 194, 196-7
King Lear, 8, 48, 52, 54, 58, 61, 64-5, 72, 82, 85, 97-8, 108, 111, 114, 117-18, 123, 144, 189, 192-3, 195
Lover's Complaint, A, 6, 103,